AMERICAN AUTO RACING

AMERICAN
AUTO RACING

*The Milestones and Personalities
of a Century of Speed*

by

J. A. Martin
and Thomas F. Saal

McFarland & Company, Inc., Publishers
Jefferson, North Carolina, and London

Library of Congress Cataloguing-in-Publication Data

Martin, J. A. (James Alva), 1944–
American auto racing : the milestones and
personalities of a century of speed /
by James A. Martin and Thomas J. Saal.
p.   cm.
Includes bibliographical references and index.

ISBN-13: 978-0-7864-1235-8
softcover : 50# alkaline paper ∞

1. Automobile racing — United States —
History — 20th century.
I. Saal, Thomas F.   II. Title.
GV1033.M37   2004   796.72'0973'0904 — dc21   2002013183

British Library cataloguing data are available

Background images ©2004 Digital Vision

Cover photographs: (top row, left to right) Teddy Tettlaff in the German Blitzen Benz at
the Utah State Fairgrounds; Frank Lockhart in the Stutz Blackhawk at Daytona Beach *(IMS
Properties);* Dan Gurney, winner of the Race of Champions at Brands Hatch *(Norman Hayes).*
Bottom, left to right: Al Unser, Sr. in the Indy Porsche *(Cliff Morgan);* Two Vipers
leading a lone Corvette at the Petit Le Mans; and Dale Earnhardt *(Ed Clayton)*

Manufactured in the United States of America

McFarland & Company, Inc., Publishers
Box 611, Jefferson, North Carolina 28640
www.mcfarlandpub.com

ACKNOWLEDGMENTS

I thank the many people in motorsports who contributed their time and resources to this effort. Special thanks are given to Larry Black, Al Dowd, John Fitch, George Follmer, Andy Granatelli, Dan Gurney, Jim Hall, Jerry Helck, Lee Holman, Parnelli Jones, Karl Kainhofer, Bud Moore, Wally Parks, Richard Petty, Carroll Shelby, Al Unser, Bobby Unser and Cale Yarborough for their memories. To the Eastern Museum of Motor Racing (EMMR) and Detroit National Automotive Historic Collection at the Detroit Public Library for making their files available. And I thank Ed Clayton, Dudley Evans, Dave Goehrig and Jerry Helck for continuing support and my family for their patience.

J.A. Martin

TABLE OF CONTENTS

PREFACE

When Jim Martin first proposed this book I begged off, telling him that I was in the process of developing a racing-based comic strip and didn't have time for such an ambitious undertaking. When he persisted I told him I would help with historical data and photo procurement, but that he would have to do the heavy work, which is what he did. I'm obliged to Jim for making me a 50/50 coauthor even though my participation was only from the sidelines, and I give him full credit for concisely summarizing the gist of American auto racing and ingeniously dividing it into just eighty-plus chapters. Also, McFarland Publishing is to be commended for having enough patience and perseverance to work with two authors whom at times they might have perceived as being from different planets instead of different cities.

Thomas F. Saal
Lakewood, Ohio
August 2003

INTRODUCTION

American auto racing is unique. It is run on different types of tracks, with different types of cars and for different reasons than the rigidly structured international motorsports system that grew from European racing and is headquartered in Europe. The unique nature of American racing is derived from the geography of the country and reflects the nature and values of its people.

At the beginning of the twentieth century America was still a predominantly agricultural country. Most roads were nothing more than wagon tracks, even in the east, and trains were the primary means of long distance travel. Rural Americans seldom ventured far from their homes, and their limited leisure time activities included local fairs where they sometimes met to see who had the fastest horse. These were everyday workhorses, not the kind bred specifically for racing, and every fair had a horse track. The tracks at the county fairgrounds were usually a quarter-mile around and those at the state fairs were mostly half-mile, the length generally measured at the inside rail.

Europe, in the meantime, had superior roads, many of them centuries old, that connected large cities in different countries and could be traversed by horse-drawn carriage in a few days, sometimes a few hours. In Europe horse racing was the sport of kings, and the steeplechase, an extension of the cross-country nature of fox hunting, was the predominant form of horse racing. Thus it's not surprising that the advent of the automobile and automobile racing took different forms in America and abroad.

At first the Europeans raced on public roads until the 1903 Paris-Madrid "race of death" forced them to use controlled road circuits such as Le Mans. The road racing influence was best expressed in America by the Vanderbilt Cup and American Grand Prize epics that ended with further loss of life at Santa Monica in 1916. American road racing was low key until the post–World War II era, but attention never veered from the horse tracks where daredevils such as Louis Chevrolet, Ralph Mulford and Barney Oldfield were already making headlines.

At first, the hayseeds out in the great plains were content to gasp in disbelief at the exhibitions staged by auto racing impresarios who traveled with cars and drivers by rail from fair to fair. But their familiarity with the Model T Ford and the

Ford's ready availability sparked a lot of local competition and introduced racing versions that gradually replaced horses on the track just as they had on the road. The emergence of the Indianapolis 500 as "the greatest spectacle in racing" further fixated the racing fraternity on oval track racing.

Another factor in the development of American auto racing was southern California. From the beginning of the motor age the West Coast had the advantage of never-ending sunshine, making it an ideal place to develop airplanes. The aircraft industry was a magnet for people with a passion for mechanical innovation, and nearby deserts provided an arena for pushing the limits of speed, both on land and in the air. The hot rod influence was a major factor in oval track racing just before and after World War II, and California cars and drivers were the dominant force at Indianapolis until the rodders' efforts were diverted into the uniquely American sport of drag racing.

While technologies have changed dramatically, the character of the people who influence American racing has remained constant. Many of the personalities of early racing would feel right at home in contemporary races after becoming familiar with speeds that were unimaginable years ago. Early drivers were like the American cowboy, rough and tumble types, who gave no quarter and chased their need for speed while barely earning enough prize money to pay for tires and gas. They were often their own mechanics and usually towed their race cars from track to track on open trailers.

Tinkering has been an American pas-time since colonial days, and that same ingenuity was later applied to race cars. Designers and constructors, from Harry Miller to Jim Hall to Dan Gurney to Don Devendorf, have taken good ideas made the cars faster.

Changes in racing are extensions of the nature of America. Europe would not have initiated the growth of influence from sponsors that is expressed today in stock cars packaged like bags of candy, but they have followed the American lead to today where Grand Prix cars, the holy grail of European influence, are colored to match a sponsor's name.

It is easy to marvel at the cars and drivers of today or to be nostalgic for the greats of a generation ago. Racers today run on one-mile circuits faster than what was once the land speed record. It is easy to think that the cars and the men who made them were primitive to our sophisticated products and that the men, while gutsy, were not as proficient as today's drivers. This is clearly not the case. Designers and drivers alike took what they had at the time and pushed it to the edge, then beyond. While it is impossible to completely compare cars and drivers of different eras it is clear that the Miller 91 was every bit as much a technological gem as the AAR Eagle Mk III, and that Ralph De-Palma could have held his own with Mario Andretti in skill, versatility and bad luck.

It is not the goal of this book to include every type of racing in America. Someone else should discuss motorcycles. Monster trucks, swamp buggies, snowmobiles, and battlebots are also not discussed.

J.A. Martin
Tom Saal

1 RACE OF THE CENTURY
Nineteenth Century That Is

By the last decade of the nineteenth century all the components that would make up the automobile had been created. The big obstacle to mobile power sources had been solved with small steam engines, electric batteries and gasoline fueled internal combustion engines, though no one knew which would become dominant. In 1889 Karl Benz of Germany had successfully joined a gas motor with a carriage. Powered surface transportation, free of tracks, was here. Various sources give credit to separate American inventors for creating the first automobile, though it was not called that for almost a decade later. However, all agree that it was created in 1893 or 1894. By the middle of the decade there were enough horseless carriages to make a race.

The first recorded race was organized in France in 1894. The French newspaper *Le Petit Journal* sponsored an over-the-road event from Paris to Rouen. Herman H. Kohlsaat, publisher of the *Chicago Times-Herald*, encouraged by pioneer auto promoter and forecaster Frederick U. Adams, saw an opportunity for a similar event

sponsored by his paper. Hailed as the "Race of the Century," the 54-mile race was to go from Chicago's Jackson Park to Evanston, Illinois, and back. The rules limited the race to vehicles with two seats and at least three wheels. The power source was the entrant's choice. The winner would receive a prize of $2,000. An amazing twenty-eight entries were submitted for the race to be held on July 4th, 1895. As a number of entries indicated that they would not be ready that soon the race was moved back to Thanksgiving Day.

Kohlstaat could organize and promote the event but he could not control the weather and on November 27, a foot of snow fell on the Chicago area. By the next day, Thanksgiving, only six of the promised eleven cars made it to the starting line. The race was delayed for half an hour in hopes that the other five would arrive. There were two electric powered vehicles and three imported Benz gasoline powered vehicles and a single vehicle built and driven by Frank Duryea.

The twenty-three-year old Frank and his brother, motorcycle builder Charles E.

Duryea, had built their first car in 1893 — it was credited with being one of the first — in Springfield, Massachusetts. It had a two-cylinder motor and a steering tiller. On the first run the automobile went for only two hundred feet, but it had run under its own power. By September 1895 Frank and Charles had advanced the vehicle enough to form the Duryea Motor Wagon Company.

On a good day the trip from Chicago to Evanston was a challenge for any 1895 vehicle, but with the snow it was a surprise that any finished the race. In many places the road was impassable, and even the clear sections were a continual series of ruts and mud bogs. Parts barely able to handle city stones broke under the impact of the road surface. By draw Duryea, with his riding umpire Arthur White, was the first off the line in car #5, leaving the others to follow in one minute intervals. Within six miles

of the start Duryea had a steering arm failure that required a 55 minute visit to the blacksmith. Jerry O'Connor's Benz was hampered by three collisions before it finally quit. Duryea, having retaken the lead, was sidelined with ignition problems. After rousting a local tinsmith for repairs he was on his way again after another 55 minute stop. Duryea won in a time of ten hours and twenty-three minutes — seven hours and fifty-three minutes of that time were actually spent on the road. Despite the repairs and stops Duryea did finish. A Benz finished ninety-five minutes later. All the electric vehicles ran out of charge before the race was over, highlighting a weakness that has yet to be fully resolved. Fewer than fifty people watched the finish. A gold medal was given to the non-finishing Electrobat for excellence in design, cleanliness and ease of control.

The win made the Duryeas famous

Past the November snow and cheering crowd the Duryea powered on to win the first organized American race. Peter Helck illustration from *Great Auto Races*, 1975.

and the first example of "win on Sunday, sell on Monday" came to be. Thirteen cars, the first production lot, were produced in 1896. However, the brothers were unable to take advantage of their fame and their lead position in auto production. By the end of the decade the company, and the relationship between the brothers, was finished.

But public interest wasn't. News of the accomplishment, promoted by the *Chicago Times-Herald*, went coast to coast as proof that the motor-car was becoming a reliable means of personal transportation. Both Henry Ford and Ransom Olds acknowledged that completion of the race reaffirmed the need for their continued work towards a practical vehicle.

2 THE MAN WHO INVENTED RACING
The Bennett Rules

Alexander Winton was frustrated at the lack of coverage he and his Winton Runabout had received for setting a new record time for travelling between New York and Cleveland. On May 22, 1899, he and reporter Charles B. Shanks set off for New York in a car of his own manufacture, arriving there in 47 hours and 34 minutes running time, a new record. Yet the response was to question why his average speed was about half that of the winner of the Paris-Bordeaux race. Winton said he could have done better if American roads were as good as French roads, thereby questioning the skill and equipment of Fernand Charron, the French winner. A reporter from the *New York Herald* made this into a challenge. American expatriate James Gordon Bennett, son of the founder of the *News Herald* and editor of the Paris edition, who had sent Henry Stanley to Africa to find Dr. Livingston, had been interested in motorsports for several years and recognized that race organization lacked standard rules. The Winton-Charron challenge presented him with the vehicle to prepare a race with a set of rules that were applicable to any form of racing.

The international race for, Bennett's *Coupe Internationale* was open to cars from every country, with the provision that the entire car, from motor to tires, was to be made in that country. To make the cars recognizable, each country was assigned a national color. American cars were red, French cars blue, Belgian cars yellow, German cars white and (later) British cars green.

To communicate to the drivers a series of colored flags was created. One set told the driver that the race started (green), stopped (red) and finished (checkered), but also that a faster car was preparing to pass (blue and yellow) or that there was danger ahead (yellow). By holding or waving the flag the drivers were told of the immediacy of the communication. The national racing colors and series of flags are still used today with no plans to change, though colored lights have often supplemented colored flags.

Bennett, following the lead of the American Cup yacht races, planned to have

The Gordon Bennett Trophy. From the collection of Tom Saal.

the country of the winning car as the host for the race the next year. The first race, conducted by the Automobile Club of France (ACF), was held on July 14, 1900, as part of their Paris-Lyon classic, a distance of 353.75 miles.

When Winton arrived in France he quickly realized how much more advanced French cars were compared to his Runabout. The premier French car was a front engine 20 hp Panhard, to be driven by Charron. The Winton had an eight horsepower engine under the driver.

Five cars started the Lyon race. The race did not go well for Winton as a wheel

collapsed. Charron, despite steering problems, went on to win in nine hours, nine minutes.

The following year the second race was won by Girardot with another Panhard.

Englishman S.F. Edge won the third race with a Napier. As England had the "Red Flag Laws" forbidding auto racing, the 1903 race was held in Ireland. Jenatzy, of Germany, won with a Mercedes. The American representative was again Alexander Winton.

France regained the trophy in 1904 when Thery won with a Richard-Brasier. Thery repeated the win in 1905, the last of the Bennett cup races.

The French pushed for racing more than three cars per country. When they were turned down the ACF withdrew and adapted the rules for their own Grand Prix, virtually ending the Bennett trophy races. The cars were entered by manufacturers rather than nations.

The demise was irrelevant to Bennett as he had by then turned his attention to aviation. He never attended a single race that bore his name.

Winton continued to build cars bearing his own name until 1924 and went into business building marine diesel engines. The descendant of that business is the Detroit Diesel Company.

3 UNIQUELY AMERICAN TRACKS
Dirt Ovals

Racing in Europe began with cross country trips along public roads. These races formed the basis for the inter-city endurance races like the Targa Florio and

closed course races at Le Mans. Simulating the open road led to closed course road racing and Formula 1 style races. Races were for the elite who could afford cars and manufacturers who built racecars to prove the reliability of their passenger cars.

In America inter-city road races never caught on but there was another type of race-track ready to accept the automobile. Every county fairground had a circular dirt track where horses had been run since the town had been settled. The same bragging rights over who had the fastest horse quickly led to who had the fastest car. The first examples of what would later be called "hot rods" were cars made into race-cars by removing everything that did not make the car go faster.

Teddy Tetzlaff on the German Blitzen Benz on a typical half-mile race-track, dirt minus the usual horses, at the Utah State Fairgrounds. From the collection of Tom Saal.

Horse tracks had everything needed for early auto racing. Stands and crowd control fences were as applicable to one type of closed course racing as another. Horse staging in the infield easily accommodated early race cars. The first race track used for auto racing was run on September 7, 1896, at the one mile Narragansett Park, Rhode Island, horse track in conjunction with the Rhode Island State Fair. Eight cars lined up for the race, including four Duryeas, one driven by Frank Duryea. Two of the cars were electric. A Riker electric won the first two heats with the final race going to an Electrobat that needed 11 minutes, 27 seconds for the five miles. Narragansett Park continued to hold auto races through 1904.

It wasn't just the little tracks that allowed auto racing. The big national horse tracks like Pimlico in Baltimore and Churchill Downs in Louisville hosted motorsports events. In 1908 Emanuel Cedrino of Italy established a new one mile closed course record, down by five seconds, to 51 seconds at Pimlico. The glory was short lived as he lost control just after passing the finish line, crashed and was killed.

Racing was brought to the people, who could sit in the stands and watch the entire race without having to get up and move around. The races were easily promotable and accessible to anyone, as compared to the European racing by factory teams for the benefit of the aristocracy.

At first the races were promoted by travelling circuses. The promoter provided the cars and drivers, and even the scoring officials. Through theatrics that would make professional wrestling proud, the crowd was presented with a motorized morality play where, despite the obstacles, the hero prevailed. When local drivers put out their own cars the competition became more real.

Oval tracks with controlled audiences made racing profitable for promoters and track operators. American racing became financially practical, independent of

The pits at the dirt half-mile Winchester (Indiana) Speedway in 1939 offered little protection to crewmembers, and this was typical. Courtesy of Bob Sheldon.

In 1950 Milwaukee was still a one-mile dirt track at the Wisconsin state fairgrounds. Courtesy of Bob Sheldon.

wealthy patrons and nobility or of the promotion department of the auto companies. The dirt ovals made the audience fans of the race rather than the cars, racing becoming more entertaining than technically interesting.

In 1916, after several spectator fatalities, racing on public roads ceased, putting more emphasis on the dirt tracks. Some state fair horse tracks, such as DuQuoin, Illinois, Syracuse, New York, and the Indianapolis State Fairgrounds, have continued to hold auto races. Milwaukee was paved in 1954 and continues to host many races.

One problem with dirt is that, when dry, it turns to dust. There were two cures. One was to continually water the track. The other was to put down a coating of oil that soon mixed with the dirt. This kept down dust, but purists didn't acknowledge the resulting surface as a dirt track.

The cars have changed but the excitement, and the dust, are unchanged in almost a hundred years. From the collection of J. A. Martin.

The best dirt tracks today are really clay, whether indigenous or trucked in from afar. When properly conditioned with water by a track superintendent who knows what he's doing, a clay surface can be fast, safe and spectacular with little or no irritating dust hanging in the air.

4 THE GREAT RACE
New York to Paris, the Long Way, 1908

Point to point racing by automobiles took the world by storm in the first decade of the twentieth century. The 1907 races had gone from city to city to across the nation then crossing the continent. The last great challenge was to go around the world and in 1908 that came to be.

Sponsored by two newspapers, *Le Matin* of France and *The New York Times*, a race was to go from New York to Paris, the long way, over land. Six cars showed up in Times Square on February 12, 1908. *Le Matin*, hoping to prove the superiority of French cars, concentrated its coverage of the three home cars. *The New York Times*

centered its attention on the lone American entrant, the *Flyer* by the Thomas Car Company, headed by E.R. Thomas, of Buffalo, NY. Thomas was not interested in entering the race but Harry Houpt, his New York agent, began the project on his own initiative. In addition, there were single car entries from Germany and Italy. All six teams were bundled up in furs and wool blankets and looked more like an arctic expedition than a motor race, but it was an expedition of endurance. Each car was equipped with tools, replacement parts and spare gas cans, as well as sleeping and cooking gear.

Around 250,000 people came to cheer

Thousands of New Yorkers lined the Manhattan streets to watch the cars leave for Paris in February 1908. From the collection of Tom Saal.

on the start. The six cars were lined up side by side in Times Square. With a shot by an official of the American Automobile Association the race was on. As a courtesy the host Flyer was the last to depart, but it was the first to the first checkpoint at Albany. The 15 hp French Sizaire-Naudin dropped out before reaching Albany.

Two days after the start Thomas Flyer driver Montague Roberts, mechanic George Schuster and reporter T. Walter Williams of *The New York Times* brought the "stock" car into the Buffalo shop where it was altered to meet the demands of the trip. From there the six cars headed across northern United States. At that time it was easier to run on frozen roads and lakes than through warmer sections with mud and swamps. Norwegian explorer Hans Hansen, who began with the French DeDion-Bouton team, changed to join the Thomas effort. After Omaha the Thomas followed

the Union Pacific right of way. Linn Mathewson took over the driving duties from Roberts in Denver. To get past a snowbound region the Flyer drove over the Union Pacific rails and ties. Fifteen hours were needed for repairs in Ogden, Utah, and Harold Brinker assumed the driving role. On one section the German Protos and French Motobloc were transported on rail cars. After three weeks the first leg was completed when the cars arrived in San Francisco with the Thomas firmly in the lead.

The rules were ambiguous. The lead by the Thomas was squandered when it was shipped to Seattle in order to attempt Alaska. When it was determined that the trail was unsuitable for wheeled vehicles the Flyer was shipped back to San Francisco, a side trip of three weeks. In arriving in San Francisco the French Motobloc was withdrawn. The Zust, Protos and DeDion were sent directly to Japan, the teams not realizing that Japan did not yet have adequate roads over the mountainous backbone of the island nation. Though the French DeDion arrived first in Vladivostok, the owners ordered the team to withdraw. Then there were three.

After nine days of rebuilding, the Protos was the first to leave for the Asian journey. In the next few days the German and American crews pulled each other out of mud traps. But the strain on the transmission of the Thomas forced a side trip by Schuster to get replacement parts. When the Flyer was moving again the Protos had a six-day lead. Still the teams came together again at Lake Baikal, though the Protos had the ferryboat. Just before Omsk, Russia, the Flyer passed the Protos. Then both cars were delayed awaiting replacement parts and repairs east of the Ural mountains. After seven days spent securing parts and making repairs the Flyer was underway again, but the Germans had the lead. By the time the Flyer reached Berlin on July 26 news reports stated that the Protos was in Paris. The beleaguered Flyer arrived two days later. However a review of

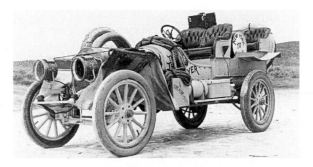

The Thomas Flyer restored to the condition in which it appeared at the end of the 1908 race. From the collection of Tom Saal.

the event resulted in the German team being penalized a total of fifteen days for the rail journey in America and not attempting the Alaska route. The Flyer was declared the winner. The Zust finally finished in mid–September. A victory celebration with the keys to the city, a parade and a visit with President Roosevelt was held for the Flyer crew in New York City and another in Buffalo. Thomas tried to bank on the fame of the Flyer but was never able to match the "Great Race." In 1912 the company went into receivership and the winning Flyer itself was lost. But by the 1970s the Flyer was found and restored to race winning condition.

5 THE RACE THAT STARTED AN EMPIRE
Henry Ford and the 999

As the twentieth century began Henry Ford was one of a large number of American mechanics who had built and were trying to sell automobiles. The field was vast and growing. Ford realized that unless he found a way to stand out from his competitors his company was probably doomed to failure.

To prove his car, Ford did what

countless other companies with perception problems have done, he went racing. Unlike the armies of cars Ford was to send into combat decades later, this effort was with one car with a mechanic/owner who had never raced a car before facing Alexander Winton, the best known race driver of the day.

Near Ford's Dearborn shop was the

one-mile oval track of the Detroit Driving Club at Grosse Pointe, Michigan, before the area became an upper class neighborhood. For the October 10, 1901, program three cars were entered for the twenty-five-mile race. One car withdrew and, due to the length of the preceding races, the Ford/Winton race was reduced to ten miles. The winner was to receive $1,000, a glass bowl and recognition.

Ford built his first internal combustion motor in 1893 and his first automobile in 1896. In 1899 he became superintendent of the Detroit Automobile Company, a business that lasted less than two years. Ford then embarked on a tour of the East, getting to know what the other automobiles were like. Back home he built a car that was smaller than the competition, weighed less than 1,600 pounds and was powered by a 540 cubic inch motor that produced 26 horsepower.

Before Ford and his riding mechanic Spider Huff went racing Ford met with bicycle racer Tom Cooper, who gave Ford a quick lesson on how to drive fast around the track. With Ford was his engineer, Oliver Barthel, who had designed the car.

As expected Winton took the early lead, at times over 300 yards. But Ford, with Huff hanging on the side, was not falling back and as he began to understand more about racing he began to catch Winton. On the straights Ford was faster though he lost ground through the turns. By the eighth lap they were even, then Ford pulled in front, winning at 44.8 mph.

The bowl, the only trophy Henry Ford won as driver, was nice. The check helped the new company. But most important was the news that was received across the nation that a car built by Henry Ford had won over the famous Winton.

The day was also significant as Cooper met with fellow bicycle racer Barney Oldfield. Cooper introduced Ford to Oldfield. Under Cooper's promotion, Ford's famous 999 race car, and Oldfield's breathtaking driving, the first legends in American racing were born.

A frozen Lake St. Claire (Michigan) was the only place Henry Ford could find to run his 999 in 1904. After a path was cleared Ford set a new speed record. Peter Helck illustration from *Great Auto Races*, 1975.

Ford left the Henry Ford Company the next year to pursue racing, though he wasn't certain how. After his name was removed the company continued, eventually becoming Cadillac.

In May 1902 Ford and Cooper, with a few employees, began work on a new race car. Two examples were built, named for famous railroad locomotives of the day, the Arrow and the 999. Both were stripped of unnecessary weight, like valve covers, and were steered by a tiller. Ford used the Arrow to set a new land speed record on a frozen Lake St. Clair. Cooper and Huff convinced Oldfield, who had never driven an automobile, to race the 999. On October 25, 1902, at Grosse Pointe, Oldfield matched up with Winton. The two were vastly superior to the rest of the field and had a tight race until Winton's car began to misfire and Oldfield won his first race. His time was a record for a five-mile race on a one-mile track. Over the next year the combination was virtually unbeatable with Oldfield recognized as a national driving champion. After 1903 Oldfield left Cooper to create his own legends. Ford stayed back at the office and built an empire.

6 THE VANDERBILT CUP
1904–1916

By 1904 motor racing in America was a growing but disorganized sport. Promoters were staging road shows at local horse tracks all across the country, sometimes with questionable results, but there was no race that defined the sport. Rules were almost non-existent.

And while racing played to crowds, most of the people in the stands could not afford an automobile, those belonged to the wealthy, a group that was not inclined to patronize local horse tracks.

Cross country road racing had not developed in America as it had in Europe where royalty had both the wealth and administrative power, making public roads accessible for racing.

Enter William Kissam Vanderbilt, Jr., of the family that built railroads and was financially and socially at the top of New York society. In 1900 the 22-year-old Willie K. as known to his friends, organized the National Automobile Racing Association. One of the first events was a hill climb at Newport, Rhode Island, which he won. By the end of the year he was the first National Champion. Following a tour in Europe, where he set speed records and competed in several races, he returned to America to organize races to compete with the best of Europe.

With the support of the social families of Long Island, the new American Automobile Association, founded in Chicago in

The original Vanderbilt Cup. From the collection of Tom Saal.

1902, and the young American auto industry, Willie K. organized a race along 28.4 miles of public road. Vanderbilt deeded a gift to the AAA of a 24 inch tall silver Tiffany cup with a ten and a half gallon capacity.

The first event had an international field of eighteen cars from four nations (United States, Germany, Italy, and France). While the Packard "Grey Wolf," was a dirt-track racer, the other American cars, the Pope-Toledo, Royal and Simplex were hardly more than modified street machines, and the 13-liter Pope was a racer, but unproven.

By comparison the French 12.8 liter DeDietrich and 15.4 liter Panhard had won major races in Europe and the Kaiser himself backed five Mercedes. In addition there were Italian FIATs and a French Renault and Bayard. After protests by local farmers and an anti-social society press were settled, the race was held on October 8, 1904. The starters were sent off in two-

George Heath on a Panhard won the 1904 Vanderbilt Cup race and finished second the following year. From the collection of Tom Saal.

minute intervals beginning at six o'clock in the morning. George Heath's Panhard won at an average of 52.2 mph.

American cars had run well but none were in contention for the win. For 1905 the American entries were racing specials, including a front drive car from Christie, a steamer by White and a 17.7-liter Loco-

The starting line at the 1904 Vanderbilt Cup Race when cars were waved off in numerical order at two minute intervals. George Heath on his 90 Panhard-Levassor was the seventh starter at 6:12 am. From the collection of Tom Saal.

mobile. A quarter of a million New Yorkers, society and common folk alike, lined the course on October 14, 1905, for the second race. The same European teams were back. Victor Hemery's Darracq won over Heath's defending Panhard with Joe Tracy's Locomobile in third, the best finish for an American car. The Darracq upped the winning speed to 61.5 mph.

Louis Wagner in the Darracq V-8 with which he won the 1906 Vanderbilt Cup race. From the collection of Tom Saal.

Success of the race was shown in the third year by the attendance; with three hundred thousand the Vanderbilt was the biggest sporting event in the country. And so many American cars were entered that an elimination round was necessary. Unlike the 24-hp Pope-Toledo of the 1904 race the new American cars were specially built for speed. The Thomas had a 10.2-liter motor while the Frayer-Millers had 16.2 liter air cooled motors. A Locomobile won the elimination round.

Europe again sent the Italian FIATs and Italas, French Panhards, Darracq, Hotchkiss and DeDietrich and the German Mercedes.

Weather delayed the start until 6:15 A.M. on October 6, 1906, but even with the delay the police were not able to completely clear the crowd from the track. During the race one spectator was killed and two injured. The Darracq of Wagner won at 61.4 mph. Due to potential safety problems no race was held in 1907.

The 1908 race was diminished by the number of European cars that passed up the Vanderbilt to race in the rival Automobile Club of America's (ACA) Grand Prize in Savannah, Georgia. The ACA had made great improvements in track safety and organization, things the European drivers had complained about at Long Island, and the Grand Prize was only for pure race machines.

The foreign cars that did compete in the Vanderbilt were a 12.1-liter Renault, a 16.3-liter Hotchkiss and a 14.4-liter Mercedes.

A new feature for 1908 was a nine mile section of the concrete Long Island Motor Parkway that ran past great estates. However, fourteen miles were still run on public dirt and gravel roads. Wire fencing had been used for crowd control, but fans had torn it away to get to the best viewing areas, usually in the areas of the wealthy. Water hoses proved to be more effective at keeping the crowds back. Twenty-three-year-old George Robertson dominated with his Locomobile, winning at 64.3 mph.

For 1909 the Cup was for production based cars of up to 10 liters and ran on a shorter course comprised of five miles on the Parkway and 7.6 on public roads. Only FIAT sent a challenger to the American stock cars. Harry Grant's long wheelbase chain driven Alco-6 won with a strategy of consistency, finishing at 62.8 mph.

A major contender was lost before the start of the 1910 race when George Robertson took a reporter with him for a demonstration lap. When the reporter panicked in a tight turn his grab caused Robertson to lose control and flip. After frantic laps by the Marquette-Buick team the win went to Grant, who again held to a careful plan for his Alco at 65.1 mph.

After so many deaths and injuries, Long Island was closed to the Vanderbilt Cup. The November 1911 race was a support event for the Savannah Grand Prize, a series begun in 1908 which is chronicled in Chapter 12. Ralph Mulford won in a Lozier over the Grand Prix Mercedes of Ralph DePalma.

Milwaukee, Wisconsin, won the rights for the 1912 Grand Prize and Vanderbilt Cup races. At 7.8 miles it was the shortest road course yet used. Eight cars started the Vanderbilt, with Ralph DePalma winning at 68.9 mph on a Mercedes. Neither race was run in 1913, and both were moved to Santa Monica, California, for 1914 where DePalma won the Vanderbilt again, outfoxing Barney Oldfield as related in the following chapter.

San Francisco was home to the 1915 races as part of the Panama-Pacific Exposition, a city's celebration of rebirth after the 1906 earthquake. The 3.8 mile course went around some of the finest houses and the Palace of Fine Arts. Crowd control was effective with the entire course patrolled. For 1915 both the Vanderbilt and the Grand Prize limited engine size to 450 cubic inches so the 30 car fields were virtually identical, as was the result. Dario Resta won both races with a Peugeot, virtually identical to the revolutionary car that had dominated at Indianapolis with a shaft drive, long stroke overhead cam motor and low slung body.

Both races returned to Santa Monica for 1916, the final year. Nineteen cars started the race at ten second intervals. The race came between the Peugeots of Resta and Aitken until the latter's motor broke an intake valve and Resta won his second straight cup at 86.98 mph.

With the war in Europe drawing off talent and the AAA championship made up, for the most part, of speedways where crowds paid to see the races, road racing was not profitable. The Cup was no longer meaningful, but Willie K.'s goals had been met. The American auto industry was competitive with Europe and racing had become organized. Willie K. continued his involvement in motorsports until his death in 1944.

7 THE FIRST SUPERSTARS
Oldfield, DePalma and Mulford

No sooner had racing begun than a group of drivers emerged that rose above the rest. Three men dominated for the first two decades.

Berna Eli "Barney" Oldfield was many things to early racing but to most Americans he was the one name they knew, the man that symbolized the early daredevil days of motorsports. From the way that early racing was conducted and the way

Oldfield managed to "control" a race it is impossible to estimate how many races he actually won.

Born June 3, 1878, in Wauseon, Ohio, Oldfield began racing bicycles in his teens, but fate intervened in his career path on October 10, 1901. One of his opponents at the Grosse Pointe, Michigan, track was Tom Cooper, a partner of Henry Ford's racing effort. Ford won the race over Alexander Winton then decided to retire as a driver. Cooper needed someone to take over Ford's new car, the 1155 cubic inch 999. Though Oldfield had never raced a car, or even driven one for that matter, he accepted the offer to drive and race.

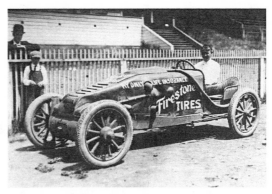

Barney Oldfield in the front drive Christie. One of the first uses of a car as a means of advertising. Courtesy of the EMMR collection.

The following October Oldfield was matched against Winton, recognized as the best racer of the early years. Oldfield easily won. Over the next year Oldfield won races across the country with the 999, becoming the first driver to complete a mile oval in under one minute and setting a new land speed record. In 1903 the AAA recognized Oldfield as National Champion. As faster cars came along Oldfield left Ford to advance his career with a variety of manufacturers. Even with all his success in later cars Oldfield's name will always be most associated with the 999.

Oldfield was a master of self promotion. Though his trademark cigar was a way to keep his teeth from clacking together, it gave him that cocky look of a winning scoundrel. He and co-promoter Bill Pickens would bring a race package to a local track that would include cars and drivers and even time keepers. Before the race he would fiddle with the motor to impress the locals, many of whom had never seen a car before. Then, in practice he would thunder around the track and set a new track record, aided by his timer if necessary. For the race Oldfield took off to lead the early laps but along the way a problem would befall the mighty Oldfield. He

would have to make a pit stop or hang over the side of the car to make a fix on the fly. While he was so engaged the field would pass him and it would look like his race was over. But like the melodramas of the day, the hero would come surging up through the pack in his now fine running race car to take the lead just before the checkered flag. The crowd was on its feet as Oldfield won again.

This may sound contrived, and it often was, but it brought paying fans to the tracks and made racing a profitable venture for many track owners. It also created fans who left under the spell of the daring speed demons, even the ones that Oldfield passed. While not pure sport, it was a winning situation for all involved.

Even the cars he drove were marketing gems. They bore such names as the "Peerless Green Dragon," the 21.1-liter "Blitzen Benz" and Harry Miller's closed cockpit "Golden Submarine."

A most unusual and unmatched victory was with the Green Dragon when he "raced" on a treadmill on a Broadway stage to win a fictional Vanderbilt Cup. In another theatrical race, promoter Bill Pickens matched Oldfield against black heavyweight fighter Jack Johnson, the latter in a Thomas-6. The AAA, fearing racial violence, promised suspension of all participants

In an early staged event Barney Oldfield raced against black boxing champion Jack Johnson, "to restore the supremacy of the white race" after Johnson had defeated white fighter Jim Jeffries for the title. Afterwards the AAA banned Oldfield and his manager for staging the exhibition. From the collection of Tom Saal.

tator at the inaugural Vanderbilt race that he found his true passion. DePalma was given his chance with four wheels by Fred Moscovics and the Allen-Kingston team. Soon he was winning races and creating international attention by earning a drive with first the factory FIAT team, then the Mercedes team. At the 1912 Indianapolis 500 he had his most famous non-win when, with a five-lap lead and four laps to go, the engine failed in his Mercedes. DePalma and mechanic Rupert Jeffkins jumped out and pushed the car. Within sight of the checkered flag Joe Dawson passed them for the win. DePalma went on to win Indianapolis in 1915 and the AAA National Championship in 1912 and 1914.

and participating tracks. Oldfield and Pickens went ahead with an easy win. AAA enforced the ban, and Oldfield's race cars were impounded. Oldfield was temporarily out of the racing and promotion business. He did return for more wins and glory but never again as the carnival promoter.

Oldfield never won the Indianapolis 500. He placed fifth in 1914 for Stutz (best-placed American car), didn't make it in 1915, and placed fifth again in 1916 in his own Delage. The fact that Oldfield knew how to promote racing, and himself, will not diminish his true ability as a driver. He raced and defeated the best of his day. Oldfield died in 1946.

Mario Andretti was not the only Italian born American race driver to have great success and great disappointment at Indianapolis.

Ralph DePalma's parents emigrated from Italy to Brooklyn, New York, in 1892. The athletic young DePalma tried racing bicycles before moving to motorcycles with limited success. But it was as a spec-

It is estimated that he won over 2,000 races on dirt, board and road tracks, including his historic 1914 Santa Monica Vanderbilt Cup win over Barney Oldfield. DePalma and Oldfield had never liked each other, and when Oldfield joined the Mercer teams where DePalma was lead driver, DePalma quit, then came back to beat his rival in a year-old privately entered Mercedes, his 1913 winning car. After several fast cars dropped out the race was between the faster but tire-consuming Oldfield and the steadier DePalma. DePalma won by indicating that he was coming in for tires. Oldfield's pit saw the signal and called him in for tires only to see that DePalma had stayed out. Despite Oldfield's furious charge DePalma won at 75.4 mph.

In the early 1920s he drove in European

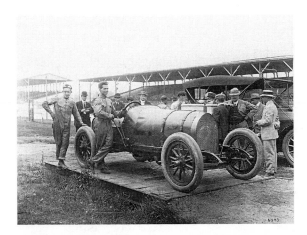

Ralph DePalma awaits tech inspection with his Mercer at Indianapolis in 1913. From the collection of Tom Saal.

Grand Prix for the Ballot team, finishing second to Jimmy Murphy at the 1921 French Grand Prix, the only 1-2 for American drivers. He remained active in racing after he retired as a driver in 1934. He died on March 31, 1956.

In 1925 Pete DePaolo, DePalma's nephew and occasional riding mechanic, won the 500 for the first repeat win within a racing family. There were to be others.

The ever-smiling Ralph Mulford built a solid racing career that lasted into the 1920s. Born in Brooklyn in 1884, he first became aware of the new mechanized vehicles ten years later and quickly learned how a gasoline motor works. By sixteen he built a marine engine that was better than the factory Lozier motor. Lozier hired the boy, and when the company began to produce cars in 1905 Mulford was the company demonstrator. The natural next step for a car company in 1907 was to go racing, and in Mulford they already had a driver who knew the car. Mulford won his first race, a hill climb, and a driver was born. He followed with a win in the international 24-hour race, with co-driver Harry Michener, at Point Breeze near Philadelphia, winning over factory sup-

ported Mercedes and Darracq cars. At the September 11-12, 1908, Brighton Beach 24-hour race Mulford and Harry Cobe won with a Lozier, again over several European factory teams, setting a new distance record.

American race cars were modified stock cars and had little chance against the pure racing cars from Europe in the first Grand Prix at Savannah, Georgia, for 1908. Yet from his second starting position Mulford led the first lap. He was quickly outclassed by the European cars but was still running at the end. Mulford led again for Lozier in the 1909 Brighton Beach 24-hour race. During the era of the 24-hour races Mulford won three times and finished second twice out of the ten races he entered.

Mulford promised his fiancé he would quit after the October 1909 24-hour race at Brighton Beach but a weather delay moved the event back to his wedding day. Contracts and commitments were equally met when he was married, raced and won, setting a new distance of 1,196 miles, retired, then went on a honeymoon. In 1910 he came out of retirement and won the Elgin National Trophy race. He was named National Stock Car Champion. Racing did not

Ralph Mulford, center, became the premier driver in the early American 24 hour races. From the collection of Tom Saal.

hurt the marriage as his wife often served as his non-riding mechanic throughout the rest of his career. Mulford may have won the inaugural Indianapolis 500. There was uncertainty as to whether a lap was counted during the confusion of a three-car accident and possibly he should have been ahead at the end. Officially he is listed as the first runner-up. It was his best finish at Indianapolis. What was certain was that he was named the 1911 National Champion by the AAA Contest Board. Later that year, though he was a 20–1 long shot, Mulford won the Vanderbilt Cup at Savannah, in a Lozier.

His return to Indianapolis was marked by another record. Drivers continued until they completed 500 miles. As the last running car in 1912 Mulford continued on in his Knox at a leisurely pace, including breaks for snacks and drink, for over nine hours, long after all but a few officials had gone home, earning tenth place and $1,200. In 1916 he also won Pikes Peak at a record time that stood for eight years and set a cross-country mark (5 days, 3 hours, 31 minutes). Two years later he was again AAA National Champion. On one day in 1921 Mulford set eight speed records at Uniontown, Pennsylvania, with a Paige. Through the teen years and into the 1920s Mulford raced for and won in cars by Mason/Duesenberg, Hudson, Frontenac and Mercedes.

A thinking driver, the mechanically-oriented Mulford constantly evaluated how much abuse his car could take and drove accordingly. When faster, more aggressively driven cars went out Mulford picked up the win. Even with a slower car Mulford would be faster. Where the Lozier was a modified stock car the European competition was usually comprised of specially built racecars. Ralph Mulford continued his involvement with cars and racing until his death on October 23, 1973.

 # A FULL DAY OF RACING
Twice Around the Clock on a Dirt Oval

In the early 1900s no one was really certain of what was the best form of racing. In Europe city to city racing over public roads was favored. Racing on dirt horse tracks was popular in America.

And what length of race? If the goal of racing in the early 1900s was to show the reliability and endurance of the car, why not go to the realistic ultimate of racing for an entire day, twice around the clock, for twenty-four hours, the automotive marathon?

The first 24-hour events were not races at all but internal engineering tests. In 1904 a Packard went 820 miles. This figure was proclaimed in advertising. The following year a Peerless was driven for 923 miles. A 40 horsepower National upped the ante to 1,094 miles in November, 1905.

The Columbus (Ohio) Auto Club was the first to formalize these tests into a racing event with spectators in July 1905. In heavy rains on a dirt track a Pope-Toledo won, achieving 828.5 miles.

To promote the new United States Motor Racing Association (USMRA) Bill Pickens organized a 24-hour race on May 25, 1907, at the one-mile Point Breeze horse track near Philadelphia. He called it the International Endurance Derby. For the night he set up arc lights with the pits opposite the main grandstand. Ten cars started. An

Much of the 24-hour race at Point Breeze was a mud bath on the dirt oval, but it didn't stop Ralph Mulford who took the win. Peter Helck illustration from *Great Auto Races*, 1975.

Autocar won, covering 791 miles. One month later Pickens held a second event. This was marked by eight solid hours of rain and a new racing hero, Ralph Mulford in his first ever 24-hour race. On the final lap the left driving chain on his Lozier broke but Mulford lurched across the line on the right chain for the win.

Pickens's race in Chicago was marked by uncertainty as the untrained scorers made incorrect car identifications and mis-scored cars through the night. For 1907 Pickens moved his races, now called "grinds," to Brighton Beach, New York. Scorers were trained and the best drivers were brought in. Fifteen stripped passenger cars were entered in the first race. Monty Roberts won but it took strong action from the AAA to obtain the winner's purse.

Twice around the clock races popped up all over the country. Though lacking the longevity of Brighton Beach, grinds at Los Angeles, Seattle, Milwaukee, and Birmingham, Alabama, proved popular for several years.

The Morris Park Motordrome Club in the Bronx was built as much to sell real estate as to prove automobiles. Nine cars began the September 1907 race with a Renault taking the win. Three weeks later nineteen cars started. After a two hour mid-race break for support races and track repair the grind resumed only to face heavy rains that lasted through the win by a FIAT.

Though the AAA declared the participants outlaws, the 1908 race was held at Brighton Beach and won by Mulford in a Lozier covering a record 1,107 miles. The record was to last for only three weeks. A Simplex survived the next event covering 1,117 miles.

Covering the track with a layer of concrete did not lead to a new distance record, nor did a mud free surface, when a month later a Renault won, covering 1,050 miles. Wrecks on the track killed the crew of a Stearns and a later crash injured a policeman.

Mulford won the 1908 Morris Park Motordrome race on his wedding day, setting a new distance of 1,196 miles before

Poole comes in for a new set of tires at the 1909 24-hour race at Brighton Beach (New York). Peter Helck illustration from *Great Auto Races*, 1975.

retiring. He came out of retirement to finish second in May of 1910.

The last Brighton Beach marathon was held in August 1910. With the advent of nearby airplane and boat races and the absence of stars DePalma and Mulford who were racing elsewhere, the once record crowds were greatly reduced. Only seven cars started with a Stearns covering 1,253 miles for the win. It was the last 24-hour race in the world until the French "discovered" round the clock racing at Le Mans in 1923. The only American "grind" today is the 24-hour race at Daytona.

9 INDIANAPOLIS MOTOR SPEEDWAY

The birth of big-time American oval track racing occurred in August 1909 with the opening of the Indianapolis Motor Speedway. Located west of the city of Indianapolis, Indiana, the track was a 2.5-mile oval, or rather a round-cornered rectangle. Unlike the European-style road courses or the modified horse tracks, this venue in the heart of America was created for high-speed auto racing.

The speedway was the fulfillment of a dream for Prest-O-Lite owner Carl G. Fisher. An early race driver, Fisher saw his future in promotion of racing. With financial help from three other Indiana businessmen, Arthur Newby of National

Motors, Frank Wheeler of Wheeler-Schebler Carburetor and Prest-O-Lite partner James Allison, a track was born.

The first race on the tar and crushed stone surface was held on August 19, 1909, before thirty thousand paying fans, fifteen thousand in seats. After time trials, known as much for the dust and potholes as speed, the inaugural races were held. Eighty entrants competed over three days culminating in a 250-mile event. Early in the race the leading car struck a pothole and crashed, killing the driver and riding mechanic. After track repairs racing resumed the next day to a larger crowd. Another mechanic and

Henry Ford (L) with the four founders of the Indianapolis Motor Speedway, (l–r) Arthur Newby, Frank Wheeler, Carl Fisher, and James Allison. Photograph used with permission of IMS Properties.

two spectators were killed as Lewis Strang won the exhibition race. Afterwards the AAA looked at having the track closed.

An aerial view of the 2.5-mile Indianapolis Motor Speedway, before the infield road course was included. Photograph used with permission of IMS Properties.

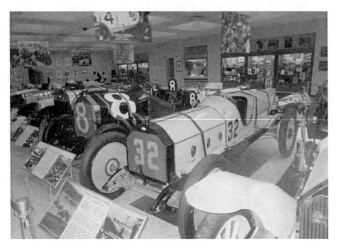

Ray Harroun's Marmon is among the cars on display at the speed-way museum. From the collection of J. A. Martin.

Lewis Strang became the first winner on the bricks with a FIAT, though the event was a time trial due to weather that was too cold for actual racing. After races on Memorial Day, July 4th and Labor Day in 1910 Fisher proposed a feature race that would rival the Vanderbilt Cup and the Grand Prix. Initial plans were for a 24-hour race but a distance of 500 miles was accepted, the approximate distance a race car could go before dark descended.

The solution to dust and potholes was to pave the entire track with 3,200,000 bricks. Work took 63 days and a second series of races was held on December 17.

Forty cars of up to 600 cubic inches lined up for the $27,550 purse, the largest in racing. The best of Mercedes and FIAT challenged American machines. In the end

The field lined up before the start of the inaugural Indy 500 in 1911. Photograph used with permission of IMS Properties.

it was the 1910 AAA champion Ray Harroun, with a one hundred mile stint by a relief driver, who won in his Marmon Wasp.

For the following year the purse was doubled to $50,000 and the field limited to 30 cars, although only 24 made the race. Ralph DePalma's Mercedes, with an eleven-minute lead, failed on lap 197, setting a pattern of late lap leader failures that are a permanent part of the legend of the speedway.

To gain credibility C.A. Sedwick, on behalf of the track, went to Europe in 1912 to secure many of the best factory Grand Prix cars and drivers. For the next five races the Europeans dominated the 500 with Peugeot taking three victories. Victories at the speedway demonstrated that European motor technology was years ahead of American.

In 1923 a new type of car came to the speedway, single seaters eliminating the riding mechanic.

After leading the speedway from a dirt field to the single most important race facility in the world, Carl Fisher sold the

Pat Flaherty takes the drink of milk and accepts the Borg Warner trophy for winning the 1956 Indianapolis 500. Courtesy of IMS.

track in 1927 to former driver and World War flying ace, Eddie Rickenbacker.

By the late twenties most of the factory backed teams had withdrawn so in January 1929, in order to encourage more private teams, rules were revised allowing 366 cubic inch motors and banning superchargers but requiring riding mechanics again. This separated Indy rules from those governing the European Grand Prix cars.

The speedway was not Rickenbacker's only concern. He was president of Eastern Air Lines and on the board for the new Roosevelt Raceway. Under his reign the track remained the premier American circuit, but as the world slipped into war the track slipped in professionalism. During the war the track was neglected, the result being broken bricks and grass growing up through the corners. The stands and buildings had become unsafe.

After the war Rickenbacker sold the track to Anton "Tony" Hulman, Jr., One of Hulman's first moves was to

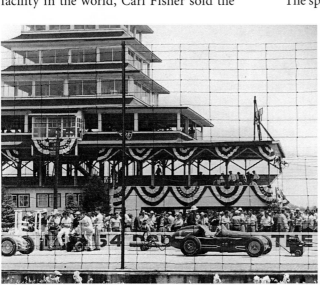

For years the Pagoda was the symbol of the speedway as here in 1954. Courtesy of Bob Sheldon.

In 1993 NASCAR tested at the Speedway in the first incursion that led to the Brickyard 400. Courtesy of Dudley Evans.

make Wilbur Shaw president and general manager. Under Shaw's leadership the track was again the premier race facility. Shaw died in 1954 but Hulman continued to reinvest in the track, adding and upgrading every year to keep the track at the forefront. By the mid–1960s the race was the largest single day sporting event in the world, hosting over 400,000 fans. Pole position day was the second most attended event, often having over 200,000 fans. The other three qualifying days, plus practice sessions, brought in several hundred thousand more.

Upon Tony Hulman's death in 1977, leadership of the track passed to several presidents and a committee of the Hulman/George family until Tony George, Hulman's grandson, took over. Under George's leadership the speedway hosts a NASCAR and IROC race, generating crowds as large as the Indy 500, and, beginning in 2000, the United States Grand Prix.

10 MERCER
America's First Great Race Car

The first great American racecar was a result of the resources of two families who joined together in 1909. The Roeblings, Washington II, F.W., and C.B., were descendants of John Roebling, the pioneering bridge designer who built the first suspension bridge over the Ohio River then began a bigger version from Brooklyn to Manhattan, though the latter was completed by his son Washington. The Roeblings were experts in metallurgy. Washington II was a founder of the Roebling-Planche Speed Car company.

John and Anthony Kuser, and William White, joined with the Roeblings to build a car. Finley R. Porter was hired as Chief En-

gineer. For a name the founders chose Mercer, the county of their Trenton, New Jersey, home. The first race was in the Wheatley Sweepstakes, a support race for the 1910 Vanderbilt Cup races featuring cars of smaller motor displacement. E.H. Sherwood finished fourth in a yellow modified "Raceabout." In the first years race cars, even at the top level, were basically road cars with fenders and other unnecessaries removed.

Two stock 300 cu. in. T-head Mercer Raceabouts ran in the inaugural 1911 Indianapolis 500, finishing 12th (Hughie Hughes) and 15th (Charles Bigelow) despite being the smallest cars in the 40-car field. In road races at Elgin, Fairmount Park, Oakland, Tacoma and Savannah they were always a threat and usually won in the light car class.

To remain competitive for 1912 a new race car was needed. Erik Delling was hired to design it, and his Type F (a long-stroke T-head) placed an amazing third in the 1912 Indianapolis 500 with Hughes driving and Eddie Pullen riding even though they lost a lot of time in running out of gas and making seven pit stops for tires.

Two of the three Mercers entered in the 1913 Indianapolis 500 were the new Model 45 with 424 cu. in. engines (Ralph DePalma and Caleb Bragg). Both broke, but Spencer Wishart placed an even more amazing second behind Goux's Peugeot in his 300 cu. in. Type 35 with relief from DePalma. In August DePalma won the light car race at Elgin in a Type 35.

DePalma's win with his old Mercedes over Oldfield's Mercer at the 1914 Santa Monica Vanderbilt was told in Chapter 7, but Eddie Pullen won for Mercer in the Grand Prize run there two days later.

The season was marred when Wishart, going for a fourth straight win in the Elgin Sweepstakes, crashed and was killed. Pullen finished the season with a win in the Corona Road Race, the fastest race ever at that time.

Eddie Pullen poses with his stock Mercer Raceabout at a period board track. From the collection of Tom Saal.

After Delage and Peugeot swept the first four places at Indianapolis in 1914 with ohc engines, Mercer followed suit. But Delling's design proved fragile, and the three cars entered in the 1915 "500" were withdrawn early. Revised for 1916 but too late for Indy, Pullen debuted one at Sheepshead Bay on September 5th but fared poorly at the final Vanderbilt and Grand Prize races at Santa Monica in November, failing to finish either. There were other feeble attempts prior to WWI, but the glory days of the Mercer were over. By the mid–1920s the Mercer motor car company had been sold into receivership and soon disappeared.

11 STUTZ
The Car That Made Good in a Day

The day that led to the company slogan was Memorial Day, 1911. A single Stutz car was entered in the Indianapolis 500, not so much to race but as a means to test rear axle transmissions, which the Stutz Auto Parts Company hoped to sell to other auto manufacturers. The Stutz did not win, but it finished eleventh when finishing at all was an accomplishment. Soon customers were ordering, not only transmissions, but entire cars.

Harry Stutz started the Stutz Manufacturing Company in Dayton, Ohio. In 1897 he adapted a gas motor for his first four-wheeled vehicle. In the earlier part of the 1900s he designed vehicles for the American Car Company and the Marion Motor Car Company before starting the Stutz Auto Parts Company in 1909.

The new Stutz car was part of the Ideal Motor Car Company. Following on the positive press of the 1911 race a line of cars was produced including a four-door roadster and a five passenger family vehicle. The most famous road car, based on 1911 racer, was the Stutz Bearcat, the first true American sportscar. The Bearcat was little more than the racecar with fenders and lights and was an immediate success.

Racing success followed in 1912 with a fourth at Indianapolis, a fourth at the Vanderbilt Cup and a third in the 300-mile American Grand Prize race. The year 1913 was great for the fledgling company. Earl Cooper won the AAA National road racing championship with wins at Santa Monica, Tacoma and Corona. Charles Merz finished third at Indianapolis with the 389.7 cubic inch T head motor. The competition board of the AAA recognized the achievement naming Stutz as the "Car of the Year." Realizing where the fame of the company was coming from, Stutz Auto Parts and the Ideal Motor Car Company merged to become the Stutz Motor Car Company.

Barney Oldfield was the lead driver in 1914, taking a fifth at Indianapolis, the first American car behind four European cars with the new overhead cam motors. For 1915 Stutz had a new motor of the revolutionary Peugeot design and the cars finished third, fourth and seventh. The most spectacular speed event was when E.G. "Cannonball" Baker drove his Stutz the 3,728 mile distance from San Diego to New York in 11 days, 7 hours and 15 minutes, setting off a national obsession for cross country driving.

Cooper took the National Championship again in 1915. But in 1916 the company got out of racing and the original owners sold the name and works.

The Stutz name did not die from racing; just a decade later Gene Schulz won the 1926 Atlantic City stock car race and the 1927 Pikes Peak Hill Climb in a stock Speedster. The following year a Stutz Blackhawk finished second in the 24-hour race at Le Mans, France, with a fifth in 1929. With light fields of special racecars, a lightly modified Stutz finished tenth in the 1930 Indianapolis 500. But the times and worsening depression were catching up with the specialty car company and in 1935 Stutz ceased to produce cars and went out of business.

12 UNITED STATES GRAND PRIX
Prewar

The United States is the most affluent and automobile oriented country in the world. There are more cars and more miles of roads than anywhere else. It is a country where the car has been not a luxury, but for many years a necessity. The U.S. also has more racetracks and more variety in kinds of tracks than any other nation.

International Grand Prix racing has been acknowledged as the pinnacle of motorsports since the inception of the series in the 1900s. While the quality of cars and drivers has varied over the years the world has recognized the Grand Prix as the best of the best. Hosting a Grand Prix, and there is only one per country unless there is a very special exception, is a matter of national pride.

Yet for all this, the history of the Grand Prix in the United States has been spotty at best.

The first American use of the term Grand Prize, Grand Prix in French, was by the Automobile Club of America (ACA) for the International Grand Prize road race. Ascribing to the Gordon Bennett rulings the entrants were associated with national auto clubs and the royalty of Europe.

Savannah: 1908–1911

In Paris new rules for weight limits were initiated for international racing. The AAA and the Vanderbilt Cup refused to go along as the rules favored the specially made European cars over the more stock American cars. The old Automobile Club of America stepped in and accepted European rules, including the use of the military for crowd

control, and was granted the Grand Prix modeled after the French Grand Prix. The rights to the race were determined by placed bids, with the Savannah Automobile Club winning for their 17 mile course. Using Georgia convict labor the length was increased to 25.3. The purse was twice what was offered for the Vanderbilt race. Six Italian, five French, three German and six semi-stock American cars were entered in the first race. Louis Wagner won in a 737 cubic inch FIAT in 6 hours, 10 minutes, 31 seconds.

The race was not run in 1909 but was resumed in Savannah in 1910, reduced to 17.3 miles per lap. Though an amateur, David Bruce-Brown won with a 920 Benz. American cars finished third through sixth after the Grand Prix cars dropped out.

An American car first led a Grand Prix in 1911 when Patschke put his Marmon up front, but at the end it was David Bruce-Brown this time with a FIAT. By the age of 21 Bruce-Brown had finished the inaugural Indianapolis 500 and in a factory FIAT led the French Grand Prix at Dieppe by over two minutes before his fuel tank was knocked loose. A member of New York society, Bruce-Brown was handsome and skilled, credited by no less than

Savannah, Georgia, hosted the first Grand Prize race in America. From the collection of Tom Saal.

Ralph DePalma as "one of the greatest drivers."

Milwaukee: 1912

On the last day of practice the 22-year-old David Bruce-Brown and his riding mechanic were killed when a worn tire let loose causing a crash. American drivers Caleb Bragg and Ralph DePalma seriously considered sitting out the race but reconsidered. For race day nine European and three American cars were waved off at the eight-mile course. Caleb Bragg won in his personally owned FIAT when DePalma crashed his Mercedes on the last lap after the flamboyant Tetzlaff's FIAT dropped out after alternating between lap records and tire stops.

Santa Monica: 1914–1916

Greater Los Angeles was on the other side of the world in 1914, but it was this oceanside suburb that hosted the Grand Prix-Vanderbilt races. The course was 8.4 miles long along city streets beginning on Ocean Avenue and winding through the

Racing was dangerous for fans as well as drivers. At the 1916 Grand Prize race at Santa Monica, California, Lewis Jackson lost control of his Marmon. Jackson, a photographer, a vendor and a spectator were killed. It was the last Grand Prize race in America. From the collection of Tom Saal.

city. Hollywood film crews recorded much of the race producing footage that found its way into several movies. The Mercer with driver Eddie Pullen won by over half an hour.

The last official Grand Prix in America for over forty years was held in Santa Monica in 1916. Dario Resta and American John Aitkin were competing for the AAA National Championship of which the Grand Prix counted for points. Resta dropped out and Aitkin won but in the Peugeot started by Wilcox. He received no points and the title went to Resta. Soon afterwards road racing in America was legally banished.

San Francisco: 1915

Like a phoenix the city of San Francisco had re-emerged from the 1906 earthquake, and to celebrate

Pullen, in his Mercedes, won the 1914 Santa Monica race by over half an hour. Peter Helck illustration from *Great Auto Races*, 1975.

San Francisco, trying to show that it recovered from the 1906 earthquake, was hit with torrential rain for the 1915 Grand Prize/Vanderbilt. Peter Helck illustration from *Great Auto Races,* 1975.

New York: 1936–1937

The Vanderbilt Cup races for 1936 and 1937 were not official Grands Prix but featured Grand Prix cars. A group of New York financiers and motorsports enthusiasts, including Indianapolis Motor Speedway owner Eddie Rickenbacker, combined to form the Motor Development Corporation in 1935 to bring the European teams back to America. Roosevelt Raceway was a specially built four-mile long road course with seats for 50,000, including VIP boxes. While American roads in urban areas were hard surface the Long Island track was made of packed dirt, limiting the speed. Only two races were held before disinterest and prewar tensions forced cancellation.

it hosted the Panama-Pacific Exposition. On a February afternoon thirty cars started the race through the wind and heavy rain. The weather reduced the projected crowd of 120,000 to under 50,000. It took five hours for newcomer Dario Resta to take the checkered flag in a Peugeot over the partially paved, partially boarded 3.84 mile course.

13 THE BROTHERS DUESENBERG

Fred (1874) and August "Augie" Duesenberg (1879) were born in Lippe, Germany, then followed their older brother Harry to America after their father died, settling in Rockford, Iowa. Fred began his mechanical career repairing farm equipment. With his introduction to the bicycle Fred found his calling and soon became known as both a builder and racer. With a bicycle built by his own company the 22-year-old Fred set world speed records in 1898. By 1900 he was installing internal combustion motors on bikes. In 1902 he began working with four wheels, starting a love affair with the automobile.

Fred and Augie began modifying and racing cars until, in 1907, a Mr. Mason hired them to make and race a car with his name. Success led to the company being bought by washing-machine magnate Frank

Maytag. The two balanced each other, with Fred being outgoing, a natural promoter and full of ideas, while the quieter Augie made Fred's ideas work. Both were workaholics before there was such a term.

Using their experience from Mason the brothers began making race cars under their own name. In addition, Fred's designs were used for aircraft and marine motors and led to the "walking-beam" engine (named for the big rocker arms and side valves). With this Fred designed the straight eight-cylinder motor that provided the standard for reliable powerful motors for the next two decades. A Formula Libre race was held at Brighton Beach, N.Y., in 1912. Against cars with much larger motors two Duesenberg-designed Masons with 350 cubic inch straight fours took first and second. The first major win under the Duesenberg name was in the 1915 Glendale Road Race.

Peugeot had first built the modern race engine for 1912. It featured dome shaped combustion chambers, gear driven overhead camshafts, cup-type cam followers, the spark plug mounted in top of the combustion chamber and knock off wheels, plus superior metallurgy. A Peugeot won the Grand Prix that year and Indianapolis the next. Mercedes followed with a similar motor and the two manufacturers dominated the mid–1910s.

After learning from race engine rebuilds, Duesenberg motors were advancing in sophistication with two, four, six and eight cylinder versions that were used by the military for marine motors and a 300 horsepower aircraft engine. Partnering with Chicago's Loew-Victor Engine Company, they produced new motors intended for a Duesenberg passenger car. During the period the new company moved from St. Paul, Minnesota, to Chicago, Illinois, to Elizabeth, New Jersey, and finally to Indianapolis, Indiana.

By 1919 Tommy Milton was team leader for Duesenberg's racing efforts. His position in the team was so secure that he could threaten to quit the team if his 23-year-old protégé Jimmy Murphy was not given a drive. Murphy got the drive.

When the 300 cid engine formula ended for 1920 Milton put two of the now obsolete motors together for a 16 cylinder land speed record car known as the "Double Duesie." While he was racing in Havana, Murphy, unknown to Milton, ran the car on the Daytona beaches at speeds up to 152 mph for a new land speed record. After cleaning the sand out of the car Milton took it back and upped the record to 156 mph.

Dissatisfaction set in between Milton, Murphy and Fred Duesenberg with Milton leaving the team to win the Indianapolis 500 in a Frontenac in 1921 and in a Miller in 1923. Murphy, winner of the French Grand Prix in 1921 and Indianapolis in 1922, died in a crash at Syracuse in 1924.

By the 1920s many technical differences between American and European cars were due to the differences in race tracks. European races were run on road circuits so a successful race car had to have superior handling and braking. Mid-range power was important. Whether dirt, boards or bricks, American racing was on oval tracks. The last road race was at Elgin in 1920. American racing motors were built for sustained high speed running. Ironically when Murphy won at France with a Duesenberg his advantage was with superior brakes.

The twenties began with a new secret Duesenberg weapon, though even the creators did not know the extent of the potential. John Boling's 1920 Indy car had a supercharger, a mechanically driven blower that forced air into the motor creating more power. The first car was noisy but not noticeably faster that year. Duesenberg would need until 1924 to release the hidden forces when Joe Boyer took over from starter L.L. Corum and quickly took the lead at the Indianapolis 500. He held on for the win with the developed supercharged 121cid straight eight. Rules only dealt with engine size, and the Duesenberg was within limits. In 1925 Pete DePaolo, nephew of Ralph DePalma, won at Indianapolis in another supercharged Duesenberg, the first to win at over 100 mph. By the seasons end he earned the AAA driving title.

The 1920s saw Duesenberg and Miller designs borrowing from each other, an innovation in one motor soon finding its way to the other and then back. The competition between the two companies, between the two designers, and even between the east coast and west coast culture produced some of the greatest leaps in motor design of any period. Both had experience with aircraft motors and by the mid-decade were well ahead of what was being done in Europe. This was a stunning reversal from how thoroughly European designers had dominated American racing a decade earlier.

After winning the French Grand Prix in a Duesenberg Jimmy Murphy installed a Miller engine in the chassis and won the 1922 Indianapolis 500. In 1927 rookie George Souders won Indy. He did not get to enjoy his win though as he died racing that same summer. Pete DePaolo's win at Altoona two weeks later was the last win for a Duesenberg and in July he was in a Miller.

Despite their many combined skills neither of the brothers were great businessmen and in 1927 the Duesenberg line was absorbed by Errett Lobban Cord who only produced passenger cars. Five years later Fred died from complications after a 1932 car crash. Augie died in 1955.

14 Duesenberg Wins at the French Grand Prix

Grand Prix racing did not immediately resume after the cessation of hostilities in 1918 and even when the races *were* held it was difficult for organizers to attract a full field of quality cars. A major problem was that the two premier prewar cars, Peugeot and Mercedes, were built by the two major antagonists of the Great War. For the organizers of the 1921 French Grand Prix, the Automobile Club of France (ACF), a solution was to invite American cars to participate. Beginning in 1921 the *Association Internationale des Automobiles Clubs Reconnus* had changed the rules for the Grand Prix: cars ran to 183 cubic inches, an identical formula to what the AAA Competition board had approved in 1920.

Subtle restrictions to American cars had kept them away before as all motors had to be tested on dynamometers, which were less than reliable, and there was little economic incentive for the cost of transporting to Europe. Ballot, the leading French race team, used substantial influence to insure that Ballot cars were favored to win.

Then the ACF made a major concession that the dyno bench test was waived. This brought interest to the Duesenberg brothers who were interested in exporting passenger cars to Europe and saw this as an opportunity to showcase their cars. Albert Champion, an American businessman who had been born in France, came forward to pay for transportation of the Duesenberg race team. George Robertson, a former Vanderbilt driver and Army material manager who stayed in France, was hired as team manager. Even the French conceded that the Duesenberg team had organization superior to the European factory teams. Four cars were sent along with drivers Jimmy Murphy, Joe Boyer, Albert Guyot, and Louis Inghibert plus Augie Duesenberg. Firestone distributor Barney Oldfield had gum-dipped tires prepared with his name on them. The French course was 10.7 miles of crushed stone over a sand bed.

Ballot entered four cars, one for American Ralph DePalma.

While unfamiliar with European style road racing it was soon apparent that the Duesenbergs had a major advantage, all using Lockheed style hydraulic brakes. When chief mechanic and Murphy's riding mechanic Ernie Olson modified the front shoes to the Ballot style of smaller front brakes, the Duesenbergs were vastly superior to the best of Europe. After calculations to show that it was better to drive back to the pits on the rim rather than stop on the course to replace a tire, the Duesenbergs went off without the normal spare tire. All did not go well though as Murphy crashed and received a broken rib. Then Inghibert had to withdraw. Andre Dubonnet, a wealthy but talented amateur, took over the car.

Thirteen cars took the green in 30-second intervals on July 25th. By the second lap Murphy took the lead. The deteriorating track surface began to take its toll and Murphy came into the pits to have his tires inspected but was quickly sent back out. Ballot driver Jean Chassagne had taken the lead until he was forced to retire on lap 17 when a stone ruptured his gas tank. Murphy retook the lead. Guyot was running second when his mechanic was hit in the head by a rock. The resulting pit stop to remove the injured man dropped Guyot back to sixth.

Meanwhile Murphy was building up his lead until the 29th lap when a tire blew and a rock went through his radiator. This forced a second pit stop. The crew watered down the motor as they replaced the tire and Murphy was back out. Despite taking it easy to keep the now air cooled motor from overheating he still had trouble when another tire blew on the last lap. Still he won the race by almost fifteen minutes at an average speed of 78.1 mph for the 321.78

Jimmy Murphy and the Duesenberg were too much for the European cars at the 1921 French Grand Prix. Peter Helck illustration from *Great Auto Races*, 1975.

miles. DePalma was second with Dubonnet fourth and Guyot sixth.

Representatives of the Ballot Company were furious, proclaiming a moral victory, for whatever morals they had in mind. Murphy received a small medal but the organizers did not, as prescribed by tradition for the nationality of the winning car, play the Star Spangled Banner at the awards ceremony. The rantings of Ballot officials continued through the victory dinner.

Champion was detained as a traitor for not having served in the French Army despite being an American citizen. He was released after intervention by the State Department.

The Duesenberg brothers advertised the accomplishment in order to promote the passenger cars and within a few weeks the Paris office was flooded with orders, so many that the company could not meet the demand, causing a loss of credibility

The following year Murphy took the same car, with a Miller motor, to victory at Indianapolis. Photograph used with permission of IMS Properties.

in Europe from which they never recovered.

The following year Murphy won the Indianapolis 500. He was killed on the dirt mile at Syracuse in 1924 in his own Miller. It would be forty-six years before another American driver would win a Grand Prix race in an American car.

15 HOLY TRINITY AND THE MIRACULOUS MOTORS
Miller, Offenhauser, Goossen

For over half a century variations of a single race engine dominated the top level of American racing and the imagination of the public. It was the result of three very different but equally talented individuals and the synthesis of their abilities and dreams. ˙

Henry Armenius Miller was born in Wisconsin in 1875. At age 13, over parental objections, he left school to become a ma-chinist. He showed an early genius for creative ideas, though he often moved on before the creation was finished. Lacking formal training, he relied on intuition for what was right. At age 18 he moved to Los Angeles where he later opened a machine shop. While working with bicycles he may have built the first motorcycle in the U.S. He is credited with the first outboard gas boat motor. He didn't bother to patent it,

A brilliant engineer but unsuccessful business-man, Harry Miller conceived and developed the Miller 91 race car and the Offy motor. Photograph used with permission of IMS Properties.

something which Olie Evinrude did and began an empire.

Miller's first interest was in carburetors and the Miller Carburetor Company was the backbone of his work.

Fred Offenhauser was born in Los Angeles in 1888. He joined Miller in 1913 and quickly took over the shop where his pragmatic sense of order mated well with Miller.

Racing history was forever changed when, because of an engine failure in 1914, Bob Burman brought his Peugeot to Miller for a rebuild. Miller and Offenhauser studied the most advanced race engine in the world and duplicated the original. The pair made changes after noticing opportunities for improvement that resulted in the finished motor having ten horsepower more than the original. One change was to reduce displacement from 345 cid to 296 to fit the new 1915 formula. They also changed to a single overhead cam, like on the Mercedes Grand Prix car. In 1916 Barney Oldfield came to Miller for an all-new car. Miller and Oldfield developed a fully enclosed race car called the "Golden Submarine." Oldfield took it to numerous races and had many wins and international closed course records.

Leo William Goossen was working as a draftsman for the Buick car company when, in 1919, health problems forced him to move to the Southwest. Fortune led him to Miller's shop. One of his first assignments was to design an engine for drivers Tommy Milton and Ira Vail to beat the winning Duesenberg straight-eight.

Cliff Durant had commissioned the straight-eight 183. By July Milton was winning races and the Miller 183 was the motor to have. Jimmy Murphy installed a Miller 183 in the chassis from his 1921 French Grand Prix winning Duesenberg to win the 1922 Indianapolis 500. Harry Hartz was second in an identical car. Murphy went on to take the 1922 AAA National Championship.

Harry Stutz also bought Miller cars which he renamed Stutz HCS Specials.

The following year Milton won the race with the ultra slim Miller 122, the first two-time champion. After his defeat, Murphy responded by requesting a front wheel drive race car. The resulting car was low and sleek. In the 1925 race, against the turbocharged Duesenbergs, a Miller "Junior Eight" finished a close second, in large part due to the excellent handling of front wheel drive.

The following year saw the introduction of the 1.5-liter formula and the supercharged Miller 91, an evolution of the Junior Eight. Considered by many as the most beautiful pure racing car ever built, the 91 had a supercharged straight-eight with 250 bhp. Over its effective life the 91 was raced in both front and rear wheel drive versions. Top speed was in excess of 170 mph. The famed French Bugatti was modeled after the 91.

In 1926 rookie Frank Lockhart won the Indianapolis 500 over Harry Hartz in another 91 as the make took the first four places. The following year Miller 91s took the top seven qualifying spots and finished with eight of the top ten finishing spots.

Leon Duray's pole time stood for nine years, a record. Louis Meyer won the 1928 Indy 500 in a Miller 91 and the following year Miller cars won all twelve AAA championship races, including a win by Ray Keech at Indianapolis. Keech did not get to enjoy the victory as he was killed in a racing accident at Altoona June 15, 1929.

The 1.5-liter formula was terminated after 1929 and with it the Miller 91. Racer and customer Frank Lockhart began modifying his Miller house car, fixing many shortcomings obvious to him until Miller told him to cease. Lockhart then bought the car outright and the improved version was competitive throughout the 1930s. The land speed record event in which Lockhart was killed was run in a Stutz Blackhawk, built around two Miller 91 motors.

A version of the straight-eight, as used by Fred Frame in winning Indianapolis in 1932, was a 4-cylinder 90 cubic inch motor that was especially suited for the USAC midget series. Versions of this Offy continued to win through the 1980s. Miller was a genius but he was not a businessman. He merged with George Scholfield to form Team RELLIMAH (H.A. Miller backward) but the business went bankrupt in 1933. After several other failed businesses, lacking an Offenhauser or Goossen to edit his ideas, Miller died in Detroit in 1943.

Goossen continued to work on a wide variety of aircraft and marine motors, each an evolution of the preceding motor. In 1943 he designed the front wheel drive transmission for Lou Moore's Blue Crown Specials that dominated early postwar Indianapolis 500s. In addition he co-designed the Novis. In 1946 Offenhauser sold the company that bore his name to Louis Meyer and Dale Drake. Drake took full control in 1966 with a prime asset being Leo Goossen.

By the mid 1950s the Offenhauser was king of American racing, in champ cars, sprint cars and midgets.

For two decades the normally aspirated Offenhauser motor dominated American open wheel racing. Variations of the motor were succesful for half a century. From the collection of J.A. Martin.

In 1963 Ford challenged for Indy supremacy with a stock block pushrod V-8 and returned in 1964 with a four-cam pure race engine not unlike the Miller dual overhead cam Ford motor of 1932.

Drake and Goossen devised another incarnation in the venerable Offy motor when they reduced the capacity to 183 cubic inches and added a turbocharger. Art Sparks designed a new narrow angle valve head that improved combustion called the SGD (Sparks-Goossen-Drake). Mounted in the rear of an Eagle or McLaren chassis the turbocharged Offy continued to win races through the late 1970s until USAC, in the interest of safety, reduced the on-board fuel allowed. As power levels were raised, the Offy used more fuel than the new Ford Cosworth V-8, and when USAC required 1.8 mpg the days of the Offy were over. Goosen and Drake also died in the mid 1970s, a symbolic end to the engine that dominated American motor racing for over half a century and was finally defeated by regulations, not power.

16 FRANK LOCKHART

Only the term nova seems to fit the career of California driver Frank Lockhart. In a life that spanned only 25 years Lockhart achieved things that few drivers do in their lifetimes.

Frank was brilliant and fast. Though he never graduated from high school, his grasp of engineering concepts got him accepted to Cal Tech. But it was applying engineering to racing that he really loved. He built his own car, though it was with other people's that he dominated southern California racing in the early 1920s.

In 1926 he went to Indianapolis looking for a ride. When Pete Kreis, a driver for the Miller team, became ill the ride was offered to rookie Lockhart. Unfamiliar with the track (he had never previously raced on pavement), he qualified back on the sev-

Frank Lockhart designed and built the twin Miller powered Stutz Blackhawk for an assault on the land speed record at Daytona Beach (Florida) for 1928. He died in the car in April 1928. Photograph used with permission of IMS Properties.

enth row. But at the green flag he showed he was a quick learner. By lap thirty he had moved into second and twenty laps later he took the lead which he held until the race was stopped by rain at 400 miles. He was a winner at 23. At the end of the season he took second in the points championship, though he missed the early races.

Lockhart wanted to fit an intercooler on the supercharger of his Miller, causing conflict between him and team owner Harry Miller. Lockhart bought the car and left the team. He converted it for land speed record attempts. His top run at the Mojave desert was 171 mph from a car with 1.5 liters. The absolute record at the time was 175 by the English 22.3 liter Bluebird.

He returned to Indianapolis for the 1927 race and led 300 miles before the engine failed. Still money from laps led was enough to help him finance a new speed record car, the Stutz Blackhawk, powered by two side by side coupled Miller motors that, with supercharging, produced over 400 horsepower from 3.0 liters. His first run was on the beach at Daytona, Florida, in February 1928 where he achieved 225 mph before the car flipped. Lockhart was uninjured. In April he returned with a repaired car. A tire blew during a run and Lockhart was killed in the crash.

The car Lockhart had built for the 1928 race was competitive, and in 1929 propelled Ray Keech to the win. The car was still competitive in 1940.

17 LAND SPEED RECORD
To 1939

Since the beginning of history, and probably before, the speed record for a manned conveyance was achieved with a horse. The nineteenth century began with a challenger, the steam powered train, and by the latter part of the nineteenth the railed monsters were able to outrun a horse and do it for an extended period.

The first personal vehicles to run at train-like speeds were bicycles with internal combustion motors. But even as motorcycles were upping the speed ante a new challenger was making its presence known, the automobile. By 1898 speed records were recorded and recognized, the first mark being 39.245 mph set in Acheres, France, by an electric Jeantayd.

The first attempt by a gasoline powered vehicle (and the first by an American) was a French Mors driven by William K. Vanderbilt, Jr., at Ablis, France, in August 1902. He attained the unheard of speed of 76.08 mph. Three months later the record was broken by another Mors. Vanderbilt returned to America and organized the Vanderbilt Cup races in 1904.

The first attempt by an American in an American car in America was by Henry Ford in 1903. His purpose was purely commercial: a record would give recognition to his Ford Motor Company. Two crude four cylinder cars were built, the 999 and the Arrow. At nearly seventy horsepower they were the most powerful American built cars to date.

Ford drove the Arrow, and Barney Oldfield drove the 999 in closed course races. To make his run Ford had a three mile section of Lake St. Clair cleared. On January 12th, with Spider Huff working the engine, Ford drove the Arrow to 91.37 mph. Since the AAA used mechanical timers rather than the electronic timers used by the Automobile Club of France the record was not acknowledged internationally. This didn't really matter to Ford as the publicity factor was exactly what he hoped for.

A frozen lake was not everyone's site for a speed record. The most popular was the Daytona-Ormond beach in Florida. It was here that Vanderbilt retook the record by going 92.30 mph in a Mercedes on January 27, 1904. Later that year Willie K., with a 90 horsepower Mercedes, became the first to top 100 mph with a run of 102.85 mph. Like Ford's record, it was not acknowledged by the international community.

Englishman Arthur MacDonald brought a Napier to Daytona in January 1905, going 104.651, only to see his record broken an hour later by American Herbert L. Bowden in a homemade twin engine Mercedes. His record of 109.756 mph was disqualified for the car's excessive weight.

The Stanley brothers, Francis E. and Freelan O., brought a steam powered vehicle to Daytona in 1906. Driver Fred Marriott took the "Bug" to 127.66 mph, then hit 121.57 mph for a measured kilometer on the return run.

Daytona Beach was the place for Americans to set records in the century's second decade. Barney Oldfield used a Benz to raise the mark to 131.267 mph on March 23, 1910. A month later Bob Burman took another Benz to 141.732. Ralph DePalma went 149.875 on February 17, 1919, and Tommy Milton hit 156.047 on April 27, 1920.

Tommy Milton built the "Double Duesey" and ran it at Daytona Beach for a new one-way land speed record in 1920. Peter Helck illustration from *Great Auto Races*, 1975.

English and French drivers split the next group of records until Ray Keech hit 207.553 on April 19, 1928. After having set four records on European runs, Sir Malcom Campbell brought his Bluebird to Daytona Beach for a record run of 246.088 on February 5, 1931.

As speeds increased it was obvious that the beach was not long enough for future runs. Campbell took his Bluebird to Bonneville, Utah, where the salt is virtually flat for almost fourteen miles, and away from any inhabited area. Campbell's first run on March 7, 1935, was good for 276.710 mph and his second on September 3, 1935, was 301.13 mph for the record. After that English drivers George Eyston and John Cobb traded marks at Bonneville with Cobb hitting 369.741 on August 23, 1939 before the war put a hold on further attempts at the record.

After the war Cobb returned to Bonneville with the same car to raise the mark to 394.20 on September 16, 1947.

18 STICKS INSTEAD OF BRICKS
Racing on the Boards

As early race speeds climbed it was obvious that the dirt of the dual-purpose horse racing tracks was not going to be an appropriate surface for the one-mile and larger tracks. Potholes were often fatal and dust was a serious factor at high speeds. For real high speed racing a solid surface was needed.

As asphalt at the beginning of the century wouldn't hold up to a race car the options were brick, or wooden boards. The Indianapolis Motor Speedway was the most famous track to use bricks.

The alternative seemed like a great idea, boards, smoother than dirt, cheaper than concrete or bricks, and fast. When the boards were new the speed potential was incredible. If only they weren't so vulnerable to the weather and termites.

Fred Moscovics' plan in 1910 was for a perfect one-mile banked track in southern California. With $20,000 from local backers he built the track of Oregon pine near Playa del Rey, a Los Angeles suburb. The shape was intended to allow drivers to top 100 mph. The first race was held on April 8, 1910. The track lasted four years until destroyed by fire. The following year a half-mile track was opened at Elmhurst, California, like Playa del Rey, designed by former British bicycle racer Jack Prince. The design was greatly influenced by bicycle and motorcycle velodromes of the times.

In 1915 the first Midwest board tracks were the mile at Des Moines and the two-mile Maywood superspeedway near Chicago. Maywood had 45 degrees of banking and in the first year outdrew the Indy 500 by 20,000 fans. A 1.25-mile track opened soon after in Omaha, Nebraska.

Of course New York had to have a track, a two-mile oval at Sheepshead Bay near Brooklyn. By 1919 these last four tracks were gone. The two-mile oval at Tacoma, Washington, lasted through 1921.

Despite their short life span, new tracks were built as fast as old ones were lost. Uniontown, Pennsylvania (1916–22), got a 1.125-mile track and Cincinnati, Ohio (1916–19), got a two-mile track.

The glamour of racing was tied to movie stars with the Beverly Hills (1920–24) track. But the land became too valuable, and the track was dismantled. Organizers tried again at Culver City but limited resources and a non-completed access highway doomed the track. The 1.25-mile tracks were built in 1921 at San Carlos and Cotati but lasted just two seasons.

Other board tracks were built at Rockingham, New Hampshire (1925–28), Charlotte, North Carolina (1924–27), Altoona, Pennsylvania (1923–31), Laurel, Maryland (1925–26), Fulford-by-the Sea near Miami, Florida (1926), Akron, Ohio (1926–30), Bridgeville, Pennsylvania (1927–30), Fresno, California (1920–27), and Kansas City, Missouri (1922–24).

New Jersey entered the era of boards with tracks at Atlantic City (1926–28) and Woodbridge (1928–31).

Jack LeCain in the No. 18 Delage easily won the 50 lap consolation race at the two mile Sheepshead Bay (NY) board track in October 1916. From the collection of Tom Saal.

Board tracks were as temporary as the speed records they encouraged. In 1915 Ralph DePalma won the Indy 500 at 89.84 mph. A month later Dario Resta won on the Chicago boards at 97.58 mph. With banking that was impossible with bricks or concrete of the 1920s, speeds were incredible.

For many years the majority of the AAA championship schedule was held on board tracks, such as 1916 with ten of nineteen races. In 1928 it was six of eight races.

Success bred failure. Banking that allowed such great speeds made driving skills almost irrelevant. Passing was nearly impossible and board races became processions.

The Depression of the early 1930s dried up funding for new board tracks, and the snows of Pennsylvania and the sun of Los Angeles were disastrous. Even during

races carpenters would pop up between boards to hammer the surface back down. With none of the modern preservatives, life expectancy was five years at most. Dirt tracks were easier to maintain. Track surfaces that once carried Millers were turned into firewood or construction of more permanent buildings. Boards of the Laurel, Maryland, track became stores that catered crabs and vegetables to tourists between Baltimore and Washington to the Chesapeake Bay beaches.

Board tracks became obsolete when improvements in concrete and blacktop made permanent hard surface roads practical. Within a few years all the boards were torn up, some becoming buildings that still stand, though not as monuments to a passing moment.

19 THE VANDERBILT TROPHY, ROOSEVELT RACEWAY REVIVAL
1936-1937

It had been twenty years since international Grand Prix teams had raced in America, a fact that the 1908 Vanderbilt winner George Robertson and the Motor Development Corporation decided to change. The means was the revival of the Vanderbilt Cup, only this time the course was a closed circuit rather than road racing of a quarter century earlier. Fences and gates provided better crowd control (including ticket lines) and reduced the risk of people being injured.

George Vanderbilt, a distant relative of Willie K., allowed the group to use the family name and a new trophy was commissioned from Cartier, one that was even larger than the original. The purse of $75,000 was almost as large as the $82,525 offered at Indianapolis.

The site was the brand new Roosevelt Raceway, on Long Island, New York. The track crossed the runways used by Lindbergh a decade before where his Paris flight had begun, as the race was to unite American and European racing. Further emphasizing the event's international flavor, the new 300-mile Vanderbilt Cup race was scheduled for October 12, 1936, Columbus Day.

The field was a wide-open assortment of international racers. The only European factory team was from Alfa Romeo of Italy. Led by team manager Enzo Ferrari, Alfa drivers began with the legendary Tazio Nuvolari plus Nino Farina and Antonio Brivio. Bugatti and Maserati also entered their Grand Prix teams. Facing the Italians were Billy Winn, in a dirt track Miller, Bob

Swanson, in a 100 horsepower midget, plus several two-seat Indianapolis cars, all of which looked primitive compared to the new Alfa Romeo 12C-36.

The race held to form, at least in the results. Nuvolari, one of history's all time great drivers, took the lead and went on to an easy victory. But behind him Winn and Swanson were throwing their cars around, and doing an amazing job of keeping up with the Alfa Romeos. Even cars built for the demands of the dirt ovals have physical limits and both drivers fell out leaving the Alfas to collect the inaugural laurels.

After the race the management looked at the results and were not pleased with what they found. Despite being a road course like those in Europe, it was relatively slow, a fact pointed out by more than one European driver. And the crowd was

Alfa Romeo driver Tuvio Nuvolari easily won the first Vanderbilt race in 1935. Courtesy of the EMMR collection.

smaller than anticipated. Changes were needed.

For 1937 the number of corners was reduced and the corner before the main straight was increased in banking. This brought the speed way up. To bring in a bigger crowd the race was moved up to July 3rd. Over 70,000 spectators paid for the only opportunity to see the Grand Prix cars.

For the 1936 Vanderbilt race Germany sent the all conquering Auto Union and Mercedes-Benz cars. They dominated practice and the race. Courtesy of the EMMR collection.

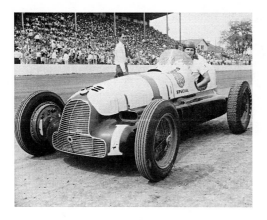

Rex Mays was the most versatile driver of his day, equally competitive at the Speedway or at the Vanderbilt race. Courtesy of Bob Sheldon.

The two German teams, Mercedes Benz and Auto Union, had not participated in the 1936 race; but for 1937, both teams sent cars. With Auto Union came Ernst Von Delius and Bernd Rosemeyer. Mercedes sent Dick Seaman and Rudolf Caracciola. This was more than a race to the two German teams, it was an opportunity to compete and yet get away from the politics in Germany.

Alfa Romeo returned but with little chance, for even their latest car was no match for the Germans. Team leader Nuvolari was back, but his heart was not into the race as his eldest son had recently died. Maserati brought the latest V8Ri then offered the car to American Wilbur Shaw. Though not a factor here, Shaw and the Maserati twice won the Indianapolis 500

in 1939 and 1940. The car was raced at Indianapolis through the mid–1950s as Bill Vukovich used it for his rookie test.

Beside the works Alfa Romeos there was a model 8C-35 that American "Hollywood" Bill White had purchased after the previous year's race and modified. Rex Mays was hired as driver. Mays won four poles in his twelve attempts at Indianapolis but his best finish was a single second.

At the start, delayed two days because of rain, Mays got the jump on Caracciola and Rosemeyer before the German cars asserted their superiority in power. When the supercharger in Caracciola's Mercedes failed Rosemeyer went on to an easy win over Seaman in the other Mercedes, Mays and Von Delius. American driving skills again were greater than American equipment. Although his car was still not up to the race, Billy Winn was a charger and passed Seaman's Mercedes while in a full-lock power slide. Mays' run so impressed the Italians that he was offered a drive with the factory team, which he declined. There was no third race. Events in Europe were moving faster than even motor racing could adjust to.

When the AAA and the CSI joined in a common set of rules beginning in 1937 American teams followed Shaw's lead and bought or copied Grand Prix cars.

Within four years Roosevelt Raceway was converted to a track for horse racing.

20 HIGH SPEEDS IN THE HIGH DESERT

Southern California had been a hotbed of speed even before World War I. The frontier spirit and year round warm weather made the area a natural venue for

those interested in speed. Early efforts were held on the streets but as speed and police enforcement increased so did the need for a place to release the horsepower.

Nearly 100 miles north of Los Angeles are a series of dry ancient lakebeds. Covered with a salt layer, these large flat areas are virtually lifeless. With the yearly rain the surface is resettled to be baked to a white tabletop-smooth finish. Measuring miles across, the lakebeds were the perfect natural location for fast cars. The largest, at 10 by 22 miles, was Muroc Dry Lake.

By the late 1920s a strong hot rod culture had developed around speed runs at Muroc. Cars were modified in Los Angeles garages by backyard mechanics to maximize their performance. Acceleration and handling were not the goal, it was top end, to see how fast a car could go. To support the early rodders specialized performance shops started customizing stock components or developing new hardware. Sponsors provided parts for recognition of assistance.

The first meets were informal runs over marked-off lines against hand held stop watches. This of course led to confusion of who was really faster. In 1931 the first organized events were held, and in 1937 the Southern California Timing Association (SCTA) was formed from several groups who wanted to see a standardized set of rules and safety regulations. The efforts of the SCTA were to promote safety for spectators and drivers alike, provide technical regulations and to work with the California Highway Patrol to encourage speed on the lakes rather than city streets. A second group, the Russetta

Timing Association (RTA), was formed to encourage the use of coupes; SCTA encouraged open racers.

The course was three miles long to gather speed, run a quarter mile timed section, then a slow down area. When the run was over the car was covered with a thin layer of fine white powder, a status symbol back in LA.

Success and the Second World War made major changes to dry lake racing. The draft took most of the participants (young males) and the military took over Muroc Dry Lake as an Army Air Force development center. After the war it was renamed Edwards Air Force Base, site of record breaking flights from Chuck Yeager's X-1 to the current.

The second largest dry lake is El Mirage. More remote and higher than Muroc, El Mirage became the postwar center for speed runs.

Due to World War II a major aircraft industry had been built in greater Los Angeles populated with engineers who had spent the last few years producing power via engines, fuels and structures for performance aircraft. With peace and relative

Terry Nish, in the Royal Purple-Nish streamliner, is pushed off the line at El Mirage Dry Lake (California), 1999. A run of 249 mph set a new A/FS record. Courtesy of Cris Schearer.

wealth their attention turned to making faster cars and more of them. By 1947 the number of entrants often exceeded five hundred. Timing clubs boomed in number, with over twenty by 1950.

Since the beginning of the lake runs the emphasis had been on running hot rods that could be driven to the lake, make a run, then be driven home. With popularity some racers were looking beyond stock to find ways to get more speed and the specialized lakester car was born. Many used war surplus aircraft tanks as effective and cheap, streamlined bodies.

The down side to this progress was that the cars were overrunning the lake. Speeds were getting higher, cutting more tracks in the dried salt. With a dry off-season the basin did not have the opportunity to rebuild itself before the next onslaught of racers.

As the speeds continued to rise it became apparent that the California lakes were too small to safely handle the racers. The fastest racers moved to the beach at Daytona, Florida, and ultimately to the salt flats at Bonneville. Meanwhile the attention of hot rodders turned to drag racing.

21 BILL FRANCE BUILDS NASCAR

Bill France began racing cars in his native Maryland in the 1920s. A consistent winner on area dirt tracks, France was able to support his family by racing. However, the mid–Atlantic racing season was limited by weather. To be able to drive full time he decided to move where racing went on all year, so he packed the family and headed to Florida.

The intention was to go to Miami, but along the way he stopped in the Daytona Beach area where land speed record runs had been made for several decades. The Frances never made it to Miami.

When the land speed record runs were moved to the Bonneville salt flats the Daytona Beach Chamber of Commerce needed a new speed event. Sig Haugdahl laid out a course that used 1.5 miles of beach then 1.5 miles of US Route A-1 with two .1 mile connecting sections. With AAA sanctioning they promoted a 250-mile race for stock cars on March 8, 1936. Entrants included several Indy drivers and the Col-

lier brothers. Milt Marion won, and his mechanic, Bill France, finished fifth.

The post World War II south was a poor region. There were none of the speed shops of the Midwest or California. Few racers could afford specially built race cars. Racing was done with a passenger car on a dirt oval cut from a farmer's field.

After the war France tried to properly organize the Daytona event. He attempted to enlist the American Automobile Association (AAA) but was turned down as stock car racing was not their priority. Not discouraged, he contacted area organizers and drivers to set up a plan for racing stock cars. They met in the Streamline Hotel in Daytona Beach on December 12, 1947, and agreed to the framework that was to become the National Association for Stock Car Auto Racing (NASCAR) with France as President. Eventually NASCAR became a private company owned by the France family.

France insisted that the premier series,

called Grand National, be for late model stock cars, machines with a minimum of alterations necessary for racing, such as adding seat belts and taping over the headlights. The standard low cost racer of the day was the modified "Jalopy," an older passenger car with modified body and engine. This led to many racers driving the car to the race, in the race, then home after the race, with barely an alteration.

Cars and fans alike had little protection in the early 1950s when NASCAR was running on open fields. Courtesy of the EMMR collection.

The first NASCAR race at Daytona was held on February 14, 1948, won by "Red" Byron. In a unique move France contracted all drivers to run exclusively with NASCAR. Eighty-five races were held that first year which climbed to 394 in 1949. Finding drivers and tracks was not a problem. Running illegal moonshine from the Carolina hills kept many families fed during the Depression. To be successful, the moonshine runners had to be faster than the police cars. Vehicles that looked like junkers on the outside often sported the most powerful motors south of Indianapolis. This led to bragging rights of who had the fastest car and who was the most skilled driver. Impromptu tracks were set up in many southern fields, some of which became actual race tracks.

In the 1950s NASCAR grew, organizing races all across the southeast. Other series were organized within NASCAR. To challenge Indianapolis NASCAR ran an open wheel series in the mid–50s with stock block V-8 powered roadsters. A convertible series was added in the mid–50s but later dropped.

Darlington, the first paved super-speedway, over a mile in length, was opened in 1949. To France superspeedways were the way to grow and to give the fans even greater speeds. In 1955 he formed the Daytona Beach Motor Speedway Corporation and by 1959 the track was ready. Lee Petty won the first Daytona 500 by mere inches.

In the years since, NASCAR has grown by adding local tracks across the country, a minor league system that continually feeds drivers to the pinnacle of stock car racing. NASCAR has also grown by adding other professional series. In 1982 the Late Model Sportsman series was added. It was later renamed Grand Nationals and when it received a full time sponsor, became the Busch Series. By the mid–1960s the original Grand National series had grown to over sixty races per year, on road courses, dirt ovals and small and large paved ovals. Races were held almost every night of the week, sometimes one on Friday evening and another, on a different track, on Sunday afternoon. The series was so varied that few drivers made every event. Even the eventual champion rarely raced in every event. This changed in 1971 when Winston cigarettes came in as primary sponsor,

Fonty Flock accepting his trophy from NASCAR official John Marcum after winning the July 8, 1951, Grand National race at Bainbridge Fairgrounds near Cleveland, Ohio. Bill France looks pleased as race promoter John Lemmo tells the story. From the collection of Tom Saal.

from the Teamsters Union, tried to form a drivers union in 1961. France faced down the union and banned Turner for life. That lasted five years. Then in response to safety concerns of the new France track at Talladega, Alabama, the Professional Drivers Association (PDA) was formed, headed by Richard Petty. Fearing that tires were inadequate for the high speeds the drivers threatened to boycott the race. To prove the track was safe, France, now age 60, got into a Ford Torino and cranked out laps at over 175 mph. The race went on with substitute and Grand American (Camaro and Mustang) drivers and mandated tire changes. Eventually NASCAR and the PDA came together, ending with the dissolution of the PDA.

changing the series to the Winston Cup. The following year the series was limited to under thirty races. Gone were Tuesday and Thursday night races, as were the tracks under a half-mile and all dirt tracks. The modern era of NASCAR had begun and will continue in 2004 as the Nextel Cup.

Bill France repelled two threats in the late sixties. Curtis Turner, with backing

Another threat came from Larry LoPatin who planned to operate a group of tracks across the country called American Raceways Inc. Riverside Raceway in California was added to his tracks in Michigan, Texas, and Atlanta. A fifth track was planned for New Jersey. LoPatin felt that owning the tracks gave him rights to challenge how France ran the events. France responded by removing NASCAR sanctioning and freezing the ARI tracks out of the new ABC-TV contract. In the end, LoPatin went bankrupt. Michigan and Atlanta became permanent parts of the NASCAR schedule as did Riverside, until the track closed in 1986. Texas International continues to operate as Texas World Speedway. The New Jersey track was never built.

The France family continues to own NASCAR. Bill France, Jr., took over from "Big

NASCAR racers came in many forms in the 1950s, like convertibles on the Daytona beach. Courtesy of the EMMR collection.

Right: In 1968 Bill France looks over his last great project, the Talladega Speedway. Courtesy of the EMMR collection.

Bill" in 1972. The France family, through the International Speedway Corporation (ISC), owns tracks from California to New York.

Death came to William Henry Getty France on June 7, 1992. Before he became a victim of Alzheimer's disease France had changed racing more than any other person in the history of motorsports.

22 BLUE CROWN SPECIALS

Few teams ever dominated their era as thoroughly as the Blue Crown Specials did between 1947 and 1950. In that four-year span at the Indianapolis Motor Speedway the Blue Crown cars finished 1-2 twice, 1-3, and 2-6-8. It is still an unparalleled record for any team, in any sport.

The team's guiding force was Lou Moore. As a driver Moore had modest but not spectacular success at Indianapolis. Over a ten year span he collected a pole, a second, and two thirds. After he retired from driving Moore entered winning cars for Floyd Roberts (1938) and Mauri Rose/Floyd Davis (1941) before the war stopped racing at the speedway.

After the war Moore was quick to understand the technological changes that the war had brought. In particular, he was interested in the 110 octane aviation gas. He reasoned that in a properly designed car a reliable high compression Offy motor on aviation gas could run the race with only one pit stop. The motor produced only 270

horsepower but pulling a lighter car made the plan realistic.

Moore turned to Leo Goossen for a front wheel drive car, a layout which allowed the driver to sit very low for reduced frontal area. With motor and the Emil Deidt built chassis the car weighed a mere 1,650 pounds.

With the design in hand Moore was able to induce the Blue Crown Spark Plug Company to become primary sponsor. Moore needed sponsorship because each car was to cost about three times the normal price of an Indy car of the period.

When two of the new cars were brought to the Speedway for 1947 Moore included Mauri Rose and rookie Bill Holland to drive. Mauri Rose started third and won in 1947 by ignoring Moore's "EZ" sign from the pits and passing rookie teammate Bill Holland with seven laps to go. Rose and Holland were 1-2 again in 1948, this time without controversy.

A rear drive Blue Crown car was built for 1949 and George Conner was added to

Away from Indianapolis, as at Goshen, NY, Bill Holland's 1947 Blue Crown special was a conventional champ car. Courtesy of Bob Sheldon.

the team. Near the end of the race, with the cars running 1-2-4, Rose in second place, as he had done in 1947, broke with team orders and challenged Holland for the lead. This time Rose's car broke down and Holland got the win. It was the last time Rose drove for Moore.

Despite being in their fourth "500," the three Blue Crown cars were running 2nd, 6th, and 8th when rain began to fall in 1950. Moore could control everything but the weather. The race was red flagged at lap 138.

Moore sold the cars after the 1950 race and moved to NASCAR. It was at a NASCAR race that Moore had a heart attack and died.

Duane Carter and Tony Bettenhausen, with Mobil Oil sponsorship, finished 8th and 9th in the 1951 race.

Mauri Rose (1) (1947 and 48 winner) and 1949 winner Bill Holland (c) in the front wheel drive Blue Crown Spark Plug specials alongside George Conner in the similar rear drive car before the 1949 race. Photograph used with permission of IMS Properties.

23 HAULIN' SHINE AND RACIN' HELL
Good Ole Boys

Bill France's new NASCAR was blessed by a unique group of characters, as diverse as they were colorful.

Stock car racing in the American southeast began in the 1930s as drivers, hauling illegal "shine," built fast stock-looking cars. This required an outlaw, devil-may-care mentality, as failure to be fastest resulted in arrest. One was driver Roy Hall. Despite his conviction for bootlegging, Hall was one of the founding fathers of NASCAR.

Tim Flock went from "haulin' shine" to leading a family of racers. Twice he won the drivers championship. From the collection of J.A. Martin.

Bob and Fonty Flock ran bootleg whiskey for their brother Carl as a way to support the family after their father died in 1928. Their uncle, Peachtree Williams, was a major figure in the Atlanta whiskey business. All the Flocks were used to high speeds. Carl had been a prewar speedboat champion and their sister Reo was an aerial daredevil. Tim, the youngest, became involved in the action after the war and with Bobby and Fonty drove in the first NASCAR sanctioned race at the three-quarter mile at Charlotte, NC. Bob took the pole position with Tim starting second. The best finishing Flock was Tim in fifth.

Tim Flock was one of the first superstars of NASCAR. In 1952, with 16 wins, and again in 1955, with 18 wins, Flock won the Grand National Championship, today's Winston Cup, title.

One of the most aggressive drivers was Curtis Turner. A timberman by family fortune, he raced for the fun of competition, not needing the winnings. When he needed money he'd sell some timber land. When he didn't need money he'd party with reckless abandon. As many as one

hundred people came to a Turner party that often lasted for several days. Turner's parties usually involved a great deal of Canadian Club whiskey, lightly clad young girls and sometimes a handgun. By party's end he would have spent tens of thousands of dollars.

Turner's driving style was no less audacious. He was all out all the way. He didn't bother with setup or trying to conserve the tires. He went for it from the green flag, and if he did not win then it was someone's fault. Turner didn't drive smart, but as team owner Ralph Moody stated "Curtis didn't have to be very smart because he was so good."

In 1961 Turner began construction of a new superspeedway at Charlotte. Needing additional capital, he turned to the Teamsters Union for help. In exchange for assistance Turner tried to form a drivers union. Bill France was so outraged that he promptly banished Turner. But when NASCAR needed public relations help in 1965 during the Chrysler boycott, Turner was allowed to come back.

Turner's favorite toy was his airplane. Long before the contemporary pilot/driver/businessman Turner would fly to races, sometimes landing on public roads for directions or a refill of Canadian Club. He lost his pilot's and driver's licenses more than once for such stunts.

On October 4, 1970, Turner set the plane on automatic pilot and took a nap in the back, leaving his friend Clarence King at the controls. When trouble began Turner awoke and tried to get to the controls. He was too late and both men died when the plane crashed into a Pennsylvania mountain.

Turner's racing buddy and party equal was Joe Weatherly. A former AAA motorcycle champion, the easy going "Little Joe" was also a pilot, former whiskey runner and skirt chaser. Many tales of pranks by early NASCAR drivers stemmed from the off track antics of Turner and Weatherly. They once parked a rental car in a swimming pool. Another time they dragged a mule up to the second floor of a motel as a joke on another driver. They'd usually get caught and have to pay a fine, but that was all right with them as long as they had a good laugh. Weatherly and Turner were rough drivers, on cars and competitors. They'd mess up a $2,000 car to win a $500 prize. They put other drivers in the wall, but the fans loved their reckless driving style. Turner won races but Weatherly also won the Grand National driver's title in 1962 then repeated in 1963. By then he was the most popular race driver in America.

Weatherly was killed at Riverside during the 1964 Motor Trend 500. Transmission problems forced him into the pits early in the race. His crew changed the hot transmission and he went back out, though not in contention. Approaching turn six Joe tried to downshift but the transmission did not catch the lower gear and he hit a retaining wall. Side nets were not then

Curtis Turner, the original hard driving, hard living "Good Ole Boy." Courtesy of Holman Moody.

mandated and Weatherly's head hit the wall.

Edward Glenn "Fireball" Roberts, Jr., was an excellent athlete. A former amateur baseball pitcher (source of the nickname), Roberts was the first driver to have a regular weight training program. But he was also superstitious and shy. From his boyhood in the Daytona Beach area Roberts

Fireball Roberts demonstrates that latest in safety equipment, a strap to keep the hood from popping open. Courtesy of Holman Moody.

wanted to race and got his first chance in 1947. By the mid 1950s he was regularly winning in both the NASCAR Grand National and Convertible divisions. In 1962 he won the Daytona 500 from the pole in a Smoky Yunick Pontiac. In 1963 he took his second Southern 500.

Roberts died in 1964 from a crash on the seventh lap of the World 600 at Charlotte Motor Speedway. Driver Ned Jarrett pulled Roberts from his burning car. Though flame retardant driving suits were available Roberts was allergic to the chemicals and never wore one. He spent the next two months in a hospital. In the end the injuries and burns were more than medicine in 1964 could handle.

The first example of safety fuel cells had been introduced, but NASCAR did not allow them for use in the Charlotte race. By late summer fiberglass fuel cells in a strengthened metal box were approved.

Counter to the Flocks, Turner and Weatherly was Lee Petty. For Lee, and all of the Pettys since, racing is a business, the family's source of livelihood. Lee was more careful knowing that only those who finished races received checks that paid family bills. For his patience Lee won 50 races, the most of any driver until his son Richard passed him. With three championships and the inaugural Daytona 500, Lee was also the model of the thinking driver. He planned and waited, letting Turner and Weatherly wear out their cars, then taking the win. But he was not a pushover to the more aggressive drivers. He'd hold his place and knew enough of their tricks to know how to keep from getting taken out, and if he had to, he knew how to return the favor, but in the manner of "don't do that again."

Lee retired after a 1961 crash at Daytona. By then Richard was ready to take over the driving side of the family business with his brother Maurice handling the wrenches. Lee remained head of Petty Enterprises and played golf until his death in 2000.

The deaths of Weatherly and Roberts brought to an end the era of pioneer "good ole boys." Junior Johnson had, like the Flocks, a moonshine background but he was a thinking driver, as shown by the success of his race team. From the early 1960s a new generation of winners was emerging, ones who knew how to set up and conserve a car to the end. Ned Jarrett won two driver's titles without pushing another driver over the wall and Fred Lorenzen was even born a Yankee. By the end of the 1960s the heroes were the introspective silver fox David Pearson, Richard Petty, the Allison Brothers: Donnie and Bobby, Bobby Isaac, Cale Yarborough and Buck Baker's boy Buddy Baker. These were the men who were to take NASCAR to the next level of national acceptance.

24 HE DID IT HIS WAY
Cunningham Challenges Europe

Sports car racing in the postwar period was entirely a European domain. The manufacturers and circuits were all in Europe, as were the drivers. American interest in sports cars was in its infancy and only the wealthy were able to afford the little imports from England and Italy. American drivers were all "gentlemen racers."

In the early 1950s one of these gentleman built a family of sports cars that seriously challenged the best of Europe.

Briggs Swift Cunningham, Jr., privately financed the cars that bore his name. Cunningham was one of the New England group that had raced at the early Watkins Glen street races, a friend of the Collier brothers and an early member of the fledgling SCCA.

In 1950 Cunningham entered two Cadillacs in the 24 Hours of Le Mans. Both cars were white with blue on the hood. In the following years the marks became the first racing stripes, a standard for American and world sports and F1 cars alike.

One Cadillac was a stock sedan, purchased retail, but the other was one of the ugliest cars to ever roar down the Mulsanne Straight. The French called it "Le Monstre," a nickname inspired by the streamlined slab-sided body, tested at the Grumann aircraft wind tunnel. Gone were the Cadillac curves. Still, the cars were successful with the sedan, driven by Sam and Miles Collier, finishing in tenth place. Cunningham and Phil Walters brought "Le Monstre" home one place behind.

Other innovations were the use of two-way radios between cars and pits and a transporter that carried the cars and supplies and also a tool shop. Not even the top European factories had transporters so fully equipped. In all, it was a very good first effort.

To compete the next year Cunningham needed his own car, not stock or re-bodied cars from another manufacturer. The resulting *Cunningham* was more in the European tradition than the Corvette a few years later. Only a few were built in the West Palm Beach, Florida, shop. Power came from a 400 horsepower Chrysler Fire Power (hemi), developed in conjunction with the Chrysler Corporation. Taking 6,000 man-hours to build with hand-beaten aluminum body panels, the car was expensive.

Cunningham entered three new Cunningham C2Rs in the 1951 edition of the classic race. One C2R crashed just before midnight, a second in the early morning. By then the Phil Walters/John Fitch car was in second place, which they held for six hours. With less than four hours to go the car developed engine trouble. After frequent stops they finished eighteenth.

Cunningham immediately returned to Florida to build a better car, a 900 pound lighter car, the C4R. Three were made for Le Mans 1952, a coupe and two roadsters. One roadster and the coupe were out by late afternoon. But the Fitch/Walters car motored on to finish in fourth place.

Cunningham and Bill Spear led the first 51 laps of the premier Sebring 12-hour race (1952) but dropped out when the axle broke on their Ferrari 340 America.

The year 1953 began with victory for Fitch and Walters in the second 12-hour Sebring race in a C4R. Cunningham cars won again in 1954 (Stirling Moss/Bill Lloyd in an Osca MT4) and 1955 (Walters/Mike Hawthorn in a Jaguar D type) race.

By summer of 1953 Cunninghams were winning sports car races across the country, showing that American equipment could win in international racing. In the best American tradition they were built

"Le Monstre" just before the start of the 1950 24 Hours of Le Mans with Briggs at the wheel. Smith Hempstone Oliver photograph from the collection of Tom Saal.

around a big V-8. It was the philosophy of the design that was picked up for the Corvette and Cobra.

For his efforts Cunningham was featured on the cover of the April 26, 1954, *Time* magazine. Such was the respect for Cunningham that Jaguar had Briggs handle their best factory cars for racing in America.

But in 1953 there was another factor. Jaguar had the best disc brakes. Though the C and D style Jaguars were not the equal of the Cunninghams in top speed, they maintained a disciplined race to take Le Mans again. Behind the Jaguars finished all three Cunninghams, Fitch/Walters third, Cunningham/Spear seventh, and the Moran/Bennett coupe tenth.

To race with higher revs Cunningham bought a Ferrari V-12 for the 1954 race. But it was the V-8 powered C4Rs of Spear and Johnson that took third and the similar car of Cunningham/Bennett was fifth after the Ferrari/Cunningham failed.

For 1955 Cunningham went to a 3-liter Offenhauser for the C6R, a combination that didn't work, thus ending the Le Mans effort with the Cunningham built cars. Mercury Marine later worked with Cunningham in developing an upside down two-stroke V-12 race motor, but that was never completed.

In 1958 Briggs Cunningham successfully skippered the "Columbia" in defense of the America's Cup with a sweep of the event. The "Cunningham," a crucial part of sailboat rigging, was also an innovation of his.

In 1960 Chevrolet made a four car run at Le Mans with stock Corvettes. Three of

John Fitch prepares to take his Cunningham C4R out for practice for the 1952 Le Mans race. Courtesy of Briggs Cunningham.

the cars were turned over to Cunningham. The big V-8s were the largest motors in the field and when rain slowed the pace the Corvettes moved up. Le Mans reality returned when the rain stopped and the high revving Ferraris took over the top spots. At the checkered flag a Corvette was running fourth behind the winning Ferrari. It was to be the highest finish to date for a GM powered car in the French racing classic but a disappointment for Cunningham and a second Corvette effort was not attempted.

Briggs returned to American racing and in the 1960s was the semi-factory Jaguar team, in blue on white. His last race was at Sebring, 1964, where he finished first in class with a Porsche 904.

Briggs Cunningham was never widely known beyond the sports car world, which is the way he wanted it. A "gentleman racer" of the old school, he shied away from publicity when later counterparts hired full time public relations staffs. He died at his home in Las Vegas on July 2, 2003, at age 96. Earlier that year he was inducted into the International Motorsports Hall of Fame in Tallladega, Alabama.

25 IT SURE SOUNDED LIKE A WINNER
Novi

No car/engine combination captured the imagination of the Indy 500 crowd or broke as many hearts as the Novi. The supercharged V-8 was powerful, blasting out a unique sound that seemed to promise that the power could be harnessed and all the years of work would be rewarded. But it was also heavy and thirsty. Though Novi powered cars set qualifying and lap records for two decades, no driver was able to make the mighty motor last long enough to get to victory lane.

The Novi was built to a different set of rules than the Offy. It was 180 cid with a supercharger in a V-8 configuration. The motor weighed 575 pounds. Because of the inefficiencies of early supercharger systems the V-8 required more fuel than the Offy, at least a gallon per lap. Novi powered cars carried as much as 110 gallons on board. Carrying that much weight at the speeds Novi powered cars ran was too much for the tires of the day so numerous pit stops were often required. This made Duke Nalon's 1948 third place finish on two pit stops all that more remarkable.

Supercharging had first been applied to an internal combustion motor in 1907. By the 1920s Duesenberg and Miller cars were supercharged. But as the Contest Board of the AAA realized that supercharging produced additional power, the motor size for non-supercharged cars was raised to 274 cid for 1938 with superchargers being banned until an equitable size relationship was established.

Most motors were straight until 1932 when Ford produced a low cost flathead V-8. A racing version won first through seventh at the 1933 Elgin National Road

Though it never won a race, the Novi rates an honored spot at the Indianapolis Speedway museum. From the collection of J.A. Martin.

Race. Two Ford V-8s were in the 1934 500. For 1935 Preston Tucker was team manager for a semi-factory Indianapolis entry in a car designed by Henry Miller.

Ford employee Lewis W. Welch began a company in Novi, Michigan, that supplied parts to Ford. Welch had been involved with the development of the Ford V-8, especially the race version.

For 1938 Leo Goossen and W.C. "Bud" Winfield created a supercharged straight 8 for Lou Meyer. During development Winfield and Welch offered each other assistance that led to a partnership for the 1940 race. After the race Winfield and Welch discussed combining the advantages of supercharging with a V-8 configuration. A silent hand in this is reported to be Henry Ford who was helping Welch and was in favor of any motor that cast a positive image to a V-8.

Welch and Winfield took the concept to Goossen who laid out the new motor. By early 1941 the new motor was ready at the Offenhauser Engineering Company. Listed as a Winfield V-8 it had three Winfield carburetors, two valves per cylinder off four camshafts and a 90-degree cylinder bank. Horsepower exceeded 450, a figure comparable to the best of the prewar supercharged Mercedes and Auto Union motors. With an intercooler the Winfield had more consistent power.

A single Winfield V-8 powered car, driven by Ralph Hepburn, was entered in the 1941 Indy 500 and finished fourth.

While still officially listed as a Winfield, the name Novi (Welch's company) soon became the popular, then accepted, name for the motor.

Against a field of rebuilt prewar cars the Novi had a new front wheel drive Kurtis chassis for 1946. Hepburn set a new qualifying lap record, though not on pole day. However, an early brake problem put Hepburn six laps down. On lap 121 his race was over due to engine failure.

A second new chassis was built for 1947. Cliff Bergere qualified second, but a stalled motor resulted in a 21st place finish. Herb Ardinger started in the second row then turned it over to Bergere, who finished fourth.

Tires were becoming a problem for the Novi. Additional weight and power, plus the long wheelbase, were placing a greater load resulting in additional pit stops.

After the 1947 race chief mechanic Jean Marcenac reconfigured the new Novi with an enclosed cockpit, streamlined tail, and a higher gear for an assault on the Class D land speed record. D.A. "Ab" Jenkins drove the car at Bonneville to a record 179.434 mph.

The 1948 race was marked with a high and a low for the Novis. After an internal disagreement Bergere left the team. Fifty-two-year old Hepburn came back as a replacement, but on practice for qualifying the car lost traction. Hepburn hit the gas and the car shot into the outside wall. Hepburn died instantly. Bergere began a

Duke Nalon and Novi in 1954. Courtesy of Bob Sheldon.

negative public relations campaign against the remaining Novi. Duke Nalon was hired for the second car. Nalon led portions of the race and finished third, the best a Novi was ever to do.

Nalon continued into 1949, taking the pole position, with Rex Mays qualifying the other Novi second. Nalon's rear axle broke early in the race, resulting in a fiery crash. Mays went out soon after with a stalled engine.

Neither car qualified for 1950.

Nalon returned in 1951 to again put the Novi on the pole. Chet Miller was third fastest qualifier but his ignition failed during the race. The plugs in Nalon's car fouled due to the slow start and he finished tenth.

Miller was the fastest qualifier in 1952 though he started twenty-seventh. Nalon started fourth. Both cars were out by lap 84. It was the last glory for the front wheel drive Novis, now almost ten years old.

For 1956 two new rear-wheel-drive cars were built. Four drivers practiced in one of them, but Paul Russo was the only qualifier in the other and was first car out. But the next year Russo was the fastest qualifier, though he began eleventh and finished fourth. Tony Bettenhausen was ninth fastest in 1957 to finish fifteenth.

Paul Russo qualified this Novi 10th and finished 4th in the 1957 "500." Courtesy of Bob Sheldon.

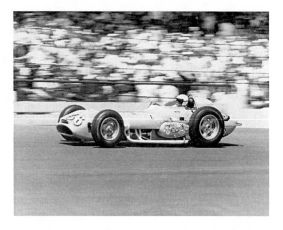

Jim Hurtubise put the Novi in the middle of the front row for the 1963 Indianapolis 500. Once again though speed did not translate into endurance and he was a DNF. Photograph used with permission of IMS Properties.

Russo started fifteenth in 1958 then was caught up in an accident on the opening lap but still continued for 122 laps. Novis were not part of the 1959 and 1960 race, failing to qualify.

Welch's businesses were failing and in 1961 he sold the Novi team to pay a ninety-day note. He tried to develop a diesel engine but industry interest was lacking.

Just when it looked like the Novis were done along came the Granatelli brothers, led by Paxton Products owner Andy. With a Paxton supercharger Novi power was increased to 640. The bright red STP sponsorship matched visual flair to the audio flair of the Novi. Three Novis made the 1963 field but could do no better than 22nd, 31st and 33rd. The most significant change for 1964 was the addition of a Formula 1 style Ferguson four wheel drive (4WD) unit driven by Bobby Unser.

Unser liked the Novi. "It was the nicest engine I ever drove, no tip in, power came in nice and easy and forgiving, but it wasn't very reliable. But it was scary because it made so much noise."

Thrilled by the handling advantages of 4WD, Granatelli planned an all-new car. When they were unable to remove enough weight from the Novi the venerable powerplant was discarded for a lighter gas turbine for the 1967 race.

Still there was the sound of the Novi. It was the screech of a true race engine and a wonderful memory to anyone who ever heard one race.

26 WILBUR SHAW
The Man Who "Owned" Indy

The last prewar American racing hero was the man who saved the "Greatest Spectacle in Racing." From 1937 through 1940 Wilbur Shaw virtually owned the Indianapolis Motor Speedway, winning three times and taking three seconds. After the war he arranged the sale to make Tony Hulman owner of the speedway.

Wilbur Shaw was born in 1902 and raised less than thirty miles from the famed brickyard. As a boy he helped around the track. The 5'7" Shaw began racing in his teens in a car he built himself and before his twenty-first birthday was winning against proven veterans. He'd drive anything, anywhere, as a driver had to do in the 1920s to make a living. He was a charger and only car failure could keep him from victory lane.

In 1927 he got his first start at Indianapolis, finishing fourth. A rear axle broke while Shaw was easily leading the 1932 race. Car failures, one trip over the outside retaining wall and two second place finishes (1933 and 1935) were his results for the next few years. Finally, in 1937, he won the 500 at 113.580 mph driving an ultra streamlined Offy powered Gilmore Special he and Myron Stevens built. He had led with the car in 1936 before loose bodywork forced a lengthy pit stop, then finished second in the same car in 1938. Mike Boyle bought Shaw a Grand Prix car, a Maserati 8CTF, with which Shaw ran away with the 1939 and 1940 races. In four years Shaw had three wins and a second. A collapsed wheel on lap 152 while leading the 1941 event prevented a third straight win.

While testing a synthetic rubber tire for the Firestone Rubber Company during World War II Shaw became aware of the

Wilbur Shaw was the dominant prewar champ car driver. After the war he arranged the resurrection of the Indianapolis Motor Speedway. Photograph used with permission of IMS Properties.

rundown condition of the speedway. World War I ace Eddie Rickenbacker owned the track but was unable to keep it up and was interested in selling it. Shaw could not buy it himself but found an interested party in Terre Haute businessman Tony Hulman.

Hulman recognized the potential of the track and made the purchase though he had no previous experience with racing. For that he turned to Shaw. Under Shaw's direction as President and General Manager the speedway was rebuilt to its former glory.

Shaw continued to manage the track until his death in a private plane crash on October 30, 1954. Few people have received, then given back, as much to a track and racing as Wilbur Shaw.

27 PIKES PEAK
The Race to the Clouds

Army Lieutenant Zebulon M. Pike first looked upon the Colorado mountain that would soon bear his name and declared in 1806 that no man would ever

A small portion of the lower Pikes Peak hill climb course. Courtesy of Mike Harrigan.

Penrose organized a hill climb race that began at 9,402 feet above sea level and ended at the summit. It was called the National Hill Climb Championship.

Pikes Peak was not the first site for a hill climb. There had been several in Europe by that time but nothing as extreme as what Penrose was proposing. This race was to begin among the grass and trees of the Colorado meadows then climb past the timberline, ending in a land without vegetation and noticeably reduced air. The road was paved gravel with no barriers to the drops that exceeded a thousand feet at places. This was not a place for driver error. The first race was held in 1915. There were two motorcycle and three car classes. Sixteen-year-old Rea Lentz won with a time of 20:55.6 for the 12½ mile course in his Romano Special powered by an aircraft engine.

reach its summit. By 1889 not only had Pikes Peak been climbed, there was a cog railway up to the top and a scrubby foot trail. A twin-cylinder steam-powered Locomobile was driven and pushed to the top in 1901. The trip took nine hours.

From the top of the 14,110 foot high mountain the view was spectacular looking down on nearby Colorado Springs and out on most of Colorado, north to Wyoming and south to New Mexico. Spencer Penrose saw the potential for a tourist site. In 1913, with $25,000 of state aid, the trail was improved into a stone road. Construction began in May 1915 and was finished five months later. For the first twenty years this was a toll road, but it never really broke even financially.

To gain publicity for his toll road

The American Automobile Association (AAA) first sanctioned the race in 1920. The association was to continue through 1956 when the AAA ceased sanctioning all forms of racing. As with Indianapolis and similar races, the new United States Auto Club (USAC) picked up sanctioning. In 1981 sanctioning switched to the Sports Car Club of America (SCCA). The Pikes Peak Hill Climb Association

Pikes Peak allows little margin for error with the emphasis in run-off areas on "off." Courtesy of Holman Moody.

took over control of the race of 1983 under the auspices of the SCCA.

In 1925 Chuck Meyers was the first to make the run in under eighteen minutes at 17:48.4. It took seven years before Glen Shultz reached the top in under seventeen minutes (16: 47.2). In 1938 Louie Unser made the first run in under sixteen minutes (15:49.9). It

Ralph Mulford takes the Hudson Super 6 up Pikes Peak in 1916 for a record setting run of 18:24.7. Peter Helck illustration from *Great Auto Races*, 1975.

was the first of many records held at Pikes Peak by the Unsers. Louie's grandson Bobby broke through fourteen minutes (13.47.9) in 1958, thirteen minutes (12.56.7) in 1961 and twelve minutes (11:54.9) in 1968. In all four generations of Unsers (so far) have raced and won in various classes. While the most well known, the Unsers are not the only family to win the race to the clouds. Three generations named Mears, including Indy 500 winning Rick, are included as well as three generations of the Daniels and Donner families. Today there are twenty classes, six bikes (one being for sidecars) and fourteen four wheelers. It isn't correct to call all four wheeled vehicles "cars" as there is a Super Stock Truck class and Class 8 Truck for the really big semis. On the other extreme is the small Pro Quad class. There is even a class for electric cars. The fastest vehicles in the 2000 race were in the Unlimited Class, an evolution of the turbo rally cars of the 1980s.

Three drivers, Parnelli Jones in 1963, Bobby Unser in 1968 and Mario Andretti in 1969 have won the two oldest American races in the same year, the other being the Indianapolis 500.

Although the actual road distance is only 12.31 miles, Pikes Peak will always be one of the most challenging races in the world. Besides the gravel road with thousand foot drop offs and series of hairpin turns, there is the nearly 6,000 foot change in elevation. It is always a compromise to set the maximum air/fuel mixture for the start and not have the engine starving for air at the top. And in the climb the weather can change dramatically. Though run near the July Fourth weekend, it is not unusual for sunshine to prevail at one end of the course and rain at the other. Twice (1967 and 1995) the race has been stopped due to treacherous conditions near the top. The 1936 race was delayed for snowplows to clear a path. Still racers from all over the world make the annual pilgrimage to the mountain.

The original "Penrose Trophy" has been refurbished and is on display in the Pikes Peak Hill Climb Museum.

28 Drag Racing
From Main Street to Mainstream

It's a very simple concept. How fast can a car go from a standing start, in a quarter of a mile? Easy to understand and with easy rules to follow, in theory it was simple. How it came about and how it was administered is not so easy.

What is now known as drag racing has been going on since before World War I when two drivers in two early cars faced off to see whose car was really the fastest. The implementation of the stop light made the start fairer for street races, although no planned distance was set. The winner was determined as the one who seemed to be ahead. Of course other drivers and local residents did not favor street racing. Injuries and deaths were not uncommon.

The legitimate "hot rodder," especially in the southern California area, took the speed challenges out to the dry lake beds. But when the courses became increasingly too limited for the ever faster cars other outlets had to be found. The Air Force provided one outlet as abandoned runways were excellent venues for speed runs. But the question soon arose as to what was the speed goal and what was to be the distance of the run?

The dry lake runs measured top speed. This required long acceleration and deceleration areas. In a limited space this was impractical.

During the late 1940s the image of the street racer was almost all negative, with speed crazed kids roaring down streets at all hours of the night. Magazine articles and several movies gave the public the idea that all those who hopped up (increased the performance of) their cars were criminals.

A group of enthusiasts and members of the southern California timing clubs met to deflect the negative publicity and save their sport. A major force was the founding of *Hot Rod* magazine in January 1948. In *Hot Rod* enthusiasts had a voice, to each other and the public. The magazine stressed safety in the cars and their operation.

In 1949 the new editor of *Hot Rod*, Wally Parks, editorialized on the steps necessary to save the sport. The first was to promote a new form of timed racing, drag racing, that could be controlled with a national body to oversee the sport. The second was to promote upright role models of safety and sportsmanship. The third was to redefine the perception of the hot rod in the public's mind.

In 1951, supported by *Hot Rod* magazine, the National Hot Rod Association (NHRA) was formed with Parks as the president. Unlike the hobby clubs, the NHRA was to be a

Nothing says drag racing like a full smoke burnout. From the collection of J.A. Martin.

national organization based on local club activities including racing and community involvement. Liaison with local and state police officers was encouraged.

Still this form of racing was not clear. Alternative forms of racing included hill climbs to encourage the braking and handling of the cars (poor on American vehicles in the 1950s), quarter mile runs with rolling starts, and races with a downhill start. By 1955 the concept of two cars in two lanes running down 1,320 feet from a standing start won over the alternatives and became the standard.

The second problem in organization was how to predict every car's performance capability. Rather than allow open competition the NHRA standardized the field into five categories and twenty-seven classes based on degree of alteration to car and motor. Safety standards for both cars and tracks were also established to protect driver and spectator alike.

In 1954 and 1955 the NHRA went on the road with "Drag Safari" to showcase the best of drag racing across the country.

NHRA founder Wally Parks (l) and Ray Brock (r) ran a 1957 Plymouth during Daytona Speedweek. From the collection of Tom Saal.

Safety was promoted along with the visual appeal of the cars.

Once the sport had been established it faced the problem of how serious drag racing was to be. The NHRA's official position was that drag racing was for the fun of competition, like a softball league. But some wanted to go faster, requiring more modifications and higher costs. To support this view the drivers needed to be

Drag racing is very basic. Two cars go head to head in a straight line and the one to the line first wins. "Thunder Valley," Bristol, Tennessee, 1978. From the collection of J.A. Martin.

Funny Cars bear a resemblance to street cars on the outside, but under the shell is a front engine pure dragster. From the collection of J.A. Martin.

The ultimate dragster, the top fuel rail. From the collection of J.A. Martin.

drivers. *Hot Rod* and the NHRA ignored the AHRA for years.

Even NASCAR tried a drag racing division in 1957 but the lack of NASCAR support for early drag racers was reason for many drivers not to switch.

Detroit was aware of the youthful demands for more powerful cars, and by the mid 1950s manufacturers were "helping" certain teams with technical and parts support.

The issues facing drag racing almost became moot in 1957 when the National Safety Council came out in opposition to drag racing. When the Automobile Manufacturers Association (AMA) placed a ban on factory support of any form of motorsports, drag racing was almost pushed back to the era of early street races. But the sport survived into the golden years of the "muscle cars."

The issue of hobby versus professional came to a head over fuel. Since the dry lake days engine builders knew that increases in horsepower were possible by replacing pump gasoline with a blend of methanol and nitro. To those going for greater speeds it was the edge of power, and to the hobbyists it was an illegitimate way of using chemistry rather than engineering for speed. In 1957 the NHRA banned special fuels. Perhaps this was the NHRA's concession to governmental concern over increased speed.

The AHRA and the Automobile Timing Association of America (ATAA) allowed special fuel.

The NHRA ban lasted until 1963, and

paid. The hobbyists were being challenged by the pros. NHRA and *Hot Rod* sided with the hobbyists and felt that those who pushed the rules for more speed were too serious. Even drag strips were to be for fun, not profit; the NHRA was almost a charity. In 1952 the NHRA had registered as a non-profit organization. The first national championship was for trophies, no cash.

The formation of the rival American Hot Road Association (AHRA) was a response by the local tracks and drivers to have more say in the national organization and to financially compensate winning it was the public that ended the ban. Fuel meant higher speeds and more exciting runs, which translated to larger crowds at meets. Sponsors gravitated to the drivers who were setting the records. Exhibition meets by professional top fuel drivers flourished while NHRA attendance stagnated. The NHRA accepted the fuels, for the stated reason that engines were now safe enough to handle the power.

In 1970 the International Hot Rod Association (IHRA) was formed. Replacing the defunct NASCAR drag racing division, the IHRA was dominant in the southeast.

By the 1980s drag racing was an accepted part of motorsports. The NHRA was a member of the international motorsports body and what used to be hot rod themes were found in design and performance of "muscle cars" bought directly from dealerships.

But the sport also faced a new set of problems. As the suburbs moved out, housing tracts surrounded many local drag strips and many strips were closed. While the professionals were doing quite well with national events and TV coverage for the three major professional classes, Top Fuel, Funny Car and Pro Stock, the hobbyists had fewer locations for racing.

The young thrill seekers of 1940–1960 found release in a hot rod. The equivalent in the 1990s is finding thrills in extreme sports and virtual reality games. The times have changed.

Although drag racing is an original form of American racing, it has caught on in England, Germany, Sweden, Japan and Australia.

29 THE BEST REVENGE IS REVENGE
The Mighty 300s

Of all the new V-8s developed after World War II none was more efficient than the Chrysler with the hemispherical combustion chambers, known as the "Hemi."

While GM and Ford supported teams in the early 1950s the Chrysler Corporation stayed out of racing. This is not to say that Chrysler was unaware of what they had produced. In 1955 a high performance Chrysler called the C300 was produced for high speed touring on public roads. Each year a suffix was added, beginning with the 1956 300B. The 300s, with the hemi motor, were powerful and heavy, perfect for cruising the new interstate highways. To Carl Kiekhaefer the 300 offered opportunity. Manufacturing Mercury marine motors had made Kiekhaefer a wealthy

man with over 2,700 dealers. Though not a large man, the cigar chomping Kiekhaefer had a dominant presence that got him results.

Kiekhaefer had begun the 1950s running Fords. But at the Pan-American race he became concerned that he was not getting access to the same equipment the factory supported teams were using. When Ford managers refused to provide for him he turned his back on Ford and went looking for the best method of revenge, beating the Fords.

When he came into NASCAR it was like an invasion, as much from the future as from his Wisconsin home. A trained engineer, Kiekhaefer brought innovations that were not to become standard within

NASCAR for a dozen, in some instances two dozen years. Even the best cars arrived at the track on trailers pulled behind a pickup in those days and some were driven to the race. Kiekhaefer's cars came in a transporter. In his shop he had a dynamometer when even many factories did not have one. It was a business decision to arrive on such a large scale as the cars were used to sponsor the marine motor business. The norm of NASCAR sponsorship in the 1950s was to include the name of a co-operative garage, usually the car owner's. The rear panels of the big Chryslers were emblazoned with graphics promoting Mercury outboard motors. Two planes were kept to run between races, or to the Wisconsin shop.

To Kiekhaefer the key to victory was testing. Besides the dyno tests, the cars were set up for each particular track. When the team arrived they already knew what rear end and gears they would use, and they were usually right.

Although Kiekhaefer was helped by Chrysler engineers this was not a factory effort. The company had never exploited their power advantage and would not do so until the mid–1960s. When the first 300 was

raced it had an automatic transmission. Five races into the 1955 season Chrysler engineers provided a manual transmission that improved what was already awesome performance.

It wasn't just the power that made the cars better. The Chryslers were heavier than the Fords and Chevys, and contact on the track, unintentional or otherwise, usually ended in favor of the heavier car.

To win with the best cars you still need the best drivers, and that was the other part of Kiekhaefer's equation. In 1955 Tim Flock won eighteen races, beginning with the Daytona beach race to start the season, and went on to take the Grand National championship. Then, for 1956, Kiekhaefer hired Flock's brothers Fonty and Bob and also Wendell Scott, Herb Thomas, Buck Baker, Speedy Thompson and Junior Johnson. Tim Flock won Daytona again to start the 1956 season, although he switched teams before the season was complete. The driver's championship was between Baker and Thomas. Baker won fourteen races and the driver's title, he would repeat the latter for 1957, though in a Chevrolet. Six different drivers were victorious in Kiekhaefer's cars. From March 25 through June 3, 1956, the team was undefeated for eighteen consecutive victories, a feat still unmatched.

Kiekhaefer was generous with his drivers, letting them keep the entire winner's purse. But he was also very controlling and ran the team like a military unit with enforced wakeup calls and curfews as well as control of many other aspects of the private lives of his employees, especially the drivers. It was this degree of con-

For two years the Chrysler 300s dominated NASCAR with power and good drivers in an era when safety was as sparse for spectators as drivers. Courtesy of Holman Moody.

trol that caused Flock to leave the best team in NASCAR.

The low point came at Road America, near Kiekhaefer's headquarters. Kiekhaefer entered six cars and provided tickets for six thousand employees, but ex-driver Tim Flock took the race in a Mercury.

Kiekhaefer left racing at the end of 1956 as quickly as he had arrived, and with him the fortunes of the Chrysler cars. He had won everything and had nothing left to prove.

Tim Flock led the Kiekhaefer team. Courtesy of the EMMR collection.

30 TONY HULMAN
IMS and USAC

The Indianapolis Motor Speedway suffered from neglect during World War II. There was no racing or testing, and the track sat unused for almost four years. Weeds grew up through the bricks where mighty race cars had once roared. The greatest racing facility in the world had been reduced to ramshackle garages and grandstands.

Eddie Rickenbacker, who had seen the track through the Depression, was no longer able to give the track the guidance it needed. He empowered track manager Wilbur Shaw to look for a buyer. It was not from the racing community but from a Terre Haute businessman that Shaw found the salvation he was seeking.

Anton "Tony" Hulman, Jr., was not from a background in racing, but he was a patriotic Hoosier who saw a need for the state to keep the track open. He was also an astute businessman who saw the potential to bring the track back to its former position at the pinnacle of the sport and show a real profit. He paid Rickenbacker $700,000 for the site then sold the concession rights, recouping almost all of his investment. Under astute management the speedway, despite yearly updates and improvements, had not gone outside for a loan.

Almost immediately Hulman began rebuilding the track. Under Shaw's management the infield was cleared, the stands rebuilt and enlarged and the racing surface paved over. And Hulman, following the lead of IMS founder Carl Fisher, paid the highest purses in racing. This attracted the top cars and drivers, which brought in ever-growing crowds.

Hulman took charge in 1955 when the American Automobile Association (AAA), allegedly because of the accidents at Le Mans, announced that it was no longer going to sanction races. Racing had been a service within the AAA, much like maps and trip planners. Professional racing

Sprints and Stock cars. Headquartered near the Speedway, USAC continues to provide rules and sanctioning for tracks across the country as well as speed records and tests for production cars.

In 1957 USAC, SCCA and NASCAR joined in creating ACCUS (American Competition Committee for the United States), later joined by the NHRA, to represent all forms of American racing with the FIA.

Hulman remained President of the speedway until his death in 1977. His heirs, headed by daughter Mari H. George (Chairman) and her son Anton H. "Tony" George (President and CEO), continue to operate the speedway, now worth many times what Hulman invested in it in 1946. Part of the success of the Speedway has been in reinvesting profits into the track and keeping the track debt free, yet at the forefront.

Above: By 1944 the Indianapolis Motor Speedway had deteriorated to a rundown facility. *Bottom:* Wilbur Shaw (r) negotiated for Tony Hulman (l) to buy the Speedway from Eddie Rickenbacker (c). Photographs used with permission of IMS properties.

needed to be run by a full time professional organization. Lacking an organizing body, American racing could easily founder. By September Hulman had organized race track operators and promoters across the country into a new sanctioning body, the United States Auto Club (USAC) to sanction Champ cars, Midgets,

From the 1950s through 1980s USAC sanctioned a stock car series through the Midwest. Courtesy of John Whipple.

31 THE TWEEDY JACKET SET
Sports Car Club of America

By the 1920s road racing in America was virtually dead. Safety issues had resulted in a ban on public road racing. The once world famous Vanderbilt Cup, the Grand Prize and the Elgin races had long since ended. Speedways, where crowds bought tickets and sat safely in grandstands, were flourishing. Race cars at the forefront of technology were built expressly for oval track racing by the famous builders of the period, Duesenberg and Miller.

In the early 1930s Ford introduced the first low cost lightweight V-8. The flathead motor was easy to work on with readily available parts. It was with a flathead Ford that Fred Frame won the reborn Elgin race in August 1933. Though the comeback for the Elgin was short lived, Mines Field at Long Beach, California, hosted the first airport race six months later. About 60,000 fans saw cars again turn right as well as left. It was the highpoint of the West Coast's road racing revival. The Ford V-8 became the backbone for the growing hot rod culture of southern California that became drag and dry lake racing and reasserted road racing in the late 1940s.

In the 1930s three wealthy brothers were hosting informal road racing events on the family estate near Briarcliff, NY. Sam, Miles and Barron, Jr. Collier constructed a three-fourths mile track for the enjoyment of themselves and a group of friends who raced their lightweight foreign cars that were recognized for excellent handling, though often lacking power in . contrast to the heavier American cars. Together they formed the Automobile Racing Club of America (ARCA). They held hill climbs and races on blocked off public roads from New England through Pennsylvania. Most of the members were amateurs as the types of courses precluded any gate receipts. The AAA invited the ARCA to join in the promotion of road races. The ARCA declined, leaving road racing unrepresented.

When America entered the Second World War the ARCA became inactive. Their last event was a race in 1940 for Grand Prix cars at the site of the 1939 Worlds Fair.

Even before World War II came to an end the group of New England sports car enthusiasts were planning for the future. On February 26, 1944, Ted Robertson, Everett Dickinson, Chapin Wallour, George Rand, George Weaver and the Collier Brothers organized the Sports Car Club of America (SCCA) as a national group. From the beginning the SCCA was to be a strictly

With a logo designed by Bill Mitchell, later head of GM design, the prewar ARCA was the first American club for sports car aficionados. Courtesy of the EMMR collection.

amateur organization where affluent (not specified in the rules) individuals could enjoy their sports cars. Early events included hill climbs, technical conferences and rallys, not races as the ARCA had held. They were gentlemen; professionals were free to race in the AAA sanctioned Indy cars.

And it wasn't just for the drivers; timers, inspectors and corner workers, all necessary to conduct a race, were volunteers. Everyone gave of themselves to make the events happen.

The early races were over blocked off country roads, but there was a need for more organized circuits. Competition Director Cameron Argetsinger, a law student from Ohio, promoted a race through the town of Watkins Glen, New York, where a relative had a lake cabin. From 1948 through 1952 the street race was the center of sportscar racing in the East, attracting over 200,000 spectators to see cars and drivers from Europe and all over the U.S. As with other unprotected street races, out of control cars caused the death of several spectators. A permanent track was built northwest of the village of Watkins Glen. Across the country other road events moved to permanent circuits in California (Riverside), Connecticut (Lime Rock) and Wisconsin (Road America). Allard driver and Air Force General, Curtis LeMay, made several air bases available for races. Crowd control was not a problem.

When the AAA withdrew from race sanctioning in 1955 several groups organized sports car racing. Besides the SCCA, the new USAC group and even NASCAR held some road races. One group had to take responsibility. Reluctantly SCCA became the logical group.

In 1955 John Bishop, a young industrial designer working in Baltimore, Maryland, was brought on full time and eventually named Executive Director. Bishop became involved by painting covers for the SCCA magazine.

By the late 1950s a crisis was developing within the SCCA. While a wealthy driver like John Fitch could afford to race for trophies, most of the hot young west coast drivers like Dan Gurney and Carroll Shelby saw driving as a vocation. They were hired by patrons who owned the best cars. The NHRA was going through the same soul searching the SCCA was forced to confront, the dilemma of driving-for-pay within a club built for driving for trophies. It was the same conflict that still agonizes the World Olympics.

The United States Road Racing Championship (USRRC), begun in 1963, provided an outlet for professional racers. The financial success of the USRRC led the SCCA to develop three distinctive professional series for 1966; the Can-Am, Trans-Am and Formula 5000.

Still the board of directors was in turmoil, and in 1969 Bishop left to form his all-professional International Motor Sports Association (IMSA), modeled after and with the support of NASCAR.

The professional series went through several bumps with only

In the early 1950s Americans discovered sports cars and sports car racing at temporary venues like the streets of Watkins Glen, New York. From the collection of Tom Saal.

the Trans-Am surviving by the mid 1980s.

Over the years the SCCA has sanctioned several race series. Race Truck, for light trucks, was a supporting player of the Trans-Am. Co-sanctioned by USAC, the Bosch Super Vee championship was a Volkswagen supported open wheel series that launched many of America's top professional drivers.

SCCA has also sanctioned pro rally events in the U.S. Though not supported by the factories to the extent of the FIA World Rally Championship, the SCCA ProRally series has survived.

The SCCA has co-sponsored the open wheel F2000 series with USAC on both road and oval tracks supporting IRL, CART and SCCA professional series.

Early post–WWII road races were often held on airports. This is Sebring (Florida) in 1960 where a Formula Vee race is about to begin. From the collection of J.A. Martin.

SCCA volunteers provide corner workers at professional CART, sports car and NASCAR events and for international races held in the U.S.

In 1972 the SCCA moved its offices from Connecticut to Englewood, Colorado, then to Topeka, Kansas.

32 CARRERA PANAMERICANA
The Pan American Road Race

In 1950 the Mexican section of the Pan American Highway was completed. To celebrate the opening the Mexican government, through the Asociacion Nacional Automovilistica, organized a 3000-km race along the lines of the great European point-to-point races, like the Italian Mille Miglia.

Though an important road, the Pan American Highway was not like an American interstate highway. Most of the time it was a two-lane road, often through desolate countryside. The hills were formidable trials, and any car that even finished

the race would be worthy of recognition. The race ran between Tuxtla Gutierrez on the border with Guatemala and Juarez bordering the United States.

The race was the first time European and American drivers faced off in the Americas and the first time sports cars and stock cars raced on an equal basis. The premiere event was run in May, 1950. The 125 drivers, including Bill France and Curtis Turner, Italian Alfa Romeo ace Piero Taruffi, Monte Carlo rally champion Jean Trevoux, Johnny Mantz in the Bill Stroppe–prepared Lincoln, and dozens of amateur

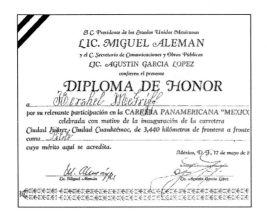

To the victors belong the spoils, a certificate. From the collection of J.A. Martin.

drivers who had no idea what they were getting into, headed south. Hershel Mc-Griff won the first race in an Oldsmobile 88 over 51 other finishers, some in a very sorry state, both cars and drivers.

Due to its similarity to the European road races, like the Targa Floria of Sicily, many European teams entered the 1951 Pan Am. Run south to north, the November race was listed on the International Sporting calendar, with classes for sedans and sports cars. Taruffi and Luigi Chinetti won the sports car class and overall in a Ferrari. Troy Ruttman and Clay Smith led much of the way in an old Mercury taken from a used car lot, but the flathead motor could not match the top speed of the Ferraris and finished fourth behind Bill Sterling's Chrysler Saratoga.

The success of the underpowered Mercury interested Ford management for 1952. It was the first time an American

manufacturer entered factory-supported cars in the race. Stroppe and Smith prepared three Lincolns to stock specs, but they were full race cars. John Holman organized the logistics of support equipment and services, from a mobile machine shop to doctors and caterers. The efforts were rewarded with a 1-2-3-4 class win for Lincoln over various Chryslers and Cadillacs. Karl Kling and Hermann Lang led 1-2 for Mercedes in the overall results.

No fewer than 22 Lincolns, prepared by Stroppe and Smith, started in 1953. The 4,300 pound cars were modified with extra large fuel tanks. Again the factory supported cars won the class. Juan Fangio won overall in a Lancia.

For 1954 Lincoln had no control of the fuel and a load of low octane gas led to failure for several of the high compression V-8s. Still, Lincolns took the top two Touring spots, three hours behind the Ferrari of Umberto Maglioli.

The racing had been good and the event popular, but at the conclusion of the 1954 event the Mexican government cancelled any further races. Crowd control was becoming impossible, bandits created road blocks, and race organization had become more than the government was able to handle. Also the road had become too important to be blocked off for several days.

For Ford the PanAmericana was a lesson in logistics. Many of the participants were later involved in Ford's next challenge in international racing, Le Mans 1964.

33 THE RACE OF TWO WORLDS
Monza 1957–1958

By the mid 1950s racing on both sides of the Atlantic had recovered from WWII,

but in different directions. Formula 1 and endurance sports cars were supreme in

It was a doubly unusual sight to fans at the Monza Autodromo with American Champ cars running counter clockwise. It was also unusual to see how much faster the American cars were. Photograph used with permission of IMS Properties.

Europe. In America USAC oval track Champ cars were dominant. How would the different types of racing compare in direct competition?

In 1956 Monza Autodrome managing director Giuseppe Bacciagaluppi invited Duane Carter, USAC Director of Competition, to visit the Italian Grand Prix. The two discussed the possibility of running the USAC Champ cars on the seldom used banked oval portion of the track. Pat O'Conner soon followed, testing the track with a Chrysler 331 powered Kurtis roadster. Results were positive so plans were made for a 1957 race. Eight USAC champ car drivers represented America.

It was the Europeans who let the Monza promoters down. The Formula 1 teams chose not to appear asserting that the race was too dangerous. The Americans said the Europeans were whining. After much persuasion the Ecurie Ecosse Jaguar team, fresh from a 1-2 finish at the 24-hour race at

Le Mans, brought three D-types. The only Formula 1 car was an old Maserati 250F.

The Europeans were further handicapped by the format. There were to be three heats of 63 laps each. The endurance capabilities of the Jaguars were negated. The race would be decided on speed and strength, both assets of the American cars.

The slowest USAC driver qualified at over 160 mph. The fastest Jaguar qualified at 152 mph.

As expected the race was an American runaway. Jimmy Bryan took two of the three heats for the overall win and $35,000. Novi driver Tony Bettenhausen set a new world's closed-course record with a competition lap of 176.818 mph. USAC success though was tempered as only three Champ cars finished.

When the race was held again in 1958 European teams took a greater interest in the event, especially with the size of the winner's check. Ferrari sent three drivers, including American Phil Hill, in his only opportunity to race against the USAC stars, to handle a single car. Maserati prepared a car for Stirling Moss. And the Jaguars returned. Fangio was entered in the USAC Dean Van Lines Special. A Ferrari took the pole but the bulk of the front positions were USAC cars, including Fangio in third.

At the green flag the Jaguars took an early lead. Once the roadsters picked up momentum the race was over.

The Ferrari came home third behind Jim Rathman and Jimmy Bryan. Moss had crashed in the Maserati at over 170 mph while holding third. The car was later re-paired and in 1959 Ralph Liguori attempted to qualify it for the Indianapolis 500 without success.

For a second time the American teams had showed their superiority on this one unique track. But the promoters lost interest and there was no third race.

An interested spectator was Formula 1 neophyte Dan Gurney. His interest in the advantages of the two worlds of racing led him to contact Ford in 1962 about bringing Formula 1 technology to America and Indianapolis. Gurney recalled, "The fact that a Jaguar could lead just because of the gearbox was an interesting thing to me."

34 RUN WHAT YOU BRUNG
Formula Libre at Lime Rock

Perhaps the most unusual race in American motorsports history occurred at Lime Rock Park on July 15, 1959. It was a true Formula *Libre* (Free Form) race, and the contestants were as *libre* as the promoters could have dreamed.

Since the beginning of racing, rules have been established in order to provide fair competition. But there was always the issue of how fast the cars of one series were compared to another. The only way to find out was to put the cars and drivers against each other in a single race with no restrictions.

The idea is easier than the reality, as anyone can figure which is the better setup and ignore the rest. That is, until USAC decided to hold a race on the road course at Lime Rock Park in Connecticut. When weather forced the race to be rescheduled from June to a month later all interested parties went looking for the best drivers and cars. Since it was a New England road course there was no problem getting the usual Ferraris and Aston Martins. As road racing, especially Eastern style, was the domain of affluent gentlemen, cost was only a small matter. One team was able to bring former World Champion Juan Manuel Fangio's Maserati Formula 1 model 250F for Chuck Daigh. Dr. Dick Thompson was in the original Corvette Sting Ray.

On July 15, 1959, the surprise of the field was recent Indy 500 winner Rodger Ward in an eleven-year-old Offy-powered Kurtis Midget. Even more of a surprise came when Ward won the pole. However, order was restored when George Constantine ran away from Ward at the start to take the first heat in his Aston Martin DBR-2.

To get more speed Ward changed to larger 16-inch rear wheels for the second heat. Ward and Constantine were the main protagonists but Ward took the win. Daigh contested Constantine and Ward in the third heat. In a single pass Ward passed

Backed by the Connecticut hills Rodger Ward emerges from his USAC Midget after winning over some of the best sports cars and their accomplished drivers. Courtesy of Joe Corbett.

both to take the lead and the win. The gentlemen with their sports cars were stunned while the crowd went wild.

Ward, encouraged by the results, entered a Kurtis Offy at Sebring for the first modern United Sates Grand Prix. The long airport straights showed the car's weaknesses and Ward was brought back to reality.

Ward saw the superiority of the winning rear engine Cooper chassis and invited designer John Cooper to Indianapolis, leading to Chapter 37.

35 ALL AMERICAN SPORTS CAR
Corvette

The Corvette C5R that came within half a lap of winning Daytona's 24-hour race in 2000 was the first factory backed team since the Grand Sport of the early 1960s. Despite having a performance image Chevrolet had been unwilling to support its sports car on the track. Although the Corvette was not the equal of the Porsche on the track, Corvettes were moving out of showrooms as fast as they were being sent. So why spend money for a race program? Because "America's sports car" was being beaten by another American sports car, the Dodge Viper, and Chevy wanted to establish Corvette as a world class sports car.

Corvette began as a response to the postwar European sports cars where price equated to speed.

· This was a traditional balance, but was it American? With the postwar awareness of sportscars and high performance engines available in affordable cars, like

the Oldsmobile Rocket and the Chrysler Hemi, the idea of an affordable American sportscar seemed a very real prospect.

The racing history of the Corvette is one of factory programs being undercut and private teams producing outstanding vehicles.

Introduced at the January 1953 Motorama, the first model was built on a shortened sedan chassis. With a 235 cid six cylinder motor, automatic transmission and hub caps, the first Corvette hardly seemed the type to challenge a Mercedes 300SL or a C type Jaguar. It was more comfortable as a two seat highway cruiser. But in 1955 the first Thunderbird proved to be a better personal car. The Corvette had to become a sports car or be dropped. And the way to prove its worth was to race.

The catalyst for the transformation was Zora Arkus-Duntov. The immigrant engineer joined GM in 1953 after seeing the Corvette at the Motorama. In a memo the 44-year-old former Le Mans class winner laid out how Chevrolet could become the car of choice for young buyers. As head of Chevrolet performance he virtually single-handedly made it a world class performer. As a driver he set a new "measured mile" record in a prototype 1955 Corvette at Daytona Beach of over 150 mph.

The addition of a 265 cid V-8 and a three speed manual transmission, then a fuel injected 283 cid with a four speed in 1957, gave muscle to the redesigned body and Corvettes were soon winning SCCA races, but not when facing factory supported Ferraris. That would take more of a car.

The Corvette SS was a way to show that the young American sports car was equal to the best of Europe. With a magnesium alloy body, fuel injection, inboard rear brakes and a deDion-type rear axle the SS was a true race car.

Two models were brought to Sebring for the 1957 12-hour race. One was a "mule" but the other was properly prepared. John Fitch and Piero Taruffi took the car out in practice and turned in respectable times against the Maseratis, Jaguars and Ferraris. At one point World driving champion Juan Fangio took the Corvette out. After a few laps he proclaimed the car to be "fantastico."

The lone Corvette SS was 6th on the first lap but lasted only 23 laps due to

The first Corvette specifically designed for racing, the Corvette SS at Sebring, 1957.

brake and ignition problems and the car was withdrawn.

Before the car could be prepared for another race General Motors, in response to the ban on performance cars by the Automobile Manufacturers Association, ceased all motorsports participation.

Three years later Briggs Cunningham campaigned three Corvettes in the 24-hour Le Mans race. Easily the biggest displacement cars in the race, the three were virtually stock. Each held its own in the speedier sections but, lacking the developed disc brakes of the Jaguars and Ferraris, lost in the handling sections. Periodic rain showers reduced the top speed of the high winding Ferraris and the Corvettes moved up to contending positions. But when the clouds left, so did the last hope of the Corvettes. The Cunningham Corvette was fourth at the conclusion. This was to be the highest a Chevrolet powered car has ever finished at Le Mans.

General Motors design chief Bill Mitchell and stylist Larry Shinoda, beginning with a sketch by Peter Brock, had a special body created over Arkus-Duntov's mechanical goodies for an unofficial Corvette race car. Primarily driven by Dr. Dick Thompson, the "Sting Ray" won SCCA races and greatly enhanced the performance image of the Corvette.

In 1962 Chevrolet had a new opportunity and a new challenge. In the fall an all-new Corvette, based on and named after the Sting Ray, was introduced. Visually it was possibly the most exciting car in the world. It was a Chevrolet to challenge the world's best.

In California Carroll Shelby had begun to race his new Cobra. As powerful as the Corvette, the Cobra was almost a thousand pounds lighter and was soon winning races over the Corvettes. Corvette engineers thought they were ready to challenge Europe, but suddenly they were not even the fastest American car.

A new racing Corvette was developed to meet the threat. Complying with FIA international rules, the Corvette Grand Sport, using a tube frame and .04" thick fiberglass, weighed half a ton less than a standard Corvette. Power came from a 377 cid aluminum alloy motor.

The plan was to build a thousand cars in coupe and roadster form to be eligible as production vehicles. But only three coupes and two roadsters had been built when GM chairman Frederic Donner ordered all divisions to cease participation in any form of racing. The project was dead.

But Arkus-Duntov did not give up. Since the factory could not race the cars they were lent to private race teams that Chevrolet had worked with.

Car #004 debuted at Marlboro, Maryland, in April 1963. While not a successful first outing, by mid-summer the car was winning in the capable hands of Jim Hall, Roger Penske, A.J. Foyt and Dr. Dick Thompson. At Watkins Glen, then at the Nassau Speed Weeks, the Corvette GS beat the best of Europe and the Cobras. By 1964, however, the Cobra program was in full swing, including an aerodynamic coupe. Although well-prepared and well-driven, the Grand Sports, classified as Prototypes because so few were made, were not contenders over the length of the season and even private teams ceased support.

All five Grand Sports still exist and are often seen at vintage racing events.

Except for the Grand Sports the only racing Corvettes were in the hands of SCCA A- and B-Production weekend racers. Then John Greenwood could stand it no more and campaigned the wildest bodied Corvettes ever made. Greenwood had won the national AP title in 1970 and 1971 in a big block Corvette and established a link with Arkus-Duntov. The BF Goodrich tire company sponsored Greenwood to race his Corvette at Le Mans on street radial tires in 1972 and 1973. When the

Capitalizing on IMSA's liberal body rules, John Greenwood created a road racing funny car. From the collection of J.A. Martin.

Trans-Am series was opened to sports cars in 1973 Greenwood won two races, and Chevrolet took the manufacturer's title. Still more was needed against the new Porsche Carerras, especially in IMSA. Greenwood and Arkus-Duntov came up with the new thing, a radically shaped Corvette with wide fenders, a shovel nose and a high mounted wing over a strengthened tube frame roll cage body. Greenwood took the 1975 Trans-Am title and numerous poles in both the Trans-Am and IMSA series. In 1978 Greg Pickett took the car to the category II Trans-Am title.

With the advent of the Porsche 935 the Greenwood Corvette was overmatched and retired.

In 1983 Chevrolet returned to the Trans-Am series with semi-factory support for the DeAtley Camaro team of David Hobbs and Willie T. Ribbs. The pair took the Camaros to the manufacturer's title and were 1-2 in the driver's title.

For 1984 DeAtley switched to the new C-4 Corvette. Unfortunately for Chevrolet 1984 was the year that Ford factory support returned. The Tom Gloy and Jack Roush teams dominated the series with the Mercury Capris and Mustangs. The favored Corvettes were soon left behind. Not until 1998 with Paul Gentilozzi would a Corvette driver again take the Trans-Am championship.

Ely Reeves Callaway III has built some of the most exotic, and fastest Corvettes. His company takes the standard Corvette and improves it with high performance accessories and body panels. Beginning in the early 1980s he had built twin turbo versions of the Corvette. When the German press described these cars as "Hammers" Callaway decided to build a "Sledgehammer." In October 1989 the 898 hp car was driven to 254.76 mph at the Ohio Transportation Research Center. To prove the roadworthiness of the car it was driven back on public roads to the shop in Connecticut.

A Callaway Corvette sits in a Daytona garage preparing for the 1996 24-hour race. Courtesy of Dudley Evans.

In the spring of 1994 a race version of the Callaway LM, the SuperNatural, was prepared to race at Le Mans. Boris Said was fastest qualifier in the GT2 class and was fighting for the lead with the Porsches before co-driver Michel Maisonneuve ran out of fuel on the course.

Supported by Callaway Competition GmbH of Germany, a Callaway won the GT2 class in the next two races at Vallelunga in Italy and Spa in Belgium. At the 1995 Le Mans race SuperNaturals qualified 1st, 4th, and 5th in class. Although the lead car was damaged while avoiding a spinning competitor after running 1-2-3 in class two, Callaways finished second and third in class, ninth and eleventh overall.

For 1996 the Callaway Corvettes were placed in the GT1 class. At the Daytona 24-hour race a Callaway finished third in class before taking the first three races in the SCCA World Challenge Series. Driver Almo Coppelli took the S2 championship.

With the introduction of the Corvette C5 Callaway prepared a new car, the C7. Originally built to FIA GT1 standards, the C7R was to compete in GT1 for overall honors. But changes in the regulations made the project impractical and Callaway was out of racing.

Zora Arkus-Duntov died in 1996. Though he had retired from GM in 1975 Duntov had remained involved with his Corvette until his death.

After 4,000 miles of testing in 1998 the Chevrolet factory returned to GT racing in 1999 with the C5-R, a 2,510 pound race version of the fifth generation Corvette. With a 365 cid/600 hp V-8 the C5-R raced in GTS class against turbo Porsches and Dodge Vipers, debuting at the Daytona 24-hour race. Corvettes began the 2000 season with 7 liters and a second overall at the Daytona 24-hour race. The return to Le Mans by a factory supported team after forty years was equally successful with a top ten finish that gave promise for more in the future. By the end of the 2000 season the Corvettes had proven to be equal to the champion Vipers.

The year 2001 began with an overall win at the Daytona 24-hour race, a 1-2 in class at Le Mans and an ALMS manufacturers championship. Corvettes repeated the Le Mans and ALMS victories in 2002.

36 A.J. FOYT
Winning Was Everything

Born January 16, 1935, in Houston, Texas, Anthony Joseph Foyt, Jr., never wanted to be anything but a race driver. His incredible record of 36 consecutive starts in the Indianapolis 500 began in 1958, a race he first won in 1961 with repeats in 1964, 1967 and 1977. In addition, Foyt is a seven-time national Indy Car champion (1960, '61, '63, '64, '67, '75 and '79), three-time USAC national stock car champion (1968, '78 and '79) and Dirt Car champion (1971), a two-time IROC champion (1976 and '77) and is the only driver in history to have won the 24 Hours of Le Mans (1967), the Daytona 500 (1972), the Daytona 24 Hours (1983 and 1985) and the Sebring 12 Hours (1985).

Foyt's race-by-race accomplishments are far too numerous to recite here, but his tenacity, his resiliency and his unwavering determination to win set him apart. Other men would have quit the game after suffering any one of the many crashes which Foyt survived over the years, but he always seemed to accept injury and pain as the inevitable consequence of being a race driver.

His first big accident happened at the Motor Trend 500, a NASCAR road race at Riverside Raceway in California, on January 17, 1965. Sudden brake loss forced him to swerve in turn 9 to miss the cars driven by Junior Johnson and Marvin Panch, sending his Holman-Moody Ford off the edge and down a bank at 140 mph, demolishing the car and giving him a broken back, a broken left heel and multiple scrapes and bruises. Recalling the details a year later in the *Los Angeles Times*, Foyt revealed that this was not his first accident,

A.J. Foyt

saying that he had been hurt "three or four times avoiding somebody I could have used as a backstop."

Even so, his injuries did not prevent him from competing in 17 of the 18 races in the 1965 USAC Championship series where he won 10 pole positions and 5 races, placing second to Mario Andretti in season points. He also ran three more NASCAR races that year, including a win in the July 4th Firecracker 400 at Daytona.

Recounting the chain of events that led to a crash at Milwaukee on June 5, 1966, while practicing in his ex–Jimmy Clark Lotus the day before the Rex Mays 100, Foyt was quoted in *Competition Press & Autoweek* 7/9/66 as saying, "I felt something break (the left rear suspension), and the car started spinning to the inside of the straightaway. I locked it up and did the best I could do, but when a driving wheel breaks like that there's not much you can do. The car hit the cement wall so hard that it tore the lines off the sump (spare) tank which holds about two and a half gallons, compressed it, and it exploded all over everything. The car was still running at 80 mph and it seemed like there were flames everywhere. I put my hands over my face, but the (his gloves) were burning away." He was back racing later that month, missing only 4 of the 16 races on the championship schedule.

The mile at Du Quoin, Illinois, the site of the first champ car win in 1960 and four other wins after that, was a track that turned nasty for Foyt in 1970 when he ended up on his head, and nearly fatal in 1972 when he left the pits too soon trying to stay in the lead. The still-connected hose spewed high octane gas all over the cockpit, and Foyt suffered burns and a broken ankle when he leaped out and the moving car ran over his left leg.

After winning one of the two 125-mile qualifiers and starting third in the 1978 Daytona 500, Foyt spun his No. 51 Valvoline-sponsored Buick into the wet grass on lap 68, causing it to roll, ending up on its roof. He spent a night in the hospital for treatment of neck and shoulder injuries. Still he went on to run all 18 championship races and 11 of the 13 stock car races in USAC that year (winning the stock car championship) plus one more NASCAR race, the May 14 Winston 500 at Talladega where he started second and finished third.

A.J. nearly lost his right arm in CART's inaugural Michigan 500 on July 25, 1981. Something caused Foyt's No. 14 Gilmore-Valvoline Coyote to veer into the wall on a lap 80 restart, shearing off the right side suspension and sidepod. His arm slashed and his elbow broken, the unconscious Foyt was flown by helicopter to the University of Michigan Hospital in Ann Arbor. He left for home the following Monday but was out of racing for the rest of the year.

The years 1982 through 1990 saw Foyt alternating between CART and NASCAR, but his only wins came in sports cars at Daytona and Sebring driving for Preston Henn. Parting with Henn in 1986, Foyt bought a used Porsche 962 and ran with the leaders in several IMSA Camel GT races in 1987 and 1988 with Copenhagen sponsorship, but he never won a race as a sports car team owner. However, he did manage to set a new closed course speed record of 257.1123 mph in an Oldsmobile Aerotech on August 27, 1987, on Firestone's 7.712 mile Fort Stockton Test Center in Texas.

Foyt's mysterious absence from CART's August 7, 1988, Marlboro 500 at Michigan is best told by this paragraph from the 8/22/88 *On Track*: "Johnny Rutherford was a last-minute replacement for A.J. Foyt, who checked into a Houston hospital on Thursday complaining of severe stomach pains. J. R. did a fine job in relief of Super Tex, but everyone's attention naturally focused on the daily updates on A.J.'s physical condition. Happily, Foyt's problem was diagnosed as a bruised kidney, most likely the result of the contortions involved in getting in and out of his stock car the previous weekend at Talladega."

The crash that led to the end of Foyt's driving career occurred on lap 24 of the Texaco/Havoline 200 at Road America near Elkhart Lake, Wisconsin, on September 23, 1990. According to a report in the 10/18/90 *On Track*, "Near-tragedy struck (on lap 26) as Foyt's Copenhagen Lola-Chevrolet plunged off the road at Turn One. The car sped across the damp grass at unabated speed, virtually cleared the sand trap and then thumped into an earth bank. Its front end badly damaged, the car vaulted the bank and came to rest amid the undergrowth — a long way from the track itself. Quick-acting corner workers extinguished a small fire in the back of the car and managed to extricate Foyt who was trapped in the car by his legs.

A follow-up notice in the same issue

said that the accident occurred because the
brake pedal assembly
apparently broke, that
Foyt was airlifted to
the Milwaukee County
Medical Complex, then
on Monday was trans-
ferred to Methodist
Hospital in Indianapo-
lis where he underwent
further surgery.

Foyt endured ex-
tensive physical therapy
on his legs to be ready
for the 1991 Indianapolis
500 where he started
second but left the race

A.J. was still the only 4-time winner of the Indianapolis 500 in 1985 when this photograph was included in the Gilmore/Copenhagen press kit.

early after a front wing on his Foyt/Gilmore Lola-Chevrolet was knocked askew by debris from a crash between Kevin Cogan and Roberto Guerrero. He soldiered on for half the CART season, scoring no points, and then put Mike Groff in the car. At season's end CART "honored" him at the awards dinner by retiring his racing number, a hint Foyt chose to ignore, placing ninth in the 1992 Indy 500 and finally retiring for good as an Indy car driver with an emotional farewell at the Speedway in 1993. Foyt's last appearance as a race driver was NASCAR's

inaugural Brickyard 400 at the Indianapolis Motor Speedway in 1994 where he started 40th and placed 30th, four laps down.

In 1996 Foyt formed a team in the new Indy Racing League, winning the series title with Scott Sharp that same year. With Kenny Brack he won the IRL title in 1998 and the 1999 Indy 500. In 2000 he formed a NASCAR team with headquarters in Mooresville, North Carolina, which is run by his son Larry. A.J. himself tends to the IRL series where grandson A.J. IV has begun a racing career of his own.

37 REAR ENGINE REVOLUTION

In 1959 the Cooper Formula 1 team won the World Championship, establishing the rear engine car as the standard for international race car design. But Cooper's dominance was short-lived as the FIA changed the engine size for 1961, thereby leaving the Cooper with nowhere to race.

Sports car racers were the first to accept the new rear engine racers. Roger Penske modified an ex–Cooper Formula 1 car with a closed body producing the Zerex Special. Even race prepared Ferraris and Jaguars were no match for the little racer. Bruce McLaren bought the Zerex Special and added a V-8 to produce the prototype for what was to become his Can-Am cars that dominated the latter part of the decade.

Cooper, seeing the success of modified Cooper Grand Prix cars, produced their own car, the Cooper Monaco. Carroll Shelby added a Cobra V-8 to produce the King Cobra for Dave MacDonald. Lotus built a similar car, the Model 19. By 1963 there were no more competitive front engined sports racing cars.

Meanwhile, American Champ car racing was at the height of the roadster era with a big front engine, usually an "Offy."

Through the 1950s Indianapolis was the only paved track on the Championship trail, and front engine "uprights" worked well in the dirt. But in the later years of the decade tracks were being paved with concrete and asphalt, a fine surface for a rear engine race car.

In 1961 Jack Brabham entered a former Formula 1 Cooper in the Indianapolis 500. Although giving away almost ninety cubic inches to the rest of the field, he qualified for the race. During the race he

The Offy roadster was a direct evolution of the first Indy race cars, the lightweight tube frame having replaced the earlier rail frame. From the collection of J.A. Martin.

held enough speed through the turns to insure decent speed down the straights. He finished ninth.

The first to take notice was Mickey Thompson. In 1962 he startled the Indy establishment with three Buick-powered rear engine cars designed by Englishman John Crosthwaite. Afer 31-year-old "rookie" Dan Gurney qualified one of them eighth on the first weekend, he called Lotus boss Colin Chapman to come over and watch the race at Gurney's expense. Gurney finished 20th (out on lap 92 with gearbox failure) and then arranged for Chapman to meet with Ford racing personnel who

The King Cobra of 1963 was typical of the early American road racing machines. A Cooper chassis housed a Shelby built Ford V-8. Carroll Shelby looks on at lead driver Dave MacDonald. Courtesy of the Lynn Park collection.

In 1961 Jack Brabham entered his (now obsolete) rear engine Cooper. With rule changes for Formula 1 the two-time world championship car had no place to race, so why not try Indy? From the collection of J.A. Martin.

were starting up the "Total Performance" race program. Ford was interested but was unsure if they should go with the revolutionary Chapman or the proven A.J. Watson who had built the last four Indy winning chassis. In the end Ford joined with Lotus. The resulting Lotus 29 was powered by a 4.2-liter version, with eight carburetors, of the Fairlane family car motor. Two cars were entered in the 1963 "500" for Gurney and Jimmy Clark. At the first round of roadster pit stops the more fuel efficient Lotuses were running 1-2. In a controversial finish Clark, who had come to within five seconds of leader Parnelli Jones, backed off to finish second after Jones' roadster started losing oil. In August Clark won the Milwaukee 200, ending a winning streak by the Offy engine that went back over one and a half decades.

Colin Chapman's Ford powered Lotus turned the race world upside down in 1963. Here Dan Gurney's Lotus sits in front of Jim Clark's similar machine. From the collection of J.A. Martin.

Despite the apparent superiority of the rear engine design most of the USAC Champ car establishment stayed with roadsters for the 1964 race. Ford produced a new four cam racing engine that powered the first four cars on the starting grid for the Indianapolis race. However, poor management by Rodger Ward, over enthusiasm by Bobby Marshman and improper tire choice by the Lotus team allowed the race to fall again to a roadster.

By 1965 even the staunchest members of the old guard were racing sitting in front of their motors, usually in former Team Lotus chassis. Jimmy Clark took the event in the superb Lotus 38.

Jim Hurtubise qualified the last roadster for the Memorial Day race in 1968. The Mallard, sporting a turbocharged Offy, did not complete the race. Roadsters continued for a few more years as a decreasing number of dirt tracks were part of the series.

Without any new standard of design, race car builders began to look for other variations on what a winning car should be. Smokey Yunick put the driver beside the motor. Mickey Thompson tried four wheel steering. Rather than commit to either engine location, one car had a Porsche motor in the front and another in the back.

Most of these ideas went nowhere. One that did make an impact was the STP turbine in 1967.

Jim Hurtubise made a last hurrah for the roadsters, with a turbo Offy, by qualifying 30th for the 1968 race, but the motor failed and he did not finish. From the collection of J.A. Martin.

38 WHEN HOLMAN AND MOODY MEANT FORD

In the 1960s John Holman and Ralph Moody, operating as the racing division of the Ford Motor Company, put together the most extensive racing organization seen until at least the late 1980s. In their heyday the H-M Shop supported up to five cars for NASCAR's top drivers, Ford GTs, plus motors for every type of racing from the Can-Am to European rallys to ocean boat racing. They employed all the best drivers of the era. They also made major contributions to safety and standardization in NASCAR car construction.

In 1956 John Holman was hired by Pete DePaolo, who headed Ford's racing efforts, to run racing on the east coast. Holman, a former truck driver, had worked in California for Bill Stroppe who continued with Ford's west coast race operations.

Ralph Moody was a capable driver in the early years of NASCAR (five poles and seven wins), but it was his mechanical skills that made his reputation.

When Ford withdrew from racing at the end of 1957 they put all their racing equipment, including cars, up for sale. Holman and Moody pooled their assets to buy as much equipment as possible and, in doing so, formed Holman and Moody. Though Ford was officially out of racing, H-M continued to field Ford cars. In addition to racing their own cars for Curtis Turner and Joe Weatherly, they began to build cars for other teams. They were the first to get a bare chassis directly from the factory to be rebuilt for racing.

In 1962 H-M stepped out to Ford motors to develop the fledgling Cobra. H-M work was to continue with Shelby through the Ford GT program, culminating with the Le Mans wins of 1966 and 1967. They also prepared the Falcons for European rallies, though the cars were run by Alan Mann of England. In 1967 they built the Honker II (John Holman was Honker I) Can-Am car for Mario Andretti.

By 1963 all racing Fords were being built by H-M. Dan Gurney, Fireball Roberts

Left: The Holman-Moody warehouse held crates of Ford 427 cubic inch engines for everything from Le Mans to drag racing. *Right:* (left to right) John Holman, Marvin Panch, Ralph Moody, Bill Amick, Joe Weatherly, Curtis Turner. Both photographs courtesy of Holman Moody.

In the mid–1950s NASCAR pit stops were leisurely affairs. Note lack of roll cage and safety in refueling equipment.

and Freddie Lorenzen won in H-M cars, while the rising Wood Brothers team used H-M engines. Ned Jarrett took the 1965 driver's title in an H-M Ford. By the mid 60s H-M was preparing Fords for Jarrett, Junior Johnson, Lorenzen and Dick Hutcherson.

H-M innovations became the standard for all of NASCAR. Moody had tried to get NASCAR to use fuel cells and a safety strap between the driver's legs. NASCAR resisted until drivers were injured in ways that the innovations could have prevented, notably the death of Fireball Roberts. H-M also created the box steel chassis that is still a NASCAR standard. By standardizing assembly of the chassis, power train and suspension, a top quality turnkey racecar was affordable for a large number of race teams. Regardless of the brand name on the outside, the contemporary NASCAR stock car is based on the principles of the H-M Ford of the 1960s.

H-M even got into drag racing, creating the first A/FX

Mustang, the forerunner of the Funny Car.

In 1967 Andretti and Lorenzen finished 1-2 at the Daytona 500. By mid-season Lorenzen retired to be replaced by David Pearson. Because of an engine dispute with NASCAR few Fords were running at the top level. To slow the Richard Petty streak (10 wins in a row) Ford hired Jimmy Clark for the Rockingham race, to be run by H-M. But it was the new H-M team of driver Bobby Allison and crew chief Lorenzen that was finally able to beat Petty on the track.

Pearson made the most of his H-M Ford, taking sixteen wins and the driver's title in 1968 and again in 1969. In a dispute with Chrysler, Richard Petty switched to a Ford for 1969, a car built by H-M.

At the end of the 1970 season the world of racing seemed to fall apart when Ford withdrew from racing. H-M was on its own with no factory contracts. All but essential services were concluded. At the end of the season Pearson left and H-M ceased to be a race team. The last H-M race entry was for Bobby Unser at the 1973 Riverside race. Ralph sold his share of the company. The company sold the Ford GTs,

Besides Ford racers for NASCAR and Le Mans, Holman Moody also made drag racing Mustangs. Courtesy of Holman Moody.

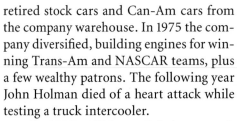

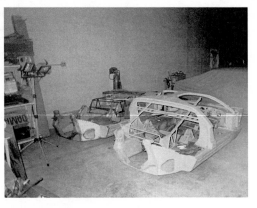

While raced by several teams, all Ford GT Mk IIs were built by Holman-Moody. Photograph used with permission of the Ford Motor Company.

Today Lee Holman builds "original" Ford GT Mk IIs using the original dies, materials and usually by the same builders. From the collection of J.A. Martin.

retired stock cars and Can-Am cars from the company warehouse. In 1975 the company diversified, building engines for winning Trans-Am and NASCAR teams, plus a few wealthy patrons. The following year John Holman died of a heart attack while testing a truck intercooler.

In 1978 Lee Holman, John's son, took over the remnants. While they continued to build NASCAR engines, he led development of a Mazda-powered sports car. Z and W Racing, which developed the Denali, raced the car as a Mazda GTP.

In 1991 Lee Holman began a new project that built upon the company's historic past. Using as many original tools and drawings as possible, plus assistance from some of the original craftsmen, a new series of Ford GT Mk IIs was built. The car was authentic to 1966 race standards, including the big 427 cubic inch motor. A brand new vintage race car appealed to enthusiasts who didn't want to spend big money for a genuine antique and then depend on thirty-year-old welds for reliability and safety.

39 Garlits Goes to the Rear

He gained national attention (in the world of drag racing) when he upset the famed Cook and Bedwell fuel dragster in 1957 and when he retired in 1987. In between, always in the top fuel class, Don Garlits won 35 NHRA national championship events, another 25 in the rival IHRA plus seven seasonal championships in the AHRA.

An advocate for unlimited speeds and higher earnings, he backed up his claim that professional drivers were not receiving enough of the winnings by forming the Professional Racers Association. Then he promoted the Pro Challenge in 1972, forever changing the winnings received by the teams, though he lost money on the event.

But his greatest contribution to the

"Big Daddy" Don Garlits. Courtesy of the EMMR collection.

While his front engine "Swamp Rats" won numerous races and titles, the rear engine cars set new standards in design for speed and safety. Courtesy of the EMMR collection.

sport may have been his push to move the engine behind the driver in rail dragsters.

While drag racing was getting started in southern California Don Garlits was living in central Florida. He thought he was going to be an accountant but an early flirtation with speed led to drag racing. By the mid 1950s he was building his own car and motor, setting records that the west coast drivers presumed came from inaccurate timing facilities. That is until he whipped them all in Texas in 1958. He acquired the nickname Swamp Rat, perhaps meant as disparaging. He accepted the name and now it's on a Garlits top rail machine in the Smithsonian Institution.

Top Fuel was always the ultimate edge of drag racing. These are the purest drag racers stripped of everything that does not help speed. In 1950 Dick Kraft created the first rail job by stripping his car to the bones. But by the mid 1950s a familiar shape was taking form. Over the years the wheelbase was increased but the layout remained.

There had been rear engine top fuel almost since the beginning. Art Arfons put his Allison aircraft engine behind him. Emory Cooks' rear engine racer was one of the first to go under nine seconds. And sports cars had already proven the advantages of rear engine racecars.

Still Garlits, and most competitors, preferred to have the motor in the center with the driver in the extreme rear.

His perspective changed after March 8, 1970. In the final round matchup the transmission blew up in Garlits' car. Garlits was thrown over a hundred feet. His leg was broken. While recuperating he realized there had to be a better way.

With the engine behind the driver an explosion would force the driver and nose away from the fiery motor, a simple fact that saved many lives and put the power where it belonged.

The new Swamp Rat appeared at the beginning of the 1971 season. It took a couple of months to set up the car but by the Winternationals he was winning, and by the end of the season he was unstoppable. With an air inlet over the driver's head, a small wing to hold the front down and a large wing over the rear wheels Garlits had created what looked like a long Grand Prix car.

As everyone was trying to catch up Garlits moved to other improvements in aerodynamics such as go-kart tires in front and an enclosed cockpit. Some ideas found more favor than others have but there is no question that the modern rail job began

with Garlits. He earned every letter of another of his nicknames, Big Daddy.

40 AMERICA'S FIRST WORLD CHAMPION
Phil Hill, 1961

Philip Toll Hill is an American contradiction. On the world racing stage he achieved greatness by becoming the first American to win the World's Driving Championship and co-drove to victory at the greatest European endurance race, Le Mans, three times. Yet in his own country he is virtually unknown.

Born in Florida and raised in Santa Monica, California, he became interested in the emerging sports car popularity, in the early 1950s, buying and racing an MG-TC that he had supercharged. He won his first race in the MG. As part of his training to sell imported cars he was sent to England. He returned with a Jaguar XK-120. In 1950, he won at Pebble Beach in a Jaguar, creating a demand for his driving services. While racing in the 1950s on both European and California tracks he quickly moved up to become a star driver.

Driving an OSCA in 1953 Hill had his first competition at Le Mans then at Rheims (France) in a Ferrari. He also drove in the Pan Americana, finishing second in 1954.

Luigi Chinetti, the Ferrari dealer who had sold Hill the first Ferrari on the west coast, recommended Hill to Enzo Ferrari for the factory endurance team. Hill responded by winning in his first season. The following spring he won the 12-hour Sebring race followed by his first Le Mans win three months later.

In 1958 he was hired to drive the ultimate European car, the Formula 1 Ferrari. After leading several races he won his first

Phil Hill prepares within himself for a race in 1961. Courtesy of Norman Hayes.

race, the last for a front engine Formula 1 car, at France.

Dan Gurney said of his fellow southern Californian, "He was almost hyper. He was racing all the time, whether he was at the track or not. He was reaching for the top. If you're going to be in a contest with him you're going to have to pull all out."

Hill, with co-driver Olivier Gendebien, began the 1961 season by again winning the Sebring and Le Mans sports car races. Hill and Gendebien won again in 1962, Hill's third win at the French classic.

When the Grand Prix formula was changed for the 1961 season the newly developed Ferrari Dino 246 was acknowledged as the best new car. There were as many as four of the shark nose Ferraris entered in an event. Hill and Wolfgang Von Trips of Germany were the acknowledged lead drivers.

Hill won at Spa Francorchamps in Belgium and when the series arrived at Monza, Ferrari's home track, Von Trips led with 34 points to Hill's 33. The race had barely started when Von Trips came together with Lotus driver Jimmy Clark. Clark survived the incident, Von Trips and six spectators did not. Hill won the race and the World Championship, but at an incredible price. Ferrari withdrew from the last race of the season, the United States Grand Prix, and Americans were denied the opportunity to honor one of their own.

In 1962 the British brought out several new cars powered by the Coventry Climax motor and the defending Ferrari team was shut out of victory lane. Hill's best finish was a second at Monaco. Since, to Enzo Ferrari, Ferrari cars could not be the fault it had to be the drivers, so Hill was released. He drove in the ill conceived ATS for parts of the 1963 season and with Cooper for 1964, then left the Grand Prix circus behind. Sports cars were his true love.

When Ford first challenged Le Mans in 1964 Hill was hired to handle the new GT40. He drove the first race laps at Nurburgring in May 1964 and led at Le Mans a month later.

For 1966 Phil signed with Jim Hall to drive the Chaparral 2D winning, with Jo Bonnier, the 1,000km Nurburgring endurance event. Then in the fall, with the rad-

A Ferrari mechanic prepares Hill's 1961 "shark nose" in which Hill won the world drivers' title. Courtesy of Norman Hayes.

ical high winged 2E, Hill edged out the boss to take the Laguna Seca Can-Am race. In his last competitive race Hill drove the Chaparral 2F at Brands Hatch, England, at the BOAC 1000. Hill and Mike Spence won what was the last race for the big V-8 powered American cars due to an FIA rules change.

Phil Hill's temperament certainly did not seem well suited for a race driver. He dreaded getting into the car and was forced to eat baby food before a race. He was quiet, almost scholarly, but very knowledgeable about what was happening with his car. After retiring from racing he collected classical music recordings and continued testing cars for magazines with insightful comments into the differences that made a car successful.

In Italy Hill is still recognized and treated as royalty, yet in his native land he is just a nice neighbor.

41 TOTAL PERFORMANCE
Ford Takes on Everyone

Through the 1960s the Ford Motor Company undertook the most ambitious motorsports program, ever, by anyone, regardless of the country. It was the motorsports version of the concurrent Saturn V Apollo moon program.

Prior to the mid 1950s Ford had been the performance car of choice, especially among young buyers. That changed with the 1955 Chevy followed by performance oriented Pontiacs and the AMA ban on racing that froze performance images at 1957 levels. By the early 1960s Ford had lost the youthful image, and new buyers.

Beyond popular opinion, this was backed up by marketing surveys, which showed that young buyers seldom thought of Fords. To young marketing and engineering managers within Ford this bode poorly for the growing youth auto market. In 1961, led by Lee Iacocca, the group approached top management for Ford's reentry into racing. There were no specific programs but still the group received the go-ahead. Quietly at first, then after the 1957 AMA ban was set aside, a race program was begun.

Before there could be a race program there had to be a counterculture within Ford Motor Company. Production cars required at least five years of planning, design, manufacturing setup and marketing before a car is introduced. Racing requires a team to be able to change entire concepts within a month. Racing requires mobility of thought and logistics. This was the hardest part, but one Ford was able to make.

In May 1962 Henry Ford II agreed with the young managers and made the necessary commitment. But it was to be more than a month before Henry went forward with the company's plan.

To make the program work Ford allied with top teams and drivers. In the east coast Holman-Moody and the Wood Brothers handled stock cars while Bill Stroppe handled the west coast. Alan Mann prepared Fords in Europe and Carroll Shelby put Ford power in his new Cobra.

Overseeing the race program was Leo Beebe, Special Vehicles Manager, who spoke directly to Henry II. Race operations were headed by Jacques Passino with John Cowley overseeing the GT and stock car programs. While listed as reporting to Cowley, Homer Perry, called "El Torro" by the teams, held the various programs together. Lew Spencer oversaw the Shelby Trans-Am and GT programs for Ford, although Shelby also had Henry's ear. Coordinating all the programs was Shelby's Al Dowd. In his administrative job Dowd, called "Greasy Slick," hired drivers and arranged for all the incidentals, including everything from the caterers to team doctors, were where they were needed.

The program first hit the tracks in 1963. The year began with a Mann prepared Ford Falcon finishing second at the Monte Carlo rally. Even before the Mustang was unveiled Alan Mann rally cars finished 1-2-3 at the Tour de France. Shelby's Cobras were beginning to take the measure of Corvettes in American sports car races and Ford backed stock cars were winning again on both the USAC and NASCAR series. And Fords and Mercurys were once again winners in drag racing.

The biggest impact on the public was

Jacques Passino (l), director of Ford's racing efforts, and John Cowlley (r), operational control of the stock car and GT program, are briefed on the day's test results. Courtesy of Holman Moody.

made when Scotsman Jimmy Clark finished second at the Indianapolis 500 in a Lotus powered by a stock based Ford V-8.

But even with the skills of Clark and the Lotus chassis it was obvious that a more powerful motor was needed if a Ford was going to win the 500. Immediately after the 1963 race work began on a full racer version, one with four overhead cams. Though defeated in 1964 by other factors the Ford Quad Cam became the dominant USAC/Indy engine, winning in turbocharged form as late as 1977.

As Indianapolis is the biggest race in the U.S., Le Mans is the biggest race in Europe. To guarantee a quick win Iacocca tried to deal with Ferrari for his cars to become Fords, but the deal fell through. Rather than develop an endurance race car from scratch, Ford worked with Lola designer Eric Broadley

to modify his Lola Mk 6. The result was the Ford GT40. The GT40 debuted at the Nurburgring in spring 1964 followed by the first Le Mans attempt. However, success did not come until Daytona 1965 after Shelby America took over the car. Shelby Cobras, especially the new Daytona coupe, were regularly winning over Ferraris in the GT wars. The Ford GTs were prepared by Shelby, Holman-Moody (who also did the stock car based motors) and Alan Mann in England. Ford GTs won Le Mans in 1966 and 1967. John Wyer's semi-private GT40s won in 1968 and 1969 after the factory cars were regulated off the track.

Creating winning exotic cars is fine for a company's image, but it needs a product to sell that conveys that image to buyers. Adding a fastback to the 1961 Galaxie made the Starliner into a NASCAR stocker for the streets. A similar treatment made the Falcon sexier, by a little. It was the April 1964 introduction of the Mustang that changed Ford. With a price like the Falcon and looks like a Ferrari, it was an instant hit and paved the way for Pony cars from other companies and the Trans-Am series, which was won by Mustang in 1966 and 1967.

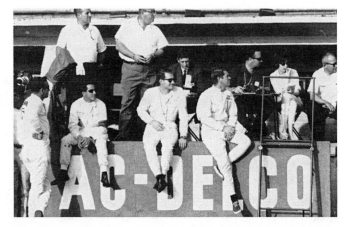

Part of the Holman Moody Ford GT team waits out a practice session. Left to right, Dick Hutcherson, a Ford engineer, Mario Andretti, John Holman, a test driver and Ronny Bucknam. Courtesy of Holman Moody.

Ford of England had had a long standing relationship with Cosworth Engineering. Through Cosworth and Lotus Ford entered Formula 1 at Zandvoort in 1967 and won. Versions of the motor would power Formula 1 winners through 1983 and turbocharged versions would win in Indy cars through 1988.

Through 1967 the Lincoln-Mercury division had its own racing division with entries in stock car and drag racing, often against Fords. In 1967 the Cougar narrowly lost to Mustang for the Trans-Am title. Rather than allow this intracompany rivalry to continue, all racing was put under one program. Since then, Mercury race victories have been only where Ford is not interested.

After the reintroduction of the hemi by Chrysler in 1964, Ford protested that they could not compete. In 1965 Ford introduced a hi-rise motor, and protesting Chrysler (Dodge and Plymouth) teams boycotted NASCAR. When the hemi was allowed back Ford teams boycotted most of the 1966 season, but the crowds were tired of boycotts and Ford was forced to come back on NASCAR terms. With the introduction of the true fastback Mercury Cyclone and Ford Torino, Ford dominated stock car racing in 1968 and 1969. Even Richard Petty switched to Ford for 1969. Though there were many Ford teams, all used engines built by Holman-Moody.

By the end of the decade Total Performance trophies included championships in NASCAR, USAC and Indy, Trans-Am, NHRA and AHRA, Le Mans and the World Manufacturers series, and even Formula 1. Al Dowd reported that in 1967, "the Golden Year," he spent $12 million, apart from the cars and drivers. Henry wanted to win, and teams were given cost plus (20%) accounts. Everyone went first class and made money.

Lincoln-Mercury supported a sports panel that included their drivers Dan Gurney and Parnelli Jones plus Jesse Owens and Al Kaline among others.

Dan Gurney recalled the politics within the Ford program. On one side were the Firestone teams led by Holman and Moody of Charlotte, North Carolina. From southern California was the Goodyear team and Shelby America. "I think, because Henry Ford had a personal relationship with Harvey Firestone a long time ago, there was always a feeling that there was a bias towards Firestone. Obviously it was not so much that it kept Goodyear from doing very well."

Ford employed probably the greatest group of drivers in the history of the sport. In NASCAR there were Ned Jarrett, Freddy Lorenzen, Tiny Lund, David Pearson, Cale Yarborough (prepared by Junior Johnson). Mario Andretti, A.J. Foyt and Al Unser won USAC titles. Dan Gurney, Jimmy Clark, Jackie Stewart and Graham Hill won in both USAC and Formula 1. Parnelli Jones, Peter Revson, Sam Posey, George Follmer, and Jerry Titus took Trans-Am wins. Sports car wins came with Bruce McLaren, Jackie Ickx, Ken Miles and Lloyd Ruby.

It all came to an end in the fall of 1970. The "Big Three" automakers announced that they were withdrawing from motorsports. However, Ford was still able to supply some support to Bud Moore for a 1971 Trans-Am effort and assistance for selected teams in NASCAR and NHRA. Ford of Europe continued in a reduced form for most of the 1970s. The decision to withdraw was made easier for Ford as they had won everything they had set out to do. There were no more worlds to conquer.

In the 1980s auto makers rediscovered motorsports, putting money and talent behind private teams from stock cars to GTP. Still the level of support paled in comparison to "Total Performance."

42 THE WHITE WINGED WARRIORS
Chaparral

James Ellis Hall was the right man in the right place at the right time. An innovative engineer, Hall came into racing in the early 1960s as the greatest era of change in race car design was about to begin and became involved in the series that offered him the opportunity to put his innovations into practice. By the end of the decade he had advanced the paradigms of race car design, beating even Colin Chapman to many innovations that are still standards of design.

Hall came from a family with the financial resources to allow him to race and build his own car. As his cars grew in innovation he developed a working relationship with other innovative engineers within the GM Technical Center.

In the early 1960s James Hall and his friend Hap Sharp established Chaparral cars in Midland, Texas. The first car was a front engine Chevrolet V-8 powered car modeled after the Scarab and built by Dick Troutman and Tom Barnes.

When they built the first rear engine car, the Chaparral 2, they used fiberglass-reinforced plastic (FRP) in an innovative box design. Through contacts with an equally young and eager Alcoa Aluminum salesman, Roger Penske, Hall was able to obtain some aluminum blocks.

The Chaparral 2 debuted on the pole at Riverside in October 1963 but retired after leading a field of international superstars. Over the winter changes were made to the nose to fix aerodynamic problems. The big innovation was the in-clusion of an experimental Chevrolet automatic transmission. This unit would remain a part of the Chaparral design and mystique through the end of the program.

Through 1964 and 1965 the Chaparral 2 was the premier sports car and Hall took the 1964 USRRC championship. Hall and Sharp co-drove a Chaparral 2 to victory at the 1964 Sebring race in a torrential downpour, beating factory cars from both Ford and Ferrari. By the end of the year the Chaparral 2C was debuted with a moveable rear flap.

Hap Sharp wanted to enter international endurance racing, and so for 1966 a roof was added to the older car and the Chaparral 2D was born. The cars (there were two) competed in seven races in 1966 and 1967. To get cooler engine air an intake box was placed on the roof. The only race they finished was the Nurburgring 1000km race in 1966 where Phil Hill and Jo Bonnier took the win.

The new Can-Am series debuted in the fall of 1966 and Hall had a new car that pushed the open spirit of the series. The Chaparral 2E was innovative beyond even Hall's past efforts. The radiators were placed

In 1965 the Chaparral 2 was the world's premier sports car, whether winning Sebring or as seen at Mid-Ohio. From the collection of J.A. Martin.

In the fall of 1966 the Can-Am Chaparral 2E changed almost every concept of racecar design. Courtesy of Chaparral Cars.

Jim Hall, Texan, driver, innovator. From the collection of J.A. Martin.

alongside the driver in the center of the car. Jim Hall says, "There were three good reasons for moving them (radiators) to the side. One was to get rid of the heat. Number two was to shorten the plumbing. Number three was to move the center of gravity more towards the center of the car." Four years later the Lotus 72 followed suit and set the standard for open wheel designs for most of the decade.

The most noticeable innovation was the high mounted rear wing. Wings in any other form of racing were still a year away. And to make it better Hall had designed a control linkage so the driver could move the wing during a race, flat for the straights and angled for cornering, providing downforce without drag. Hall says, "When we started running with the wing everyone pooh-poohed us, saying that it was a crutch that Hall is having to use because there's something else wrong with the car. Even the sophisticated people didn't make the connection."

There were teething problems and Phil Hill's win at Laguna Seca was the season's high point.

The original Chaparral chassis was constructed to allow modifications and the 2F showed how many changes could be included. A high wing and mid radiators were added, as was a roof leading to a squared off tail. In addition power came from a Chevrolet 427 cid V-8. Other innovations in air

control showed how much thought Hall was giving to aerodynamics; a still hit-and-miss science in most of the auto industry but one in which Hall and Sharp were becoming very knowledgeable. A nose trap door controlled air pressure in the front. A single 2F debuted at Daytona. The transmission failed because of a faulty bearing. An improved bearing was not ready until the last race of the season at Brands Hatch which Hill won with Mike Spence.

The 2G for the 1967 Can-Am season was an extension of the 2E with a 427 motor. The year 1968 was no better and at Stardust Raceway at Las Vegas Hall came together with Lothar Motschenbacher. The resulting accident broke both of Hall's legs and effectively ended his driving career.

Not all innovations are advancements. For 1969 Hall designed the Chaparral 2H. The criteria was to reduce frontal area. All appendages except the rear wing were removed. Small side windows were added so driver John Surtees could see and be seen. The car was a failure, and by mid season Chaparral was racing a McLaren 8. It was no match for the McLaren factory cars, ironically mounting Chaparral-like high wings, though not moveable.

The Chaparral 2J was a cooperative

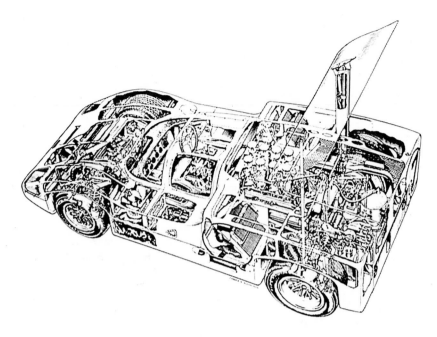

Exploded view of the Chaparral 2F endurance racer. Courtesy of Shell Oil.

effort with the GM tech group but fit within Hall's philosophy. Rather than using a wing to gain traction by pushing the car into the track, it created a low pressure under the car that pulled the car down. The "sucker," driven by Jackie Stewart, debuted at Watkins Glen in 1970. Although it qualified only third behind the McLarens it was the main topic of conversation. Drivers complained that the internal fan was sucking stones off the road and shooting them back.

After the first race Vic Elford took over the driving, he was also handling the Chaparral Trans-Am Camaro. Though he set lap records at every track, the 2J never won a race. At the end of the season the FIA banned all moveable air control devices ending the career of the 2J.

It also ended Hall's involvement in Group 7/Can-Am racing. From 1973 through 1980 Hall and Carl Haas campaigned Lolas in F-5000 and the reborn Can-Am series earning seven driver's titles.

Hall entered the USAC Champ car series in 1978 with a Lola Cosworth and driver Al Unser. As a rookie team they won all three 500 mile races.

The following year Hall debuted the John Bernard designed Chaparral 2K, the

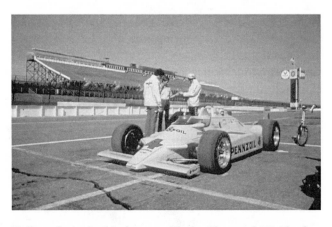

Hall revolutionized Indy cars with the Chaparral 2K. The first true ground effects car, seen at Pocono, won Indianapolis and the 1980 driver's title for Johnny Rutherford. Courtesy of Dave Kneebone.

first ground effects car for Indianapolis. Unser led early. The following year Johnny Rutherford won the Indy 500 and the dri-

vers championship with the same car. Hall continued to campaign in CART through 1996 before he retired.

43 KARTING
If You Don't Have Kart Experience, You Don't Have a Prayer

The origins of many forms of racing are lost in myth or are a result of little changes by so many pioneers that no one can truly be given the credit of creation. Not so for karting. In 1957 Art Ingels, a mechanic in the Frank Kurtis race car shop, first combined a light steel tube frame, four small scooter wheels, a very basic seat and a gas engine from a chain saw. Add a chain drive and some gears and you have the first go-kart.

The first karts had set the driver sitting upright, and for a while all similar karts followed the style. Others saw a good idea, and within a few years karting, both as a toy for around the neighborhood or as a serious first step racer, went from Los Angeles to around the world. Neophyte racers from Europe to Australia quickly recognized the tremendous potential for real racing, especially in relation to the cost. By weight and power classes could be drawn up to fit the local environment and the size and experience of the drivers.

Previous to karting the first step for an aspiring young driver was Quarter Midgets, a miniature in the sprint car/roadster fashion with a front mounted motor under a closed body. This restricted racing to pre-teenage drivers.

Adults could drive and race the karts, too, because they had no enveloping bodywork to cramp their knees and elbows.

Quickly the potential for serious racing was realized. A 1961 periodical chron-

icles a kart race in Mexico featuring two young brothers, Pedro and Ricardo Rodriquez. Both brothers went on to careers in professional Grand Prix and international endurance racing. Reports of the 1974 Barnesville Olympics includes the following drivers: Mark Dismore, Scott Goodyear, and Lake Speed. Four years later Speed won the world driving title for karts before moving on to NASCAR.

In 1960 Oregon's Larry Eyerly challenged the accepted style of Kart with a lay down version. The lower center of gravity and reduced frontal area made it an instant winner. Of course the style was quickly banned, then reinstated as a separate class. The upright Kart is called a Sprint. Most racing is done on tight road courses of less than half a mile. The laydown kart is called an Endurance. The driver is fitted into the kart, looking out between his feet. Speeds are higher and most racing is done on permanent courses like Road Atlanta or Watkins Glen. Endurance karts are longer and slightly heavier, give attention to aerodynamics and have wider tires. Both styles are segmented by driver/chassis weight and motor size with some classes allowing dual motors. Karts have not been restricted to paved courses. Sprint karts also race on dirt ovals with special tires.

The original sanctioning body for karting was the Go Kart Club of America. It was replaced by the International Kart

Shifter karts, like this 6 speed Italian built 125cc KGB, were so sophisticated that many professional drivers used these to keep sharp. They are an excellent step to a real race vehicle. Courtesy of Rick Scuteri for the Bob Bondurant School.

Federation for west coast karters. The World Karting Association, headquartered in Florida, races mostly on bigger east coast tracks like Daytona and Watkins Glen. Both groups sanction events and provide insurance for competitors. Shifter karts appeared in the 1990s, making them more like larger race cars that many hope to be moving into.

Much has been made of how champions like Ayrton Senna and Michael Andretti began with karts, but the list is so long it would be like naming all professional baseball players who began in Little League. By the 1980s it was essential for an aspiring driver to get into karts as soon as possible. If the talent, attitude and support were there, karting was the jumping off point for almost any form of racing.

Still, karting has been the motorsport of economy in America rather than the first step towards the top as it is in much of the world.

44 CARROLL SHELBY'S GREATEST PRODUCT, AND THE COBRA

Think performance and the name Shelby comes to mind, although it has been 35 years since the Cobras raced. That is because Shelby has kept his name and his cars in the public eye since his days with Aston Martin. In a time when even pro sports had no public relations Shelby had a personal PR agent and a photographer to record everything he and his team did, and what they did was fantastic.

One of the most American ways of making things happen is go all out. And when you want to go fast, put the biggest power source in the smallest body. From the P-38 fighter to the hydroplane racers, it has been a sure-fire, and uniquely American way of design.

So it was with the Shelby Cobra; put

Carroll Shelby. Courtesy of the Lynn Park collection.

The Shelby American shop maintained Cobras, Ford GTs and GT 350 Mustangs. Courtesy of the Lynn Park collection.

a big Ford V-8 motor in a small AC Ace two seat sports car, remove all accessories that do not help speed and send it on its way to challenge the world.

But to do this simple act and to give America its first World's Manufacturer's title it took one man with vision, drive, and a flair for publicity, Carroll Shelby. Shelby was an instant celebrity when he arrived in Europe in the early 1950s to drive the Cadillac powered Allards. To the Europeans he was the quintessential American, tall and lanky with a Texas drawl that remains today. He dressed like an American with a cowboy hat and bib overalls and he drove like the best.

He drove Formula 1 for Maserati before being asked to join the Aston Martin team in 1958. While the Formula 1 car was ineffective, Shelby and co-driver Roy Salvadori won the 1959 24-hour race at Le Mans in an Aston Martin DBR-1. The two-car team of Shelby/Salvadori and Stirling Moss/Tony Brooks finished the season

by winning the World Manufacturer's championship for Aston Martin. But a heart condition (eventually he had a transplant) put an end to his racing career.

Timing is everything. In 1961 the English Bristol Company was ending its business of making motors for AC cars. John Willment added a Holman-Moody developed Ford V-8. Shelby drove the car then approached AC about the possibility of putting an American V-8 in the light AC chassis on a production basis. Shelby had already developed a good relationship with the Goodyear Tire and Rubber Company, which was becoming more involved in racing. When Ford announced a new casting process that allowed them to make a lightweight V-8 the elements were ready.

Ford sent one of the early 260 cubic inch models to Shelby's Santa Fe Springs, California, shop while Shelby went to England to bring over the first chassis. The first complete car, built in Dean Moon's speed shop, was listed as CSX0001.

Shelby claims that the name Cobra came to him in dream. By the fall of 1962 Cobras were in production and seventy had been sold. The racing heritage began with CSX0002 at Riverside in September

From the first race (Riverside 1962) Cobras were all over the new Corvettes. Courtesy of the Lynn Park collection.

1962. Billy Krause easily led until a rear hub snapped. No win but the potential had certainly been shown. The year 1963 was for learning, especially about what can fail. Shelby entered two or three cars in the major endurance races, mostly to DNFs (Did Not Finish) for a wide variety of mechanical reasons. Back home the Cobras were running away from the new Corvette Sting Ray and the exotic (expensive) Ferrari GTOs when they first appeared; even as far as winning the 1963 U.S. Manufacturer's Championship. Recalled driver Dan Gurney, "For a southern California hot rodder it was something we all understood. It was looked down on by the established marques."

Cobras so dominated the 1965 USRRC series that they often drove together to prove the point as at Mid-Ohio, 1965. From the collection of J.A. Martin.

Internationally the Ferrari GTO with its high revving V-12 motor and aerodynamic body, capable of sustained speeds in excess of 180 miles per hour, was the class of any field. It was a formidable champion.

The Cobra challenged at the three-hour Daytona Continental. A Cobra finished fourth behind two GTOs and a Corvette. Le Mans, the only European race in which the Cobra challenged, was again a Ferrari win. The first international class win came at Bridgehampton, New York, in September 1963. There were no Ferrari entrants.

For 1964 Cobras were ready to take on the world for the Manufacturer's Championship for Grand Touring (GT) cars. While the AC body had worked well on sprint races a sleeker shell was needed for the high-speed circuits of Europe. Peter Brock designed the body for what became known as the Daytona coupe. By FIA rules the car is still in production, even with a different body, if the chassis and drive train are production. A fire sidelined the Daytona coupe at the Daytona Continental but the roadsters finished well. At Sebring the Daytona coupe finished first in class, fourth behind three Ferrari Prototypes.

To win the world title though you had

to defeat a Ferrari in Europe. Despite the rough road Dan Gurney brought a Cobra home first in the GT-3 class in the Targa Florio. The Daytona Coupe driven by Phil Hill was the fastest car at Spa Francorchamps, though finishing behind the winning Ferrari GTO. Gurney and Bob Bondurant took fourth overall and first in GT at Le Mans followed by another win at Goodwood (England). Rather than allow his magnificent cars to be beaten by an American hot rod, Enzo Ferrari forced the last race of the season, Monza in Italy, to be cancelled, preserving the thin points lead for Ferrari. Winning the season's final race at Bridgehampton was too late.

Despite not winning the championship the Cobra team had come closer than

In the hands of a top driver, like Ken Miles, the 427 Cobra was a dangerous and effective racing machine. Courtesy of the EMMR collection.

Above left: The contours of the Cobra Daytona coupe begin to take shape. *Right;* While retaining the standard chassis and small block Ford V-8 the aerodynamic Daytona coupe was able to stay with the high revving Ferraris on the fast European circuits. Both photographs courtesy of the Lynn Park collection.

any new car in its first year of international competition.

Cobra won again at the United States Road Racing Championship (USRRC). The Corvettes were hardly a factor. As a response Corvette installed a 427 cubic inch V-8 in some 1965 models. Cobra responded by adding a 427 cubic inch Ford V-8, with few other changes in Cobra models. The 1965 USRRC championship was again no contest.

The Cobras challenged the Ferraris again for 1965. Three Daytonas finished in the first five positions of the Daytona Continental followed by a fourth overall at Sebring, both class GT victories.

Ford, eager to see the Cobra win the international championship, enlisted English team manager Alan Mann to run most of the European events. Monza was the first event where the two Cobra coupes took first and second in class. Ferrari and Cobra traded heat wins at Oulton Park, England, with Cobra taking the overall win. Ferrari took Spa, Belgium, but Cobra came back to take Nurburgring and the Rossfeld, Germany, hill climb. Dan Gurney and Jerry Grant ran their Daytona coupe with the fastest prototype cars at Le Mans but fate settled on the Ferraris, which took the class win. The last European race was at Rheims, France, and was another Cobra

class win. Bob Bondurant took the last European race at Enna in Sicily, leading the event for many laps. As special bodies were not allowed for the 1966 season and the Manufacturer's title was assured to Cobra, this was the last race for the Daytona coupe. Three Cobra roadsters, both 289 and 427 cubic inch versions, finished in the top five at Bridgehampton.

The factory supported three 427 cubic inch Cobras and again won the GT championship in the USRRC.

The Cobras were not to run again in international racing. Shelby's attention was on making the Ford GT a winner, which was accomplished in 1966 and 1967. American professional sports car racing, the USRRC, had become centered on the Group 7 cars. In short, there was no place for the Cobras to race. They finished on top.

The influence of the Cobra extended far beyond the cars. King Cobras were one of the first true sports prototype cars, the type that became the Can-Am series. Cobra-ized Mustangs, the GT-350s, became championship winning sports cars over the small-engined Corvettes. Ford owns the Cobra name and has continued to use it on several models, including the anemic Mustang II based Cobra II, a NASCAR idea car, and most recently on a hot set-up Mustang. Shelby worked with Lee Iacocca on the Cobra and teamed up again with the latter when he headed the Chrysler Corporation on Shelby tweaked Dodge cars, including the turbo Omni GLH and the original V-10 powered Viper.

45 LINDA VAUGHN
Racing's Big Sister

One of the most recognizable personalities in all of American racing has never handled a race car at 200 miles per hour or put a wheel through a power slide. But Linda Vaughn is held in high esteem in virtually all forms of racing in America, and has been for nearly four decades, outlasting many of the "winners" in the hearts of race fans.

Linda Faye Vaughn was born in Dalton, Georgia, in 1943. Raised in a broken home and envious of her glamorous older sister, Linda planned to be a dental technician. To earn extra income for the family she was persuaded to enter local beauty contests.

Her first racing title was "Miss Queen of Speed at Atlanta International Raceway." She was just 18 and at 5'7" was already a noticeably attractive woman. Pontiac recognized her talent and her public appeal, and in 1962 she was made "Miss Pontiac," the personal symbol of Pontiac in southern racing. The Pure Oil Company hired Linda as one of the "Firebirds" then the lead "Miss Firebird." This led to recognition beyond stock cars as she was featured in *Esquire* magazine. When *Hot Rod* magazine conducted a national search in 1966 for a female personality to represent the Hurst Company, manufacturer of high performance automotive products, Linda was the easy win-

ner. Founder George Hurst became her unofficial father/mentor. Called "Miss Hurst Golden Shifter," she quickly became a regular fixture at events as diverse as the U.S. Grand Prix, NHRA Summernationals, Can-Am, sprint cars, and NASCAR races. Linda, in her gold outfit, posing next to a giant shifter on the back of a Hurst Oldsmobile convertible, has to be one of the strongest memories for anyone who saw her, or a picture of her, in American racing history. She has continued to work with Hurst and in 1983 was promoted to Vice President of Public Relations.

Along the way she has been linked romantically with drivers and race personalities all across the motorsports spectrum.

As the visual symbol of the Hurst Shift, Linda Vaughn became more known than most drivers. Courtesy of the EMMR collection.

Reports of special relationships with Carroll Shelby, James Garner, Fireball Roberts, Jimmy Clark and Joe Namath were whispered.

She has continued to work as an ambassador for racing and has been recognized by several racing hall of fame sites and SEMA (Specialty Equipment Market Association).

Through the years and her work Linda as maintained a visual presence that cannot be overlooked. Her blond hair still hangs over her shoulders and her figure has been described as statuesque. With sophistication and humor learned from experience, she has handled over the years what could be awkward references by over-

Even away from a race Linda was visually memorable. From the J.A. Martin collection.

anxious male race fans, as easily as tributes to much that is good about the sport.

46 ANDY GRANATELLI AND THE "WHOOSHMOBILE"
STP Turbine

No car ever has caused as much fuss and achieved so little as the turbine powered STP cars that competed at Indianapolis in 1967 and 1968.

In an effort to keep the Indianapolis Speedway an arena of automotive innovation USAC rules provided for powerplants as diverse as diesel motors, supercharged and turbocharged and gas turbines. In the early 1960s the Chrysler Corporation had seriously explored turbine-powered sedans and turbines had already replaced piston motors in aircraft, so it was a serious alternative. In 1962 Jack Zink brought a turbine-powered roadster to the Brickyard, but with no success.

In the early 1960s Andy Granatelli began racing the powerful but fragile Novis. He incorporated a Ferguson Four Wheel Drive (4WD) system in a car for Bobby Unser for 1964. Despite being almost a thousand pounds heavier than the rest of the field the Ferguson Novi was competitive. Says Granatelli, "I could see that four wheel drive had a lot of benefits. So I decided I wanted four wheel drive and a lighter car. All the cars had the same problem, all this fuel in the rear of the car. When you came in for a pit stop and got gas the car handled differently. So I decided to put the fuel down the center and you can't do that unless you put the engine on one side and the driver on the other. The car lent itself to a long engine and I found that a turbine was the perfect engine."

Ken Wallis, an aeronautical engineer with Douglas Aircraft began to lay out the car in the fall of 1965. The car was built in secret at the Granatelli brothers business, Paxton Products (Santa Monica, CA). "If they did, they would find a way to ban it or build one themselves," recalls Granatelli.

Several attempts, including in 1964, had been made to put turbine power in an Indy car, but none were successful. From the J.A. Martin collection.

Andy Granatelli (dark suit), Parnelli Jones (seated), the outlandish uniforms and the "whooshmobile." Photograph used with permission of IMS Properties.

Parnelli Jones was lured out of retirement when Granatelli assured him the car was capable of winning.

In the spring of 1967 the car was taken to Phoenix where a new track record was set within a few laps of practice. As the motor could not be used to help slow the car down a retractable air brake was added on the tail.

Jones qualified only sixth for the 500 and immediately there were cries that he was not showing the car's potential. Recalled Granatelli, "the turbine car was not sandbagging. At 480 horsepower it had fewer horsepower than the other cars, but what the car did have was perfect balance and the smooth turbine engine that he could drive anywhere." Jones added, "what the turbine did, it would jump across the short straightaway, it would jump down the long straightaway, then it would fall on its face ... and that's when they'd drive by me."

The Indy railbirds called it the "Whooshmobile," and the other drivers claimed it was unsafe. Granatelli again said, "They said that when you drove behind the turbine car the heat was so stifling that it made their radiator cores go up, they couldn't breathe and the heat waves coming out of the tail pipe were so blurry they couldn't see. They did everything they could to ban the car."

Dan Gurney said, "First, I didn't like the sound. Second, it was an off the shelf engine that you don't have to lean on so it should be able to go the distance. I didn't feel it was a fair shot."

Without the special qualifying motors the five leading Fords quickly gave way and Jones, who had begun sixth, took the lead coming out of turn one. Except for pit stops Jones led the race until lap 196 when, within a hundred yards of lapping second place Foyt, a gearbox bearing broke and the race was over.

It was not a complete loss for Granatelli. "As it worked out for me the best thing was losing that race as it became the most popular race car in the world and it got more publicity than any other race car ever had."

Immediately after the race USAC banned the retractable air brake and reduced turbine air inlets from 45 square inches to 15. USAC thought the turbine challenge was over. Granatelli thought otherwise.

STP also sponsored Team Lotus. The

The STP Lotus 56 turbine was almost as startling in 1968 as the "whooshmobile" the previous year. From the collection of Tom Saal.

challenge was given to Lotus boss Colin Chapman to design and build a 4WD turbine powered car of equal weight to the Fords. Chapman and designer Maurice Phillippe responded with the Lotus 56. In addition to the features Granatelli wanted, Chapman and Phillippe made the design a wedge that pushed the car onto the track for additional stability.

Tragedy struck even before qualifying was to begin for the 1968 race. Jimmy Clark was killed in a Formula 2 race accident in Germany. Then Mike Spence was killed while practicing in the first model 56. Two American drivers, Joe Leonard and Art Pollard, were hired to join Graham Hill in the three-car effort.

In a reversal of the previous year the turbines outqualified the piston cars as Leonard took the pole with Hill alongside. The front row was completed with Bobby Unser in a turbocharged Offy powered Eagle.

The race became a two-way battle between Leonard and Unser. This time the turbine, 4WD and all, did not run away from the field. Hill lost a wheel and crashed into the wall, eliminating one turbine. When Carl Williams crashed on the 181st lap the scattered debris made many think the race, with Leonard in the lead, would end under yellow. But the race went green again on lap 192. When Leonard went back to full power the turbine flamed out, and he coasted to a stop just as Art Pollard in the remaining turbine also pulled out with the same problem. Bobby Unser led the last eight laps to take his first of three Indy 500 wins.

After the 500 the turbines were campaigned for the remainder of Champ car season but none were able to complete a single race. At the end of the season USAC reduced the air inlet size again, to 12 square inches. This time the turbine threat was truly over.

Lotus continued development of the model 56, competing in several European Grands Prix in 1971. The model 63 was a Ford powered 4WD Grand Prix car in the 1969 season.

A new Lotus 65, with Ford powering the 4WD unit, was built for Mario Andretti for the 1969 race but a crash in practice sidelined the car. Andretti was forced to go to his conventional backup Hawk and won his only Indy 500 and a third driver's championship. At the end of the 1969 season USAC banned four wheel drive.

The wedge shape of the Lotus 56 served as the basis for the design of the Lotus 72 that became the model for Grand Prix cars into the mid–1970s and for the McLaren M16 and Eagle that dominated USAC champ car racing throughout the decade.

47 THE GREATEST FIELD IN THE HISTORY OF RACING
1967 Indianapolis 500

The drama of the 1967 race was in the participants. Probably no field in the history of racing ever had the variety and depth of champions entered that year. The rear engine revolution had opened the race to drivers and chassis designers who had never driven a Champ car on dirt; now they came on an equal basis.

After the victory of Jimmy Clark in the Lotus in 1965 and Graham Hill in the Lola the following year more Formula 1 drivers came to compete. Two, Denny Hulme and Jochen Rindt, drove Dan Gurney's Eagles. Rindt's car had the experimental Trans-Am based Ford pushrod motor with Gurney Weslake heads. Jackie Stewart, who led at lap 190 in 1966, was back in a John Mecom Lola. Hill had joined Clark in the STP sponsored Team Lotus, but they were not factors in this race. Ferrari driver Chris Amon tried the speedway but left with no effort to qualify but with a new wife. Including Mario Andretti, the field held six past or future world driving champions. (By contrast, the Formula 1 field during the 2000 season included only three world champions.)

A major incentive for the Formula 1 drivers to compete on the 2.5-mile oval was the winner's check. Clark and Hill earned almost as much in one afternoon as they had in an entire season of Formula 1. Carl Fisher's original plan to entice the best drivers from around the world with

Mario Andretti steps in front of 65 winner Jimmy Clark to accept recognition as the pole winner for the 1967 race. Behind him, in various stages of attention, were the best collection of drivers in the history of racing. Photograph used with permission of IMS Properties.

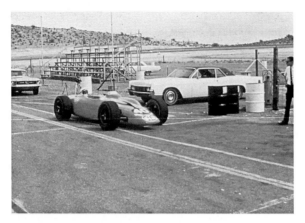

Fearing that USAC might change the rules, the Granatellis developed the turbine car in secret with tests at Phoenix. From the collection of J.A. Martin.

Two young NASCAR drivers who had yet to prove their ability, Cale Yarborough and Lee Roy Yarbrough, skipped most of the stock car races in May to enter the Champ car race.

There was Dan Gurney who had encouraged Colin Chapman to meet with Ford managers in 1962 and now headed his own All American Racing, which built the Eagles.

And there was a group of emerging new USAC stars, Andretti, the Unser brothers Bobby and Al, plus Roger McCluskey, Joe Leonard, Johnny Rutherford, and Gordon Johncock. All had arrived at the Brickyard after 1960, replacing the road-

the largest payoff in racing was proving to be just as workable in 1967 as it had been in 1911.

By turn two Parnelli Jones had pushed the turbine past everyone except pole winner Andretti who he passed before entering turn three. Photograph used with permission of IMS Properties.

ster champions that were the legends of the 1950s. Although trained in front engine sprint cars, the new group of drivers proved adaptable to all forms of racing and dominated the USAC/CART series well into the mid 1980s.

Andretti was the defending USAC Champ car champion repeating from his 1965 title. A.J. Foyt on the other hand had gone over a year without winning a race. He was in an all new car, the Lotus design based Coyote.

The race was a play in three acts. In qualifying Mario Andretti won his second straight pole with Gurney and Johncock completing the front row. The first five cars were all Ford powered, with team mates Foyt and Leonard fourth and fifth fastest. The sixth fastest driver was Parnelli Jones in the turbine, his lowest qualifying position in seven races.

Jones and the turbine, over two days due to rain at lap 14, dominated the second act of the race. As the Ford cars had to back off their race set ups from qualifying setups the turbine whooshed past. Andretti never led a lap. Only on pit stops was Jones out of the lead.

Andretti, Clark, Hill, and Lloyd Ruby were out by lap 58. Gurney was the fastest Ford, but a stuck fuel valve forced the Eagle to fly on only right side fuel tanks. The lean running motor eventually burned a valve and was out.

Jones was in a race by himself, passing where and when he wanted. The handling on the 4WD car was unmatched.

The third act began on lap 196 when a $6 gearbox bearing failed, sidelining the silent screamer. Foyt in second place, but within a hundred yards of being lapped, inherited the lead. It then looked like an easy win for Foyt until a group of cars came together in turn four on the last lap. Foyt backed off and picked his way through the debris to take the checkered flag over Al Unser and Leonard (third). Hulme finished fourth and was awarded Rookie of the Year. It was Foyt's third in seven years, making him the only driver to win the Indianapolis 500 in both a roadster and rear engine car. It was also the third straight win for Ford and the first for Goodyear Tire and Rubber.

---

48 IF YOU CAN'T BUY 'EM, BEAT 'EM
Ford Takes Le Mans

From the onset of Ford's Total Performance incursion into racing one of the key goals was to establish the name in endurance racing, particularly at the French 24-hour race at Le Mans, France. The first effort was to buy the current hot team in international endurance racing, Ferrari. But when the deal fell through, Ford Motor Company made an unparalleled commitment to win the endurance race, virtually at any cost.

Rather than begin with a completely clean sheet of design paper, Eric Broadley, of Lola Cars, was brought in to design a car based on his 1963 model Lola GT. The resultant car was the Ford GT40 (40" high). Originally it was powered by the pushrod V-8, similar to the one used in the Lotus Ford that finished second at the 1963 Indianapolis 500.

Early tests showed the car had a

tendency for the tail to rise at speed. The addition of a "ducktail" pushed the tail down and the car was ready to race. Driven by Phil Hill, the car made its racing debut at the Nurburgring, Germany in May, 1964. At Le Mans Hill led early, but the little Ford could not last the entire day. Ferrari won again.

By the end of 1964 it was obvious that the car in its original form was not up to beating Ferrari.

Two revised GT40s were entered at the 1965 Daytona Continental. Drivers Ken Miles and Bruce McLaren brought the car home to its first win. At Sebring a GT40 finished second overall behind the Chaparral sports car, first in GT. But Daytona and Sebring are not Le Mans.

Several variations of the GT40 were entered in the French June classic race. A longer nose was tried, a variation of which became the standard for the GT. A Mk II was entered with a 427 cubic inch stock car motor.

Again Ford came, saw and watched as another Ferrari took the checkered flag, although this Ferrari had an American driver (Masten Gregory), was on American tires (Goodyear) and was entered by the North American Racing Team (NART).

After that race efforts became centered exclusively on the Mk II. JW Engineering of England took over the GT40 to produce the Mk I customer car. When Ford arrived for the Daytona race, now a 24-hour event that began the 1966 season, they brought refined GT Mk IIs. Ken Miles and Lloyd Ruby led the race to take the winner's flag. At Sebring Miles and Ruby were in an open Mk II and spent most of the afternoon chasing Gurney and Jerry Grant in the leading Mk II. When Gurney's car quit on the final lap Miles swept by to take the win. Three Ford teams brought Mk IIs to Le Mans: Alan Mann of England, who had prepared the Cobras for the European races, Holman-Moody, who had prepared the big stock block motors and crewed cars, and Shelby American with three cars for Gurney/Grant, McLaren/Chris Amon, and Miles/Denny Hulme. Gurney and Grant set the early pace, forcing one Ferrari 330P3 after another to fall out. Then at the 17th hour the Gurney/Grant car had to be retired because it needed radiator water, and the rules did not allow adding water so soon after water was added in a routine pit stop. Fords were still running 1, 2, 3. Miles and Hulme were in the lead and would have finished as such until a

By early 1965 the Ford GT was becoming a winner as #11 takes second overall, first in Prototype class, at Sebring, Courtesy of the Lynn Park collection.

With the failure of the Mk II at Daytona Ford engineers quickly redesigned the J-Car into the Mk IV in time to win Sebring. Photograph used with permission of the Ford Motor Company.

Ford executive thought it would be a good advertising picture to have the three cars cross the line side by side. He ordered the drivers to get in line and cross in a tie. But Le Mans rules required that in the event of an apparent tie, the car that began further down the grid, as it went further, was to be the winner. Not one to play the marketing game, Miles backed off a few feet from the finish line allowing McLaren ahead. Ford still got their picture. All the Ford team put on a happy face, for they had vanquished Ferrari and won Le Mans.

A second Ford was brought to the 1966 race called the J-Car. It was designed entirely by Ford, using nothing from the Broadley design. Radically different in design, with a chopped tail and a narrow cabin and built on a fiberglass tub, the J-Car was not ready to race that year but would the next year.

To develop the J-Car design Ken Miles was slated to drive an open version in the 1966 Can-Am races. On August 17, during a test at the Riverside track, Miles crashed and was killed. Driver error was eliminated and no specific cause was found so the J-Car design was under a cloud of suspicion.

To enter the 1967 season the GT Mk II had to be improved. While the Ferrari challenger, the 330P4, was lighter, the Mk IIB was heavier with a stock car roll cage, bigger brakes and cast iron heads. At 3,100 lbs. it was half a ton heavier than the Ferraris.

Daytona 1967 was a disaster. Not only were the Fords not able to keep up with the Ferraris in the race but the half shafts had not been heat treated properly, and one by one they failed. Only one Ford, McLaren/Lucien Bianchi, finished, in seventh place.

The following Tuesday Ford management met to discuss the future of the Le Mans challenge. It was quickly agreed that the Mk II could not be de-

The steady drive of Dan Gurney and A.J. Foyt won the 1967 Le Mans for Ford in the Mk IV. Photograph used with permission of the Ford Motor Company.

veloped further; it would have to be with a J-Car or not at all. A design team led by Phil Remington began to redesign the car.

Two weeks later the new design, called the Mk IV, was ready for testing. After only three laps at Daytona the Mk IV was turning laps three seconds faster than the pole speed of the race a month earlier.

A single Mk IV was prepared for Sebring, to be driven by Mario Andretti and Bruce McLaren. Preparation was divided between Holman-Moody and Shelby American

Ford arrived with an armada of Mk IIs and Mk IVs plus spare drivers, mechanics, caterers and managers galore for Le Mans 1967. In the end it was a single red Mk IV that mattered. Photograph used with permission of the Ford Motor Company.

Gurney and Foyt share the thrill of a Le Mans victory. Gurney was so caught up in the ceremony that he shook his champagne, then began spraying every dignitary within reach, thus beginning a tradition for every international podium since. Photograph used with permission of the Ford Motor Company.

crew members. A revised Mk II was sent for Foyt and Ruby. Ferrari skipped the race so the only real competition was from Chaparral. Andretti took the pole, then with McLaren took the race by 12 laps over Foyt/Ruby.

Ford brought four Mk IVs and three MK IIBs, 14 drivers and an army of support technicians for the 1967 running of the French 24-hour classic. Practice looked good for Ford until the windshields began to crack. A new batch was airshipped from the Corning Glass company.

McLaren took the pole position but it was the Gurney/Foyt rabbit that was soon in the lead. As the sun set Fords were one, two and three. Then at 3:00 AM Andretti, with new brakes, spun just after exiting the pits. Ford drivers Roger McCluskey and Jo Schlesser tried to avoid broadsiding the Andretti car only to put their GTs in the sandbanks. Three Fords were out in a single incident.

Foyt and Gurney motored on, the big V8 never missing a beat. In second and

third were two Ferraris waiting for the Ford to fail. Several times Ferrari drivers tried to provoke the Ford drivers to race only to be turned aside. At one point Gurney pulled to the side and stopped, encouraging the Ferrari to go on its way. The two Americans were setting a pace and holding it. The leading Ferrari of Parkes/Scarfiotti became the chaser, setting laps ten seconds faster than the Ford, faster than any car had ever run at Le Mans. Still Parkes was told to go faster, but the exhausted driver indicated that neither he nor his car had any more to give. The fate of Ford #1 was beyond outside influences.

The only problem left for the Fords was when the second GT Mk IV of McLaren/Mark Donohue had the tail come off. McLaren had to go back around and retrieve the tail holding it in place until he returned to the pits for a proper repair. The pair finished fourth.

Carroll Shelby recalls, "two drivers (Gurney and Foyt) who they thought didn't stand a chance and would blow up. Gurney was absolutely brilliant. Gurney went a lot slower than he could so Foyt wouldn't compete with him. They brought the car home. Everyone had dysentery when it was left to those two guys to finish the race with that long to go."

At the end of the 1967 season the CSI, the competition division of the Federation International de Automobile (FIA), changed the rules, outlawing race engines over three liters. A clause was added that semi production cars (50 units per year) were allowed motors of up to five liters. This allowed the Ford GT Mk I to race with the 305 V8, a clause that would haunt the European officials who thought the rules would end the Ford threat. Raced by JW Engineering, a pair of Gulf Ford GT40s won the manufacturer's championship in 1968, taking Le Mans in 1968 and again in 1969.

49 THE EAGLE FLIES AT SPA

Goodyear Tire and Rubber supported Dan Gurney and Carroll Shelby in the establishment of All American Racing (AAR) in 1964 to develop cars to win the Indianapolis 500. After Gurney drove the first Goodyear shod F1 car, he took the opportunity to fulfill his dream, to build an American Formula 1 car that was able to win in the Grand Prix series.

Len Terry laid out the chassis so that the design of the Indy Eagle would be the basis for a car to fit the new 3-liter Grand Prix formula that was to begin in 1966. Cars for both series were constructed in AAR's Santa Ana, California, facility.

A support site was established in England called Anglo-American Racers. Gurney contracted Weslake Engineering of Rye in South Essex, England, to design and build a V12 motor, their only F1 motor. Gurney and Harry Weslake had first worked together on heads for the Ford 289/302 V8.

The season began before the V12 was ready so for most of 1966 the 2.7-liter four-cylinder Coventry motor powered the Eagle, making its debut at Spa, Belgium. Finally at Monza, Italy, the V12 was in the American racing blue car.

But it still lacked reliability and was set aside for the season's final race and opening round of the 1967 season.

The first race in Europe was the non-championship race at Brands Hatch, England, on February 26. Dan Gurney said of the potential for the team, "We had quite a few more unknowns than you would normally have because we had a low budget operation. But we were not that far off." Gurney and his new teammate Richie Ginther were entered in a pair of V12 Eagles. The cars shared the front row with Gurney on the pole. Although Ginther led early in the first heat, Gurney later came on to take both heats and the overall race.

The points races at Monte Carlo and Zandvoort, Holland, were hardly encores

The year 1967 began well when Gurney easily won the Race of Champions at Brands Hatch. Courtesy of Norman Hayes.

On one June day in 1967 the Eagle was the best in Formula 1. Courtesy of All American Racers.

The smiles, the garland, Dan Gurney upon winning the Belgian Grand Prix, June 18, 1967. Courtesy of All American Racers.

to Brands Hatch. Despite bringing a lightened model AAR 104 — the first F1 car to have a magnesium chassis and titanium suspension and exhausts — to Holland, both races were Eagle DNFs. Ginther was no longer on the team since he had retired from racing.

After a winning debut at Zandvoort for the Lotus 49, Jimmy Clark was the favorite for the Belgian Grand Prix at Spa-Francorchamps. It looked like a good choice as Clark took the pole, with Gurney second and Graham Hill in another Lotus 49 making the third car on the grid.

Dan Gurney in the Eagle Weslake at Mosport, 1967, Courtesy of Joe Calli.

Hill's engine faltered at the start. Gurney, watching for Hill, misread the start and began the race in the middle of the field as Clark drove away from everyone. On lap 12, just behind second place Jackie Stewart's BRM, Gurney followed Clark into the pits. According to Ford Public Relations, Clark had lost a plug wire and his day was over. After a very brief discussion about an apparent lack of oil pressure Gurney reentered the race. Soon he was behind Stewart again. Recalls Gurney, "I had some kind of a fuel starvation problem at maximum revs. After Jackie passed me I thought, 'there's not much use conserving it when I'm not going to win so go for it.' Once Stewart fell back we had pretty easy going." Gurney proceeded to set the fastest lap speed and went on to take the victory, the fastest ever Grand Prix at the time. The Star Spangled Banner played for both driver and manufacturer. It was the first international Grand Prix win for an American car since Jimmy Murphy's 1921 victory in France. Later that afternoon Gurney was airlifted to a nearby stadium filled with cheering American servicemen.

There were no more Grand Prix victories for the Eagle, though Gurney led the German Grand Prix until a universal joint failed within two laps of victory. By mid–1968 Gurney had a ride in a private McLaren Grand Prix car. The last race for the Eagle was at Monza. Recalls Gurney, "Because it was done in less than ideal conditions I felt there would be other opportunities, but as it turned out that was the last.

"I knew how delicate our financial condition was and the Weslake guys were performing five or six miracles each week. You couldn't sustain that. Weslake built a twin cylinder 500cc research motor. Had we been able to utilize that configuration in our V12 we would have been making another 60hp. It was a woulda, coulda, but it didn't happen."

Gurney's accomplishment was more than Murphy's in that he won in a car of his own construction. With the incredible costs of F1 today it is doubtful an individual, American or otherwise, will ever again be able to lead development of a car and then drive it on to victory. But in June 1967 one American did.

50 RICHARD PETTY BECOMES "KING RICHARD," 1967

By the mid 1960s the original "good ole boys" that fans of NASCAR cheered for were gone. Then, at the end of 1966, champion Ned Jarrett, Marvin Panch and Junior Johnson retired. NASCAR had no superstar to attract the crowds. There were plenty of hard driving young kids — David Pearson, Lee Petty's boy Richard, Buck Baker's boy Buddy, the tough little Cale Yarborough, "I'll race anything" Bobby Allison and the blonde Yankee Freddie Lorenzen — but none of these seemed able to reach the level of superstar that Turner, Weatherly and Roberts had been. Things didn't look good at the beginning of 1967. USAC aces Parnelli Jones and Mario Andretti won the Riverside and Daytona races. Petty, Pearson, Allison and Yarborough each won early races swapping wins between Plymouth, Dodges, Chevrolet and Ford. Pearson quit Cotton Owen's team, then Lorenzen, citing health reasons, retired. Pearson took over Lorenzen's Ford and Allison took over Pearson's Dodge.

Petty took a brief run beginning in mid–April when he won three in a row, then two consecutive wins in early June, yet he was still second in points to consistent James Hylton. But with four more consecutive wins in July he took the lead. After early April Petty put together 15 wins in 23 races.

After a poor showing at the 1967 Daytona 500 the Petty family/team brought out the 1966, "ole blue" Plymouth and reskinned it as a 1967. Even Richard cannot explain the differences, but the older car was a winner. The same car won on superspeedways, short tracks and even dirt tracks. In an era when 40 to 50 races per season were common, as many as three races were held each week so a team had to be ready to run Darlington on Sunday, the paved half mile of Beltsville in Maryland on Saturday, then the dirt .4 mile at Tidewater in Virginia the following afternoon. Petty took two wins and a second in those three races. By winning Darlington Petty

Richard Petty (l) at the beginning of his career and Lee Petty (r) nearing the end of his with the 1960 edition of Plymouth No. 43. Courtesy of Goodyear Tire and Rubber.

passed his father for most NASCAR wins with 55.

No one gave special thought that Petty won at quarter-mile Winston-Salem on August 12. The hoopla of his win five days later at Columbia Speedway was that it was his 18th, setting a new season record. Through the October 1st win at North Wilkesboro Petty was the only winner taking ten straight.

Ford was so desperate to break the Petty streak that they hired Allison to pair with Pearson and brought in Formula 1 ace Jimmy Clark. Top priority was given to having a Ford finish ahead of Petty, and numerous top racing executives headed south.

At the Charlotte Motor Speedway Petty's streak was broken when the engine in the blue #43 let go. But it was no help for Ford as Buddy Baker won in a Dodge.

Things did look up for Ford as Allison won the last two races of 1967 and the 1968 opener with Petty second.

But by the end of 1967 NASCAR now had a new superstar that press and fans alike were calling "The King." Richard Petty had ten straight wins and took 27 of the 48 races of the season. Petty says, "We'd go run a race, win the thing, then we'd get ready for the next one. We never thought about adding them up or nothing. NASCAR was the way we made a living, and I was the main breadwinner because I was the driver. Why me? I wasn't that much more talented than anybody else. I was just in the right place at the right time under the right circumstances to be able to accomplish what we did."

But it was more than wins that made Petty the King. His easy-going manner and quick smile were a promoter's dream. When most Americans still thought of stock car drivers as greasy hell raisers, on and off the track Petty was a role model. He was always available to the fans. As Richard said, "Common sense told me that the tracks paid me nothing. The people that were buying tickets were the ones who were

By the 1970s Richard Petty was acknowledged as "the King" though he had yet to discover his later ever present cowboy hat. Courtesy of Ed Clayton.

paying me. Without the fans, who's interested in Richard Petty? Nobody."

Petty's clean image and fan accessibility became cornerstones for what NASCAR later became.

Even "ole blue" became a celebrity. The year 1967 was the first that Petty ran exclusively with #43. In contemporary NASCAR a car's number is sometimes more important than the sponsor. Another gift from Petty Racing.

In 1971 Petty Racing signed a contract with STP for sponsorship and their colors, mated of course with Petty blue. This was the first long-term use of stock car racing for product promotion and car graphics for sponsor identity, another cornerstone of NASCAR.

By the time Richard Petty retired in 1992 he had won 200 races and seven titles and had changed American racing forever.

51 UNLIMITED DREAMS, DOMINANT REALITY
Can-Am

In nostalgic rear vision, no racing series had the appeal that the Canadian-American Challenge Series, the Can-Am, did. These Sports Car Club of America races are looked back upon as great, unrestricted racing. From 1966 through 1974 the Can-Am seemed supreme and held the imagination of the motor racing fan as few other series have.

The Can-Am is remembered as great racing with world class drivers in closed wheel sports racing cars almost unlimited in design freedom. Just about anything that could make a race car go faster was legal, including some of the most powerful engines ever intended to be raced for more than six seconds.

The reality is a bit different. Only in the initial year was there a sense of competition as the series became the domain of one manufacturer, then another: McLaren 1967–71, Porsche 1972–73, and Shadow 1974 after the Porsches were virtually outlawed. When the series had only six races in the fall teams included the great drivers of all racing worlds, but when the series went a full season, drivers who had commitments

to USAC or F1 could not take part. Except for the two Porsche years, the series was the domain of the Chevrolet V-8, small and large block. Except for a single Ford win by Dan Gurney, no other engine manufacturer ever saw victory lane, and few tried.

Still the image persists, and the name conjures up big racing beasts. The seeds of the Can-Am series were in sports car racing in the early 1960s. Americans had always been willing to try different chassis-motor combinations and to put big V-8s in little European racers. Roger Penske went the next step with the Zerex Special, a wheel covered Formula 1 Cooper. His success led Cooper, Lotus and Scarab to create two-seat rear engine race cars. By 1963 the best of the European factory racers were no match for the American hot rods. Eventually the FIA sanctioned the cars, making them the Group 7 class.

SCCA created the United States Road Racing Championship (USRRC) in 1963 for Group 7 and sports cars. Bob Holbert won the first title, racing in both a Porsche R61 and a Cobra. The USRRC continued through 1968 when many of the races were merged into the extended Can-Am series.

Beginning in 1958 the *Los Angeles Times* newspaper had sponsored a fall race at Riverside Raceway. Top drivers from around the world in the fastest sports cars brought attention to racing without limits.

In 1966 the SCCA combined the Riverside race with USRRC cars and, with support from Johnson Wax, produced the highest paying road racing series in the world, the Canadian-American Challenge. Of course everyone wanted to take part.

It was a series that begged to be dominated and Lola Cars Ltd happily obliged in the inaugural year of 1966. The two-year-old T70 was used in five of the six wins with factory driver John Surtees taking the championship. Surtees won one race in 1967 then endured three years of being overshadowed by McLaren.

The sole 1966 non–Lola win was by Phil Hill in a Chaparral 2E. The revolutionary car set design standards that are still used. However, it was also fragile. The 2G was built for 1967 but the 427-cid motor put too much strain on components and two second place finishes were the team's best. The year 1968 was a repeat until Jim Hall had both legs broken in a race accident. He retired and hired Surtees

to drive the new 2H for 1969. Ultra low and narrow, the car proved that innovation can go too far.

With the assistance of GM Hall entered the 2J, the "sucker car," in 1970. An internal motor, aided by Lexan sliding skirts, sucked the car onto the track. Still, despite the driving efforts of Jackie Stewart and Vic Elford, the car failed to win a single race. Regardless, at the end of 1970 the SCCA outlawed moveable air control devices (i.e., wings and fans).

The second domination began at Road America in August 1967 with the McLaren M6. For the next five years the Gulf orange cars were the class of the field.

Bruce McLaren had raced in the 1966 series with an M1B, a Chevrolet-powered version of 1965's Oldsmobile-powered car. He and teammate Chris Amon had three second place finishes but no wins that year.

Bruce and 1967 teammate Denny Hulme took five of the six wins and finished 1-2 respectively in driver's points. Afterwards everyone had to have an M6. Mark Donohue took his M6 to the 1968 USRRC title and a Can-Am win.

But the M6 was obsolete when McLaren entered the 1968 season with the wedge shaped M8. McLaren cars took all eight wins, two by customers, with Hulme taking the title. For 1969 Bruce won six races and the championship with Hulme winning five in the high wing M8B. The series was eleven races long. It was "the Bruce and Denny Show."

Bruce McLaren was testing the 1970 car, the M8D, when he was killed in a crash. Dan Gurney was brought in for two wins before an oil sponsorship conflict forced him out. Peter Gethin took over for one win. Hulme won six and a second driver's title. Peter Revson replaced Gethin in 1971 in the M8F, an updated M8D. Fearing the Lola challenge from

Beginning in 1967, the second year of the Can-Am series, Bruce McLaren, as here at Mosport (Canada), was the best of the best. From the collection of J.A. Martin.

Jackie Stewart, Revson was not held to team orders and won five races and the championship.

The M20 was an all new car for Revson and Hulme in 1972. It was similar to the M8F but with side radiators and a front mounted wing. The car was good, but the era of the third dominator, Porsche, was about to begin. Hulme won two races but the M20 was no match for the turbocharged "Panzers." McLaren cars packed up and went home to focus on Formula 1.

By 1969 the "Bruce and Denny Show" thoroughly dominated the Can-Am series. From the collection of J.A. Martin.

The most radical cars of the series were raced in 1970. Trevor Harris designed the revolutionary AVS Shadow in an attempt to reduce frontal area. Firestone made smaller tires to fit. The car was so small that there was no room for a radiator or sufficient brakes. In its original form driver George Follmer lay down like in a go-kart. Later he was moved more upright. The car never finished a race.

The Autocoast Ti22 first raced in late 1969. Designer Peter Bryant made a wedge shape for maximum downforce. The major innovation was the use of titanium (Ti22 is titanium's atomic symbol and weight) which was lighter and stronger than steel or aluminum. The chassis was destroyed early in the season, but driver Jackie Oliver came home second three times. The Ti22 was not a factor in 1971.

The new March car company, fresh from success in Formula 1, built the 707 with twin adjustable canards in the nose. Low and wide, the car was overweight. No factory follow-up was made.

Ferrari was the first European manufacturer to look at the Can-Am series. In 1967 a lightened version of the 330P4 was entered in several races. The world champion was no match for the new McLaren M6. Ferrari returned with a six-liter full racing engine for 1968 and 1969. They came back in 1971 and 1972 with a seven-liter wedge shaped car but the 612Ps and 712 were under-developed and Ferrari discontinued the project.

For all their success elsewhere, winning the Can-Am should have been easy for Ford, but it wasn't. The only Ford success was a single win by Dan Gurney in the inaugural season with a Lola. For 1967 Ford supported the Holman-Moody, Len Bailey designed Honker II. Despite the driving skills of Mario Andretti the car qualified only twice.

A second program was begun in 1967 using the chassis of the Le Mans winning Ford GT Mk IV called the G7A. It had an articulated rear wing but even in the hands of Sir Jack Brabham it was never competitive.

BRM also tried a Can-Am car but it was not a serious effort.

Peter Revson drove Carl Haas' factory Lola for 1970. The T222 was a match for anyone, except for team McLaren. Jackie Stewart drove the 1971 stubby T260 to two wins. The final factory car was the T310, a long low car for David Hobbs.

Though expensive, Porsche 917-10 turbos were the best cars to chase the Penske 917-30. Peter Gregg (#59) did not enjoy the success in Can-Am he did in the Trans-Am and returned to sports cars. From the collection of J.A. Martin.

Porsche had no more than introduced the 917 to World Endurance racing than an open, light weight version was made for the Can-Am and the European Interserie. With the 4.4-liter motor it was no match for the 7-liter McLarens. When their 917 was outlawed from international racing Porsche engineers looked at how it could be made competitive for the Can-Am. They could not further enlarge the engine. The answer was a turbocharger. And rather than race it as a factory effort Penske Racing was hired to run the car. Mark Donohue worked extensively with Porsche engineers to develop the car. They knew they had McLaren beat before the first race even began. The new McLaren M20 featured a dual wing nose design. Porsche had tried the same design then moved past it. They were ahead of McLaren in design and power. The one thing they did not factor in was an accident. Donohue flipped his 917-10 at Road Atlanta. He would miss races. Penske brought in former teammate George Follmer. After two early McLaren wins Follmer, and later Donohue, dominated the series, with Follmer taking the championship. At the end of the season McLaren left the series.

In 1973 Penske/Porsche dominated. Bobby Rinzler bought the 1972 Porsches from Penske and other 917-10s were made available to Hurley Haywood and Jody Scheckter. But Donohue had the ultimate beast, a car that is still popular on posters. So dominant was the 917-30 that the SCCA limited the boost on the turbocharger, and Porsche and Penske left the series. Donohue took the 917/30 out once more in 1975 for a speed record run of 221 mph.

More important to the SCCA than the domination of competition by the Porsches was the escalating cost. McLarens and Lolas were affordable to the majority of private teams. Very few could afford a Porsche, and without a Porsche, a driver was just putting in laps.

After 1970 the principals of the Ti22 and AVS Shadow joined forces with sponsorship by Universal Oil Products (UOP). The 1971 Shadow was more conventional in shape but still used small tires. For 1972 they went to conventional size tires.

Don Nicholls and the Shadow team were the only ones to respond to the rules limitations with a new car for 1974, the light but conventionally shaped DN4. Though not always the friendliest

In 1974, the last year of the original series it was the Shadow team that dominated. From the collection of J.A. Martin.

of teammates, George Follmer and series champion Jackie Oliver dominated the 1974 season, although Scooter Patrick won the last race in a McLaren M20.

Without the excitement of the Mc-Larens or Porsches and with fields that, at best, looked like a local event, the SCCA pulled the plug on the series at the end of 1974. The King was dead but the legend was born.

52 MOVIES GO RACING, AND A FEW GET IT RIGHT

Racing was a natural subject for early Hollywood films. Cars were faster and more predictable than a horse and more versatile than a train. They had action and were big enough for comic antics or fights on running boards or back seats.

Even before "talkies" were able to capture the sound of a racing engine, or the colors of racing were fixed to celluloid, racing was part of the movies. Charlie Chaplin used the 1912 Grand Prize at Santa Monica as a movie backdrop. An average of three racing-oriented movies per year, though some were single reelers, were released between 1915 and the advent of sound in 1930. Titles like *Speedway* (1929), *Greased Lightning* (1919) and *The Checkered Flag* (1922) were repeated in the 1960s, but all the films were original. *Super Speed* (1930), *Speed Maniac* (1919), *Road Demon* (1921), *Racing for Life* (1924) and *Roaring Road* (1926) left little for the fans to wonder about the topic of the movie.

Once sound was added more of the excitement of racing was brought to neighborhood theaters. In 1932 Jimmy Cagney and Joan Blondell took to the Indianapolis Motor Speedway in *The Crowd Roars*, and the cars and crowd did roar. Six years later Pat O'Brien and Ann Sheridan·used the same background for *Indianapolis Speedway*. Actual tracks were used in *10 Laps to Go* (Gilmore), *Burn Em Up O'Connor* (At-lantic Stadium), *The Big Wheel* (Culver City), and *Born to Speed* (Saugus).

After the war a new generation of movies featured racing themes. *Buck Privates Come Home* featured film from Gilmore Stadium. The King of Hollywood, Clark Gable, took to the sprint car tracks in 1951 to win Barbara Stanwyck in the predictable *To Please a Lady*. Four years later Kirk Douglas, with appropriate back-drops, ran the GP circuit in *The Racers*.

The 1959 moonshiner classic *Thunder Road*, starring Robert Mitchum, had the soul of speed if not any actual track racing. Rory Calhoun looked to be in actual stock car races in 1960's *Hard Drivin*, as did James Caan in 1964's *Redline 7000*. *The Checkered Flag* (1963) was more a checkered plot than a race, as a wife tried to kill her race driving husband.

Hollywood served up a series of Grade B drag racing movies as symbolic of teenage rebelliousness in the late 1950s. Beginning with the big name *Rebel Without a Cause* (1955) through *Drag Strip Girl* and *Hot Rod Rumble* (1957) to *High School Confidential* (1958), these movies showed teenagers as crazed for speed and thrills regardless of the risks.

Elvis Presley put racing to music in two movies, *Viva Las Vegas* (1963) and *Speedway* (1968). Numerous other movies of the Frankie and Annette genre in the

Movie stars have long been attracted to the excitement of racing. In 1947 Clark Gable joined Tony Hulman at the Indianapolis 500. Courtesy of Bob Sheldon.

enheimer's *Grand Prix*. The Cinemascope film with on-board cameras and stars like Jim Garner and Yves Montand doing their own driving brought the viewer into racing as never before. And there was an actual story relating to racing.

The Indianapolis 500 based film *Winning* was meant to be a TV movie until Paul Newman became involved. Using many techniques pioneered in *Grand Prix*, *Winning* showed the great race from the inside in a way unsurpassed until the advent of the on-board TV camera in the 1980s.

Newman and Garner became so involved in racing from their film experiences that they became actively involved in racing in real life through driving and team ownership.

Steve McQueen went the reverse. He had raced about everything on wheels before he produced and starred in a movie putting the 1970 French 24-hour classic on film, *Le Mans*. The drivers were less interesting than the cars, but then, how do you upstage a Porsche 917?

Tom Wolfe's story, *The Last American Hero*, based on the life of Junior Johnson, became a 1973 movie starring Jeff Bridges. Richard Pryor and Beau Bridges made a 1977 biographical movie of black stock car driver Wendell Scott, *Greased Lightning*. *Heart Like a Wheel*, 1983, starred Bonnie Bedelia, as drag race champion Shirley Muldowney.

Even Disney's *Love Bug* series went racing in the 1977 *Herbie Goes to Monte Carlo*. In the same year Al Pacino was a soulless Formula 1 driver in *Bobby Deerfield*.

On the surface Burt Reynolds' 1983 movie *Stroker Ace* seemed to be the silliest race move ever made, yet most of the incidents were based on true exploits by the

1960s included cool surfers, safe music, hot chicks and fast cars. The races, like the waves, were there to give a young southern California spirit to a predictable boy meets girl story.

A more mature love story was the 1966 French film *A Man and a Woman*. Jean-Louis Trintignant was a Ford of France driver from the Monte Carlo rally to Le Mans trying to rediscover love with Anouk Aimee.

Tony Curtis was the hero of two 1960s movies that humorosly tried to recreate races of the 1920s. Jack Lemmon was the villain and Natalie Wood was the beautiful heroine in the 1966 *The Great Race*. Terry Thomas and Susan Hampshire had the equivalent parts in the 1969 *Those Daring Young Men in their Daunting Jalopies*.

The quality of racing movies took a great step forward in 1966 with John Frank-

"good ole boys" of early NASCAR racing.

In 1988 Joseph Bottoms saved beautiful engineer Marla Heasly, who had invented a better racing motor, in *Born to Race*.

A heavily-hyped racing movie was the 1990 Tom Cruise vehicle *Days of Thunder* repackaging the *Top Gun* formula to NASCAR. While the story seemed to be a prediction of the career of Jeff Gordon, it was loosely based on the short mercurial career of Tim Richmond with Harry Hyde.

Two of the movie cars from *Days of Thunder*. The Chevrolet Luminas were prepared by Hendrick Racing. Courtesy of Ed Clayton.

Racing has occasionally been interjected into the plot of several TV programs. To bring the hero into the race background the plot would have him jumping into a stock car to race at the top professional level to chase down a clue or bad guy. The *Dukes of Hazard* (Dodge Charger) did their racing on country roads though an occasional stock car driver found his way to Hazard County, while *Miami Vice* cops (Ferrari) raced on the night roads of Miami. Several proposals have been pitched for a dramatic series with NASCAR and/or CART as the background but nothing has come of them.

After an attempt to make a film about Formula 1, Sylvester Stallone returned to America in 2000 to make a film about CART racing. *Driven* was a confusing movie which demonstrated dramatic special effects if nothing else.

Actors have also raced off screen. Big powerful cars were part of every male star's wardrobe in the 1930s. James Dean and Steve McQueen took their driving seriously, winning sports car races in the 1950s and 1960s respectively. Country singer Marty Robbins raced in the Winston Cup through the 1980s. Though never a winner, he actually led one lap. Celebrity races have attracted stars such as Ted Nuggent and various Playmates of the Year. Cruise, Gene Hackman and Jason Priestley briefly tried more serious racing with Priestley also providing IRL TV commentary.

53 SPRINTS AND MIDGETS

The origins of Sprint cars have been lost in the mythology of racing. Most of the first closed course races were for only a few laps, often because that was the level

Zenon Bardowski prepares to take his Riley out for practice at Williams Grove in 1938. Courtesy of the EMMR collection.

of reliability. Then as promoters were able to depend on the cars the length of races increased to hundreds of miles and up to twenty-four hours. Big name drivers and manufacturers kept moving up to bigger and bigger races, and more sophisticated and more expensive race cars like the exquisite Miller 91 were the result. The Miller was expensive so few drivers could afford one. Less expensive cars were needed for local racers.

Louis, Arthur, and Gaston Chevrolet developed the Frontenac racing head for the Ford Model T. Known as the Model R, the conversion cost much less than the Miller and was ideal for the local racer.

The ascendancy of the Offenhauser, a 220 cid version of the four cylinder Miller, offered dependable power for a bit more money. Several versions of the Offy were made, tailored to the needs of specific types of racing. One type was for the half-mile dirt ovals that dotted the Midwest. Rules, both local and AAA, allowed stock motors, but even the flathead Ford, the first performance engine financially available to anyone, lacked the power to weight ratio of the Offy.

In the early 1930s a new class was begun: Midgets. The first one was built by Californian Ken Brenneman, though other smaller versions of Championship cars had been made earlier. Similar in design to the big cars, Midgets were smaller, more powerful and much less expensive. They were

A field of Sprint cars comes around the fourth turn at Williams Grove (Pennsylvania) in 1939. Courtesy of the EMMR collection.

also the first step for weekend and serious racer alike.

At the end of the Second World War Southern California was filled with mechanics, metallurgists and fabricators who had built the planes of war, but now were without a customer. Many turned their expertise to building race cars. Where local prewar race cars were home built, one of a kind, these new builders standardized the design. They offered chassis that were safer, faster and cost less. What more could a local racer want?

Blimply Blimp's Sprint car at Williams Grove, 1945. Courtesy of the EMMR collection.

When USAC replaced AAA as the primary sanctioning body a formal class was made between the big Champ Cars and the small powered Midget class called Sprint Cars. Less powerful and intended for smaller tracks than the Champ cars, Sprint cars were the natural evolution that led to Champ Cars. That is until the advent of the rear engine racer in the 1960s. By the end of the decade the skills refined on small dirt ovals were almost irrelevant to the top class. Tom Sneva was the last Indy 500 winner to be trained in Sprint cars and he came up in 1973.

There was a price to be paid for aggressive Sprint car driving, close contact between open wheeled vehicles that often resulted in injuries and death. Many drivers disdained seat belts, preferring to be thrown from the car. But rollovers and crashes through wood barriers and into the crowd were fatal to driver and spectator alike.

In the 1950s retaining walls were increased for the fans and roll bars were added for the drivers. In the 1970s roll cages, modeled after those in NASCAR, were added. They were at first optional then later mandatory. By the 1980s

deaths were not an accepted part of Sprint car racing.

Muscle cars of the 1960s were built around big, powerful and inexpensive V-8s. Sprint car drivers had always been allowed to use these motors but now they were viable alternatives to the Offy. As the popularity of the V-8s grew special aluminum racing versions were produced. Today V-8s of up to 410 cubic inches are allowed by USAC and other groups.

There are two national sprint car series, USAC (non-wing) and World of Outlaws (wings), and dozens of regional and local associations with their own rules,

By the 1960s most Sprint cars were running with roll cages. Courtesy of the EMMR collection.

though usually paralleling the national series. Local drivers match off against the touring pros in hot Sprint car regions like Pennsylvania, Ohio and Indiana, sometimes to the chagrin of the pros.

Sprint cars no longer lead directly to Indy, but there is a definite place for close dirt-throwing racing.

54 SPORTS CARS OR STOCK CARS?
Trans-Am

In 1966, bowing to increasing pressure to allow professional race drivers to compete in SCCA events, the governing board created three new series; the Can-Am, Formula A and the Trans-American Sedan Championship, better known as the Trans-Am. The general plan was that all three series would use American cars with up to 5-liter V-8 stock blocks for power.

The Trans-Am series grew out of the public's fascination with what became known as "Pony Cars," a name taken from the Ford Mustang, a car which set a precedent copied by Chrysler with their Barracuda/Challenger and GM with their Camaro/Firebird.

An under 2 liter (U-2) classification was also established. Despite giving away three liters in motor size the nimble Alfa Romeos and Ford Cortinas were nearly as quick as the new American racers.

Chrysler Corporation and Ford provided limited support for several teams the first season. The first race was held at Sebring prior to the 12-hour race. Jochen Rindt took the overall victory in an Alfa Romeo, but Bob Tullius won for large caliber (O-2) in a Dart. Tullius is quick to point out that winning the class, not overall, was his goal. The manufacturers' point race was too close for Ford as the season was coming to an end, so they brought in Carroll Shelby to field a car. The Shelby Mustangs won the last two races and Ford earned the first Trans-Am title.

Ford Motor Company jumped in with full factory support for the second season, with the Bud Moore prepared Mercury Cougars instead of the Mustangs. Chevrolet joined in with Roger Penske and a pair of

NASCAR created the Grand American series, as here at Richmond in 1969, along the lines of the Trans Am. Tiny Lund won the first driver's title in a Bud Moore Cougar that was raced in the 1967 Trans-Am. From the collection of J.A. Martin.

Camaros. Shelby's semi-factory Mustang team edged out the Cougars for the manufacturers' title despite the driving talents of Cougar pilots Dan Gurney, Parnelli Jones, Peter Revson and David Pearson. But by the end of the season the hot combination was Mark Donohue in the Camaro.

Cougar did not return but Donohue did, taking ten of the twelve 1968 races, including eight in a row. American Motors entered the series with the new Javelin.

The next two seasons were pure fan ecstasy. Bud Moore was back with a pair of Mustangs and the battles between drivers George Follmer and Parnelli Jones with Donohue were as intense as any in racing. Donohue won eight races in 1969 and Chevrolet had another title.

The players changed, but the action continued into 1970. Penske switched to run the Javelins for 1970. Jim Hall took over the Camaros and former Shelby driver Jerry Titus fielded a Pontiac Firebird. Chrysler rejoined with a pair of All-American Racing Barracudas, a single Dodge Challenger and the P-69 aborted Indy program engine. All the players were in attendance, but the drama was a continuation of 1969, Follmer and Jones against Donohue. This time the Mustangs won.

The glory was brief as, at the end of 1970, the factories withdrew from racing. Moore returned with a private Mustang team in 1971 but was limited in trying to match the last factory team, Donohue's Javelin. Donohue took eight of the ten events and the first drivers' title.

Mark Donahue dominated the Trans-Am series in 1968 and 1969 (shown) with a Penske prepared Camaro.

Penske Racing left for 1972 and Follmer took over the Javelin, now being run by Roy Woods Racing. Against a field of independents Follmer took four of the seven events, winning both the manufacturers' and drivers' title.

While the big iron was making headlines former Shelby designer Peter Brock was campaigning a pair of Datsun 510s in the U-2.5 series (enlarged from two liter). With driver John Morton the BRE team gave Datsun its first performance image in America after winning the manufacturer's title in 1971 and '72.

By 1973 the series was living on past

In 1970 the Trans-Am series was contested by factory teams from six American campanies. From the collection of J.A. Martin.

When the American factories dropped out after 1972 foreign cars became the center of the Trans-Am. From the collection of J.A. Martin.

tube frame cars. SCCA rules balanced the cars by a power handicap eliminating the need for high tech/expensive racers. At first the series looked like a good SCCA A sedan series, but by 1982 specially built cars with top level drivers were returning to the series. Pontiac, who was paying the SCCA to use the Trans-Am name, finally won the manufacturers' title led by drivers' champion Elliott Forbes-Robinson. Chevrolet returned to championship form the following year with David Hobbs and Willy T. Ribbs in the DeAtely Camaros.

The series was again a success and in 1984 there were sixteen races.

Seventeen years after the Cougars almost won the 1967 manufacturers' title, Tom Gloy in a Capri won Lincoln-Mercury a title.

The year 1984 was also when Jack Roush entered the series. In both the

glory and had lost its way. Following the lead of the European Group 4 and the new American rival IMSA, the Trans-Am was opened to European cars while enlarging motor capacity to virtually unlimited for American machines. The results were exotic but hardly satisfying, and in 1974 there were only three races, all won by Porsches.

Through the end of the seventies the Trans-Am was a clone of the IMSA GT series, each one fighting for entrants but most often racing the same cars with the same drivers. In 1975 exotic Group 5 cars were allowed.

As the power race escalated, fueled by Porsche playing IMSA and SCCA against each other to promote the model 935, a second layer of Trans-Am was created in 1976, Category I, for less modified cars, again similar to the IMSA GTO series. For 1977 and 1978 Bob Tullius brought Jaguar the first championship of any form since the mid–1950s.

In 1980 the exotic era ended when the SCCA allowed

By the mid–1980s the Trans-Am became an ongoing battle between semi-factory teams of Camaros and Mustangs. Courtesy of Dudley Evans.

Trans-Am and the IMSA GTO series, often with the same drivers and similar cars, a Roush prepared Ford or Mercury was at the top of the series. A series of young drivers were carried to victory and championships in Roush cars. Wally Dallenbach, Jr., won in a Capri in 1984; Scott Pruett followed in a Merkur XR4Ti two years later, with Dorsey Schroeder taking the title in 1989. Tommy Kendall won three straight titles in a Roush Mustang from 1995 through 1997. In 1997 he scored eleven consecutive wins, a record in any professional series.

The all American image of the Trans-Am took a big hit in 1988 when Bob Tullius fielded a pair of factory developed four wheel drive turbo Audi 100s. Though visually boxy compared to the sleek Corvettes, the cars handled incredibly well, winning eight times and earning a driver's title for Hurley Haywood. After the season the SCCA revised the rules, limiting the series to American cars with V-6 or V-8 motors driving two rear wheels.

The 1990s were an ongoing battle between the Mustang and Camaro teams. Scott Sharp and Jack Baldwin took early titles in Camaros before the 1995–97 sweep.

The changing face of the Trans-Am as non–American cars were again allowed. Paul Gentilozzi, 2001 champion, heads for victory at Road America 2000 in a tube frame V-8 Jaguar. Gentilozzi won the drivers' title in the car with Corvette (1998), Mustang (1999), then Jaguar (2001) sheet metal. Courtesy of Dave Goehrig.

Racing in the Trans-Am was excellent, with many cars vying for the lead. As a commercial success the results weren't as great. Factories have come and gone with the viability of the series being dependent on private semi-amateur teams. Sponsors never jumped on the metal billboards as they did with Winston Cup.

In 2000, Don Panoz/Ralph Sanchez acquired the lease rights for the series, then resold to longtime competitor Paul Gentilozzi at the conclusion of 2002.

55 EVERYONE'S MR. SPEED
Mickey Thompson

Nobody ever had as much impact on so many different forms of racing as Mickey Thompson. Over a career that lasted until his death in 1988, Thompson was a major influence in drag racing, track safety, economy runs, land speed records, Indy cars and off-road races. His influence is still being felt through the Mickey Thompson line of performance accessories from the company he founded.

Marion Lee Thompson, Jr., was born in San Fernando, California, in 1928. The boy, nicknamed Mickey for his red hair, showed an early genius for mechanics, even fixing his teacher's cars long before he could drive himself. In the early 1950s

Mickey Thompson was the first American to take up the rear engine challenge at Indy. Despite being first, his cars were never successful, often pushing innovation too far and too fast for technology and the rule makers. From the collection of J.A. Martin.

he drove on the dry lakes and drag strips of southern California with an occasional sports car race, including the Pan-American Road Race. His first significant contribution was in popularizing the sling-shot-dragster. He began the sixties with an attempt on the land speed record at Bonneville with Challenger I, powered by four Pontiac motors. He made the first run at 406 mph and became the first person to top 400 on land, but a broken drive shaft prevented a return run so his mark was not official. Still the fame helped him create Mickey Thompson Enterprises selling performance parts and operating the Lions' Drag Strip in Long Beach.

Jack Brabham's success with the rear engined Cooper at Indianapolis fascinated Thompson, and for 1962 he entered a rear engined car powered by a stock block Buick driven by Dan Gurney. Gurney saw the potential and introduced Mr. Ford to Colin Chapman of Lotus. Mickey returned to Indianapolis in 1963 and 1964 with even more radical cars, dubbed by the Indy establishment as "roller skates." However, after small tires were banned, and Dave MacDonald was killed in the 1964 fire, Thompson lost interest in the Brickyard.

The formation of the National Off-Road Racing Association (NORRA) and the Baja 1000 in 1967 brought Mickey into a new area of racing. The first off-road event had been held in a riverbed near Riverside International Raceway in 1964 to enthusiastic support by the participants. Thompson ran a Bill Stroppe prepared Ford truck and was hooked. SNORE (Southern Nevada Off Road Enthusiasts) began conducting races from the Las Vegas area. A third organization, HDRA (High Desert Racing Association), began holding similar events.

Mickey Thompson did not think small, and he saw much greater potential for off-road racing than the three series were delivering. After NORRA lost promotion of the Baja race Thompson created SCORE (Short Course Off Road Events) and brought Mexican races to even greater glory. Soon SCORE was the major sanctioning body for cross desert racing, though Thompson had given control to Sal Fish as he had a new vision, a way to bring off-road racing to the public.

His first effort was to transform part of Riverside International Raceway into a six mile mini–Baja with jumps and ruts. Despite the negative predictions of the "experts," the mini–Baja was a commercial success. Still this was not what Thompson envisioned. In 1979 he held the Mickey Thompson Off-Road Championship Grand Prix in the Los Angeles Coliseum. The first few years were off and on but Mickey persisted through the Mickey Thompson Entertainment Group. Soon stadium racing was being held in the Houston Astrodome, Pontiac Silverdome, Denver Mile High Stadium and the Rose Bowl. By the late 1980s stadium racing, under Mickey's direction, was growing through ESPN coverage. Without Thompson the series died.

Other than the racing oriented businesses, Thompson operated a boxing gym, a hamburger restaurant, and an ice cream company and supported several orphanages.

Stadium racing was everything that Mickey Thompson was about. It was unique, had non-stop thrills, and brought racing up close to the fans. From the collection of J.A. Martin.

His achievements were recognized with his induction into the Motorsports Hall of Fame, the SEMA Hall of Fame for specialty equipment manufacturers, the International Motorsports Hall of Fame, the International Drag Racing Hall of Fame, and the D-A Mechanical Achievement Award in both Indy car and drag racing. In racing he also won the Mobil gas Economy Run and the Baja 1000.

Innovations included a water safety wall, nitrogen gas shocks, and the starting light system (Christmas tree) for drag racing.

The life of Mickey Thompson, which had been filled with great success and excitement, ended on March 16, 1988, when two gunmen murdered Mickey and his wife Trudy in front of their home and then escaped on bicycles, a crime that has never been solved. Six months after his death the California State Senate and Assembly honored Thompson by declaring October 21st "Off Road Enthusiast Day."

56 IT SURE SOUNDED GOOD ON PAPER
Formula 5000

It should have been one of the great racing series of all times. They were pure racing cars with loud stock block American motors. Top professional domestic and foreign drivers handled them over the best road courses in the Western Hemisphere; many went on to even greater fame else-where. At the time they were as fast as any Formula 1 or Indy car. But it didn't happen, and the F-5000 series is just a not-so-great memory.

The SCCA founders were always suspicious of open wheeled/formula race cars. The SCCA was still dominated by the

In 1971 the F-5000 series was fought between Sam Posey (l) and David Hobbs (r). From the collection of J.A. Martin.

gentleman racers, and formula cars seemed too much like professional racing. Still, when the SCCA provided three series for professional racers one was for open wheel cars. The top class was the SCCA Grand Prix Championship for Formula A cars with a minimum weight of 1,200 pounds powered by true racing engines of up to 3 liters, like the new Formula 1 cars, or modified stock blocks of up to 5 liters. USAC also raised the stock block engine size to 5 liters. This meant that a motor manufacturer could produce a single car for three different professional series.

While the Can-Am series, drawing on the strength of the USRRC series, and the stock car–based Trans-Am series, gained immediate acceptance, Formula A initially floundered.

By 1968 a few teams had figured out that a combination of an Indy Eagle with a Trans-Am Chevrolet motor could be an effective race car. Dr. Lou Sell, sponsored by Dick Smothers, of the Smothers Brothers comedy team, ran away with the 1968 championship with such a combination. With only minor modifications Sell was able to run the same car in USAC road races.

There were thirteen races in 1969 plus a great deal of enthusiasm for the series, now renamed the Continental Cham-

pionship. Sporting high mounted Formula 1 style rear wings, the Formula A cars were the fastest cars in the world on many tracks. Tony Adamowicz took the title in an Eagle Chevrolet.

The new decade began with more top drivers entering the series. Mark Donohue, David Hobbs, Sam Posey, George Follmer and Gus Hutchinson were winners, the latter in the same car in which he competed in the U.S. Grand Prix. But it was John Cannon who took the title in a McLaren Chevrolet owned by Malcom Starr and Carl Hogan.

The future seemed bright for 1971. David Hobbs took the title in the Starr/ Hogan McLaren M10 over several new factory cars. New Zealander Graham McRae was dominant in 1972, taking the title, along with the F-5000 title in New Zealand and Europe, in a Leda Chevrolet. With the prize money he bought the company and renamed the cars McRaes.

Jody Scheckter of South Africa was a wild young driver when he joined the series, now sponsored by L & M cigarettes, in 1973. With the Trojan Chevrolet he won all the early races on his way to his series title. Before the season was over he was offered a ride in the Formula 1 McLaren team. This led eventually to Ferrari and the 1979 World driving championship.

It was a great season for Scheckter but not for the series as L & M moved their sponsorship funds elsewhere.

By 1974 there were new cars from Eagle and Lola built just for the series and new drivers that were to dominate the remainder of the series' life. USAC co-sanctioned the series, allowing Indy drivers and even Indy cars. Several drivers had identical Indy Eagles and Formula A Lolas.

In 1973 Jim Hall of Chaparral fame teamed up with Lola importer Carl Haas. Sports car ace Brian Redman was hired to drive. For 1974, 1975 and 1976 Redman was series champion in the ultimate F-5000 car, the Lola T332.

There was competition, major competition. Mario Andretti, looking forward to his future in Formula 1, persuaded team owner Parnelli Jones to field an F-5000 car. Andretti finished second to Redman in the championship but gained valuable road-racing experience. The Vels-Parnelli team returned for 1975 and '76 with Andretti and Al Unser, both of whom recorded victories.

With the demise of the Can-Am series after 1974 the F-5000 series was the fastest series in SCCA, yet it was still unable to generate the type of fan enthusiasm the Can-Am had. SCCA made a compromise that gave the F-5000 teams an extension of life while bringing back the Can-Am name. For 1977 the Can-Am was reborn using 5

The dominant driver of the series was Brian Redman in the Haas/Hall Lola T332. From the collection of J.A. Martin.

liter single seaters or, in other words, F-5000 cars with bodies over the open wheels. Redman retired but the Haas/Hall Lola team continued to win, taking the titles in 1977 (Patrick Tambay), 1978 (Alan Jones), 1979 (Jackie Ickx) and 1980 (Tambay again). By 1981 new cars, with true ground effects, were made for the series, and the days of the F-5000 based Lola were done. Still, two of the new cars, the Frisbee and the Prophet, were evolutions of the Formula-5000 Lola.

57 RECORDS WITHOUT LIMITATIONS
Land Speed Record, Postwar

The debris of World War II had no sooner settled than it was back to the Bonneville salt flats in Utah and new assaults on the Land Speed Record.

The first new record was set by a familiar name. Driver John Cobb had set the prewar record in the Railton at Bonneville one week before the outbreak of war. Eight years and one month later Cobb returned to Bonneville with the Railton. He topped his old mark by 24.455 mph, up to 394.196 mph. The record stood for almost twenty

years before three Americans, two brothers and a third man, brought the jet age to the record attempts.

In the postwar demilitarization powerful surplus aircraft and later jet engines were bought for drag and speed run vehicles.

Southern Californian Craig Breedlove's *Spirit of America* was a jet engine mounted on three wheels with the driver in front of the motor. On August 5, 1963, Breedlove took the Spirit to a 2-way average of 407.45 mph. But FIA rules only recognized wheel driven vehicles so the run was not an official record.

By the next year the rules had been expanded, and American Tom Green set a new record of 413.199 mph in Walt Arfons' jet-powered car, with afterburner, called the *Wingfoot Express*. Sponsors were becoming more involved as Goodyear Tire and Rubber gave the vehicle its name.

Green had barely slowed down when Art Arfons took his J-79 jet engine powered *Green Monster* out to raise the record to 434.002 mph. Art had invested $10,000 in the car, a paltry sum compared to what the Campbells had spent.

The Arfons brothers were former drag racers from Akron, Ohio. While competing in many of the same events they worked separately, creating an automotive sibling rivalry. Though the NHRA had never given the jet cars the recognition of a professional class, the brothers were great crowd pleasers and became experts in jet powered land speed vehicles. Art had developed the use of the full roll cage and braking parachute. When NHRA banned aircraft engined cars the brothers joined the top speed quest.

Breedlove returned with *Spirit of America* and took the record up to 468.719 mph, then followed two days later with a run 526.277 mph. The run was the last for the *Spirit* and almost the last for Breedlove. After passing the last course markers, Breedlove pulled the cord to release the drag parachute. The chute did not catch. Breedlove stood on the brakes but this was more than the brakes were meant to handle and they quickly lost effectiveness. As big as Bonneville is, there is a size limit, and Breedlove was about to find it. The car hit a drainage ditch on the edge of the lake bed and went into a canal. The *Spirit* sank so that only the exhaust and tail fin were out of the water. Breedlove escaped injury and eventually the car was restored, but it never raced again.

When Breedlove returned in 1965 it was with a J-79 powered four wheel vehicle, *Spirit of America, Sonic 1*. On November 2nd *Sonic 1* averaged 555.485 mph. Art Arfons responded on the 7th with an average of 576.553 mph. But Breedlove came back on November 14 to retake the record with a 2-way average of 600.601 mph for the mile, 600.841 for the kilometer, the first to go over 600 mph.

On November 12, 1965, Bob Summers set a new record for wheel driven internal combustion engine cars with the *Golden Rod*, a car he built with his brother Bill.

Art Arfons went to the direct approach for his Green Monster land speed record vehicle, put four wheels on a jet engine and hang on. Courtesy of the EMMR collection.

Craig Breedlove and the J-79 jet engine powered second *Spirit of America*. Courtesy of Goodyear Tire and Rubber.

The Blue Flame rocket powered record setter of 1970. Courtesy of Goodyear Tire and Rubber.

Powered by four blown Chrysler hemi motors driving all four wheels, Summers averaged a comparatively sedate 409.277 for the mile and 409.685 for the kilometer.

If a jet goes fast, how fast will a rocket go? To find out, the natural gas industry sponsored the *Blue Flame*, a rocket powered three-wheeled vehicle. Gary Gabelich, whom Breedlove had recommended, was the driver. On October 13, 1970, he shot to 622.407 mph.

In 1979 Hollywood action director Hal Needham sponsored a rocket car for stunt driver Stan Barrett. Unofficially Barrett went through the sound barrier as bystanders claimed to have heard the telltale sonic boom. However, there was no official timing agency present so there was no record.

After failing to exceed 340 mph Art Arfons, in a lightweight car, retired, putting his efforts into the development of tractor pulls.

In 1983 and again in 1997 British drivers retook the record. As Bonneville was breaking up from wear and weather the next attempts were made at the Black Rock Desert in Nevada. Richard Noble in the *Thrust 2* jet powered car averaged 633.470 in 1983. In 1997 the team returned with the twin jet engine *Thrust SSC* with rear steering. Andy Green drove the car to 763.035 mph, a new record and the first time a land car had officially exceeded the sound barrier.

The Budweiser rocket car lights up the early morning at the Bonneville Salt Flats.

In the meantime, the real aficionados of speed on salt, the run-for-fun hot rodders, continue to gather at Bonneville every August for a week of record attempts.

58 WE'RE JUST RACING FOR TROPHIES
The SCCA Runoffs

Since the beginning, SCCA drivers have argued over who was the best in each class. In 1951 the title of National Champion was awarded to the driver who accumulated the most points in races across the country, as was done by most other professional racing series. But few drivers could expend the time and money to continually crisscross the country collecting points. After all, these were amateur drivers who received no monetary rewards for their efforts and few if they won.

A better system was developed beginning in 1964. All the regional champions would meet at one place to race head-to-head, with the winner proclaimed National Champion. The official title was not pre-sented for the first two years. The American Road Race of Champions, the original name, was the Olympics of amateur racing. Like the famed Greek games, all the competitors were already acknowledged champions, having won races and earned points from races in their respective regions, the best amateur sports car drivers facing each other.

The first head-to-head competition was held at Riverside Raceway in 1984. The top 183 cars were entered in 17 classes. The following year the competition was held at the Daytona International Speedway, and the first six events alternated between these two courses on opposite sides of the country.

In 1970 the championships, now nicknamed "the Runoffs," were moved to the new Road Atlanta which continued as host until 1994 when the event was moved to Mid-Ohio.

A sign of the growing importance of the event came in 1973 when it was renamed the Champion Spark Plug Road Racing Classic. Valvoline Oil bought the right to be primary sponsor in 1985 for the Valvoline Road Racing Classic, then shortened to

Close racing was the rule in spec series racing at every runoff. Courtesy of Ed Clayton.

the Valvoline Runoffs in 1987. NAPA Auto Parts joined as co-primary sponsor in 1997 to become the Valvoline Runoffs presented by NAPA Auto Parts.

In 1995 participation had grown to 692 entries. For 1999 the Speedvision cable network televised most of the races live.

Road Atlanta hosted the runoffs from 1970 through 1993. Courtesy of Ed Clayton.

SCCA racers fall into two categories, although many participants may not know in which they belong at the time. Most are content to have a separate career and race on weekends. Others are looking to the runoffs as a way to gain experience and notoriety to move into professional racing ranks. Former Runoff winners who moved to professional careers have included Bob Tullius, Mark Donohue, Peter Gregg, Paul Newman, Bob and Scott Sharp, Bobby Rahal, and 1999 ALMS champion Elliott Forbes-Robinson. Other champions, like Don Devendorf (Nissan), Doug Peterson (Acura) and Roger Penske (just about everything), have used their championships as a springboard to build a racing business.

Racers are divided into 24 classes: Formula (open wheel), Sports Racer (closed wheel special built) and production based. Classes within are generally established by motor size (speed potential). Production based cars are classified on level of modifications from Showroom Stock to Grand Touring (tube frame pure race cars that barely look like the street counterpart). By size and modification this allows for about every form from street legal Dodge Neons to Trans-Am style Mustangs.

Several Formula and Sports Racers are "spec" classes where all cars are identical with preparation and driving skill being the difference.

Many classes have been dropped as the nature of amateur racing has changed.

Runoff Poster. From the collection of J.A. Martin.

In the early years, the winners drove Ferraris and Cobras, often prepared by the factory. Many of the Sedan and Production classes were renamed as the rules were changed to meet the definition of what a production race car was. A Sports Racing and Formula A were Can-Am and Formula-5000 respectively, and the drivers alternated between running amateur and professional events with the same car, often winning in both.

The all-time champion of the Runoffs is Jerry Hansen. Between 1975 and 1984 he won ten straight A Sports Racing and from 1971 to 1976 six straight Formula A titles. In addition he won in six other categories between 1968 and 1984 for a total of 27 championships.

59 More Than Acting Like a Racer
Paul Newman

For most men, celebrating their 70th birthday means a leisurely cruise or a visit by the grandchildren. For Paul Newman it meant being nominated for an Academy Award and a class win at the 24-hour race at Daytona.

Newman was not the first celebrity to take up racing. Studio heads cringed every weekend for James Dean and Steve McQueen. McQueen, in an underpowered Porsche with his foot in a cast, finished second overall at the 1970 Sebring 12-hour race.

Prior to 1968 Paul Newman had no special interest in racing. He was a top money making movie actor and part time social activist. With the movie *Winning* a new dimension was added to his life. *Winning* was originally slated to be a TV movie, but the inclusion of Newman and his wife Joanne Woodward elevated it to big screen status. Following the advances made by John Frankenheimer's 1966 race classic *Grand Prix*, *Winning* was centered on American racing, specifically the Indianapolis 500. James Garner, star of *Grand Prix*, warned Newman that racing gets into your blood once you try it. Garner knew this well, and after *Grand Prix* he formed (financed) a team that competed with a pair of Lolas at Daytona and Sebring plus an F-5000 series car.

Garner was right, and soon Newman was taking part in celebrity races and race movie voice-overs.

His big step was his association with fellow Connecticut resident Bob Sharp. In 1972, going by the transparent alias P.L. Newman, he scored two firsts and two seconds in four races with Sharp's Datsun 510 sedan. The following year he obtained a national license and in 1976 won the SCCA national C-production championship, his first of four. By 1978, approaching 50 years old, he was running Sharp's Nissan 280ZX in SCCA National races, winning eight of thirteen starts. For 1979 he took 14 of 16 SCCA races, the Watkins Glen 6-hour race and finished second overall at Le Mans. Then he turned pro.

By now he was a partner with Sharp as the factory team for Datsun in professional IMSA racing. To compete in the new Prototype series Sharp built a one of a kind turbo powered 280ZX for Newman to drive. Even IMSA owner John Bishop commented on how brave Newman had to be to drive that car.

His driving style is much like his acting style, restrained and coolly in control. He never seemed to be working, yet he continued to win. In 1983 he entered the Trans-Am series at Brainerd, Minnesota, and won. The same world famous eyes that melted Elizabeth Taylor twenty years before were still as intense with world-class concentration. Professional drivers who have raced against him have stated that had he taken up driving when he was in his twenties he certainly could have gone to Indy or Formula 1.

"More than a pretty face" was never truer than when Paul Newman won races as at Summit Point, West Virginia, in 1980. From the collection of J.A. Martin.

Along with driving, he became co-owner, with Bill Freeman, of the March Can-Am team for Bobby Rahal, Al Unser and Teo Fabi. With the demise of the Can-Am series he joined with Lola importer Carl Haas to field the most glamorous team to ever hit the CART Indy car series with driver Mario Andretti. Andretti took the Newman-Haas Lola to the drivers' championship. Michael Andretti in 1991 and Nigel Mansell in 1993 and Cristiano da Matte in 2002 won additional titles for Newman-Haas Racing.

Approaching his seventieth birthday, Newman made the movie *Nobody's Fool*. For promotion he approached the studio to sponsor a car in the 1995 Daytona 24-hour race with Newman as a co-driver. Reluctantly they accepted. The next step was to have Jack Roush field a GTS class Mustang. The only car available was a Trans-Am Mustang lacking the full tricks of a GTS car. Still Newman, Tom Kendall, Mark Martin and Mike Brockman took the car to the line. Because of reduced night vision Newman drove only in daylight hours, his only concession to age, yet still put in a driving stint as the quartet ran a steady race to finish first in class, third overall. Newman is the oldest driver to win his class in America's longest race. Five years later he raced again but the Porsche was not up to the class standards, unusual for a man who was always (racing, acting or selling salad dressing) the standard for the class.

60 WINGS AND WIDE TIRES EXPLOIT THE WIND
McLarens and Eagles

By 1967 a new standard of design had been established in open wheel racing. From Formula 1 to Indianapolis the best cars were all rear engine in a streamlined body that easily slipped through the wind. After the upheavals of the 1960s it looked like designers were going to be able to put the emphasis once again on slowly evolving a proven set of design parameters.

The period of quiet lasted less than a year. In 1968 Formula 1 cars began to sprout wings, first small, but by the end of the season over six feet high like on the Can-Am Chaparral 2E. Accidents in 1969 forced the FIA to reduce the height of the wing struts but the wing that forced the car down for greater traction would not go away. USAC disallowed the high wings by restricting overall car height, but teams found ways to add plates on the back, listed as exhaust supports, that accomplished the same thing, added traction.

While the focus of attention on the 1968 Lotus 56 (the STP turbine) was on the powerplant, the car's shape showed another way to add traction. Colin Chapman and designer Maurice Phillippe shaped the entire body as a wedge, a wing that was the body. The turbine was effectively outlawed, but the gains of the wedge were not lost on Chapman and Phillippe.

In 1970 Lotus unveiled the car that was to set the design standard for most of the decade, the model 72. Not only was the body a wedge, but the radiators were moved back beside the driver giving the car a clean nose and locating radiator weight in the center of the car. Jochen Rindt won the 1970 driver's title in a Lotus 72, and Emerson Fittipaldi, who had taken over after Rindt's death, won the U.S. Grand Prix in a Lotus 72.

For Formula 1 it was build a Lotus 72 copy or don't place. One of the other teams was McLaren cars. For designer Gordon Coppuck the Lotus shape offered possibilities for McLaren's excursion into Indianapolis racing. The 1970 McLaren M15 had been a conventional shape. A new car would adapt the best of the Lotus 72 for American speedway racing.

McLaren had three of the new model M16s ready for the 1971 Memorial Day race. Two factory efforts were in Gulf orange for Denny Hulme and Peter Revson with a third, for Penske racing, in Sunoco blue for Mark Donohue. Rather than looking like after-thought appendages, which they often were, the front and rear wings blended in with the mid-radiator wedge shape.

Revson took the pole for the 500 at 178.696, over eight mph faster than Al Unser's 1970 pole winning speed. Donohue started second but took an early lead until he parked the car with a blown engine. Revson finished second behind Al Unser, due more to the lack of understanding of the rules by Revson and the McLaren team than to speed difference to Unser's Lola Colt.

Donohue won at Michigan that summer, and the orders started pouring in for copies of the McLaren M16.

Just as in the mid–1960s, designers were now offered an opportunity to reframe the paradigms of race car design. What design could beat the McLaren M16? Phillippe, now working for the Parnelli Jones superteam of Al Unser, Joe Leonard and Mario Andretti, winners of the last three USAC driver's titles and Indianapolis 500s, made a new style of car that angled the sides with prominent mid-mounted radiator/wings. By qualifying day the mid wings were gone but the slanted sides stayed to give the Viceroy and Samsonite cars a softer look. Unser finished second with Leonard third and Andretti seventh. Leonard won the Pocono 500 and the 1972 driver's title, mostly by perseverance and luck. The Parnelli was not the equal of the McLaren M16, neither was the new Coyote of A.J. Foyt, the Atlanta of Lloyd Ruby nor the Antares of Roger McCluskey.

But one car was ready to challenge the McLarens. Dan Gurney recalls, "We knew we were going to have to come up with something fresh because the year before McLaren had upped the ante. We knew we

Bobby Unser in an Eagle (r) and Gordon Joncock in a McLaren M16 (c) and Mario Andretti (Parnelli) led the rest of the field at Pocono, 1972. From the collection of J.A. Martin.

were going to have to come up with something, even if it was not right. We had no concept of what was needed to be done. We talked a lot about how we should do it. It (Indy) was a notorious engine test, so we had to have good cooling and this and that, and with a package that took advantage of some of the things we'd run into. When we looked back we were a little closer to what was needed than we realized."

Roman Slobodynski, chief designer for Dan Gurney's All American Racers, modified the nose from a true wedge and moved the two radiators forward of the Lotus/McLaren design.

Another innovation came from Gurney himself (Gurney had already innovated the use of full face helmets and spraying champagne [see Le Mans chapter). A small vertical flap was added to the rear of the wing. Lap times immediately improved, though for the 1972 season none of the other teams understood the function and could not repeat the performance. Eventually it became a standard and is often

called a "wickerbill" but most often a "Gurney."

Using the wider rear wing, with a "Gurney," allowed by USAC, and new gumball tires developed by Goodyear, driver Bobby Unser and the new Eagle hit Indianapolis like nothing in recent memory. Unser shattered all previous records, qualifying on the pole at 195.94 mph, 17.244 mph faster than Revson's 1971 speed. It was the greatest speed increase in the history of the Speedway. Donohue and Revson started second and third in McLaren M16s.

Unser unleashed the Eagle at the green flag, setting new speed records at every lap, but the engine expired shortly into the race. Penske driver Gary Bettenhausen took over then before his turbo expired. Donohue was now in the lead but challenged by the second AAR car of Jerry Grant. Debris punctured one of Grant's tires forcing an immediate pit stop. In the confusion fuel was drawn from Bobby Unser's tank, a violation of USAC rules, and officially Grant's race was done. Donohue took the win.

Grant came back to take the pole for the Ontario 500, although teammate Bobby Unser set a faster time. In 1972 Unser set eight fastest times and took four of the ten races. If he finished, he won. The Eagle was that much better than anything else. However, it was Roger McCluskey in a 1971 McLaren M16 who took the driver's championship.

A difference between the Eagle and the McLaren program was that Gurney was willing to sell a brand new car to any buyer, not one of last year's team cars. Even in 1972 there were new customer Eagles in the lineup, with rookie Sam Posey finishing fifth. Unser's priority was to go fast and win races. Gurney's priority was to sell cars. Sometimes the two were in conflict as Unser made an improvement only to see Gurney sell it to competing customers. The one advantage Unser could maintain was the powerful engine provided by John Miller. Unser stated, "He could get horsepower that others couldn't." But this edge often meant DNFs.

There were 19 Eagles and seven McLarens in the 1973 Indianapolis race. Parnelli Jones abandoned the diagonal sided car for a car that was very Eagle-like. This car was less successful than the 1972 car, so for 1974 the Parnelli was a virtual clone of the Eagle, and the superteam drove real Eagles in some races. Bobby Unser was again on the pole with a new record and again went out while leading. After a 500 that saw two days of rain and the death of Swede Savage, Gordon Johncock took the checkered flag in his Eagle for the shortened race. His teammate Wally Dallenbach won the Ontario race in another Eagle.

Again in 1974 Eagles and McLarens shared the spotlight. Johnny Rutherford, now the #1 driver for Team McLaren in USAC, grabbed the pole and the win at the Indianapolis 500 in an updated M16D sharing the semi wedge side shape of the Eagle. Bobby Unser, finding some reliability to go with the Eagle's speed, took the Ontario 500 and the driver's championship. Rutherford came back to take the 1976 Indy 500 in an M16D.

In 1975 Bobby Unser was in the lead when rain made the track undriveable and took the win in his light blue Jorgensen Eagle.

Penske driver Tom Sneva grabbed the spotlight from 1976 winner Rutherford when his McLaren M16D went airborne in turn two. Despite the spray of burning fuel and car body parts Sneva received only minor injuries, a testament to the built-in safety of the McLaren.

Part of the success of the McLarens and Eagles was the effective use of the turbo Offy motor. The narrow straight four fit nicely behind the driver, giving clean airflow, and Meyer Drake had continued development, increasing power each year. But each power increase reduced fuel mileage.

After the fires of 1973 USAC mandated on board fuel capacity be reduced. This mandated more fuel stops and put a greater emphasis on fuel mileage. In 1976 there was a new challenger. The Parnelli Jones Grand Prix effort had been a failure, but by the addition of a turbocharger to a destroked Cosworth Formula 1 motor, plus a few changes in suspension and tires, a new Parnelli was ready for USAC Champ car racing. Al Unser started the new car at the 500. While the Cosworth was not originally as powerful as the Offy, when turbo boost limits were reduced the motor used less fuel.

McLaren and Penske followed the lead of the Parnelli and by the 1977 season each had a Formula 1 derived Champ car powered by a turbo Coswoth. Eagle produced their own car built around the Cosworth. The days of the McLaren M16 and Eagle were fast coming to an end. Edged out, not by a more powerful package, but one that gave better gas mileage. Still in the hands of smaller independent teams

McLaren 16s and Eagles were raced into the early 1980s. By then new ground effects cars were replacing the F1 based cars.

The wedge-shaped M16 and Eagle were the first Champ cars to effectively use the air rather than trying to force their way through it. The angled body and wings pushed the car into the track for greater traction. But there was a price in increased drag. Ground effects pulled the car down and created very little additional drag — downforce for free.

61 IMCA
Racing Within ($) Limits

They are not the only ones doing it, but the International Motor Contest Association (IMCA) of Vinton, Iowa, the oldest continuous racing sanctioning body (since 1915), is solidly committed to what can best be described as "cookie cutter" race cars. It makes sense to have every car at every track the same as every other car in any particular class. It makes for honest racing, with attention to detail, chassis setup and driver skill making the difference. It works for NASCAR, but so far for IMCA it hasn't taken the country by storm. IMCA president Kathy Root says it is because they have no national sponsor.

J. Alex Sloan and William Pickens began the century organizing races across the Midwest with early driving stars such as Louis Chevrolet and Barney Oldfield. After moving the races around to meet the demand Sloan moved to Chicago and established IMCA. Sloan continued to run IMCA until his death in 1937 when his son John took over the sanctioning body. Over time IMCA sanc-

tioned Hobby Stock, Late Model and Sprint classes.

The big change came in 1978 when Keith Knaack took over IMCA. He immediately addressed a problem common to all forms of racing, how to control costs. In racing there is usually a direct correlation between how much is spent and how many races are won. More powerful motors, better gripping tires and trick suspension parts all contribute to more speed, but they all cost. Those who cannot spend are therefore relegated to the back of the field and, drivers being competitive by nature, eventually decide it does not make sense to race in that series. Knaack saw the escalation of costs as a serious threat to weekend racers.

Knaack's plan was to limit the cost of

Whether built from recycled parts or from a kit, an IMCA modified is a relatively low-cost way to go racing on short paved or dirt oval tracks. Tom Saal drawing.

the motor by placing a claim on the motor for the top four finishing cars in the Modified series. Any driver could, for $300, claim the motor from a top four finisher. The top finisher either sold the motor, or lost his position. In addition, Knaack limited all IMCA racers to a single tire brand, eliminating potential tire wars. This removed all incentive to add costly components to the motor. Winning would have to come from setup and superior driving.

The new rules took effect in 1979 and caught on immediately. Within a decade membership in IMCA rose over 300 percent, and tracks sanctioned for IMCA events jumped 80 percent with races in thirty-two states.

Kathy and Brett Root, who had been hired by Knaack several years before he died in 1992, bought IMCA from Knaack who was planning to retire anyway. Knowing it was a good thing, they have continued Knaack's vision and IMCA has continued to grow.

62 NEW TRACKS BUILT
1949–1971

For motorsports to grow after World War II new tracks were needed. The Indianapolis Motor Speedway was in disrepair and would not be able to sustain the industry by itself. Under the leadership of new owner Tony Hulman IMS was quickly reestablished as the premier track in the United States. The remainder of American tracks were dirt ovals or blocked off public roads.

The first new big track came in one of the least prosperous areas of the country, central South Carolina. In 1949 developer Harold Brasington opened a 1.25-mile track near Darlington. To accommodate a local minnow pond outside turn 2 the two ends of the track were built on different radii. This has led to setup difficulties and great respect by NASCAR drivers ever since. Though the oldest track on the NASCAR circuit, "The Lady in Black" has maintained a reputation of intimidation with the drivers, and to win at Darlington is still regarded with awe by even the best.

A half mile dirt track was opened near Martinsville, VA, in 1948.

Five years later a half-mile dirt oval was opened near Richmond, VA. Fifteen years later the surface was paved and then enlarged to three quarters of a mile in 1988.

In the 1950s most of the new tracks were road courses. Races started in the late 1940s were run on public roads. For safety and crowd control permanent road courses were constructed instead. Unlike the prewar road tracks these were paved. Watkins Glen continued in the tradition of racing that had begun with through the town races. Led by Cameron Argetsinger, the permanent track opened in 1956, and in 1961 Watkins Glen became the home of the United States Grand Prix until 1980.

General Curtis LeMay, besides heading the Air Force Strategic Air command, was a race fan and made several military fields available for SCCA sports car events. Hendricks Field, near Sebring, Florida, became a permanent course in 1950 while still an operating airfield. Developer Alec Ulmann brought the best of European sports cars for a 12-hour race. Despite numerous changes of shape and sanctioning body, the Sebring 12-hour is still the most demanding road race in the United States.

Other areas moved road races to races on road courses. Road America, under the direction of Cliff Tufte, opened in 1955. Five years earlier races were first run on Wisconsin roads. In 1956 RA hosted the only NASCAR Grand National (Winston Cup) race run in the rain. Since then the four-mile track has hosted the best in Can-Am, CART, IMSA and vintage events.

Lime Rock, in northwest Connecticut and Laguna Seca, organized by the Sports Car Racing Association of the Monterey Peninsula (SCRAMP), were constructed in 1957. By the SCRAMP charter Laguna Seca is a non-profit entity with profits going to charities.

Bill France had recognized the importance of Darlington and saw that the future of NASCAR was on large superspeedways. With NASCAR having established itself as a viable sanctioning body, France took the next step and built the fastest superspeedway in the world. In 1959 the Daytona International Speedway opened with the first Daytona 500. About 40,000 people paid to see the first "500." Included in the layout was a road course through the infield that was to host the Daytona Continental, the 24-hour race that attracts international factory sports car teams. The track is also used for Bike Week in March.

The following year the 1.5-mile superspeedway was opened south of Atlanta, Georgia.

Curtis Turner and developer Bruton Smith were also planning a new superspeedway to be built northeast of Charlotte, NC. Problems in excavating the infield and financing almost ended the 1.5 mile track before it was opened. Turner went to the Teamsters union for additional financing in return for help on organizing NASCAR drivers, a move that resulted in Bill France suspending Turner from NASCAR. The

The norm for NASCAR, full stands of paying fans, in this race, Atlanta. Courtesy of Ed Clayton.

lifetime suspension lasted until 1965 when France needed all the name drivers he could find as Chrysler Corporation boycotted NASCAR.

In 1960 a group of Portland, Oregon, promoters made a road course out of an abandoned Army housing site to complement the annual rose festival. The track is now owned and operated by the city of Portland, Department of Parks and Recreation.

In Ohio in 1961 a 2.5-mile road course was cut through the countryside near Mansfield. Named Mid-Ohio, from the beginning the track has seemed as much like a picnic field as a race track.

On the Virginia/Tennessee line a .5 mile track was opened at Bristol. The 22-degree banking was repaved to a .533 mile track with 36 degrees of banking in 1969.

Indianapolis Raceway Park was opened in 1963 as the sport's first multi-racing complex. The outer track is a 2.5-mile road course of which the front straight is a drag strip, home of the NHRA U.S. Nationals. The road course has hosted Champ car, IMSA and local SCCA events. Inside the road course is a .686 mile oval. Since 1979 the NHRA has owned the complex.

Three years after Charlotte a second superspeedway was built in North Carolina near the town of Rockingham. Darlington builder Harold Brasington, who enlisted a group of local developers, conceived the one-mile track, called the North Carolina Motor Speedway. In 1969 new owner L.G. DeWitt repaved the originally flat track it to 22–25 degree banking.

The traditional USAC Champ car tracks at Trenton, Phoenix, and Langhorne were paved in the 1960s, just when the rear engine cars were replacing the roadsters. Milwaukee, the oldest continuous used race track in America, first raced cars at the Wisconsin State Fairgrounds in 1908, three years before the inaugural Indy 500. It was paved in 1954.

Robert Marshall, Jr., and Jim Coleman opened Sears Point in 1968 as a combination road course/drag strip. The following year it was sold to the first of several owners. Over the years USAC, SCCA, IMSA, AMA, NHRA and NASCAR have held professional events at the Napa valley course.

The year 1969 was a big year for superspeedway construction. Four new tracks opened. Michigan International Speedway, near Brooklyn, Michigan, is a 2-mile oval with a road course that went outside the track. At 2⅔ miles Talladega is the biggest and fastest speedway in the world. It was also at the epicenter of a 1969 boycott by NASCAR drivers who felt tire technology was not yet up to the demands of the G forces imposed by the steeply banked track. By contrast, the 1969 opening of the two-mile Texas World Speedway near Houston was politically routine although only 23,000 people turned out for the rain-soaked event.

Dover Downs International Speedway, with 24 degrees of banking and long sweeping turns, has become "the Monster Mile." Inside the paved track is a dirt track for horse racing.

Atlanta got a second major track with the opening of Road Atlanta north of the city in 1970. In its first year the 2.4 mile road course hosted a Can-Am race and in 1971 became the home of the SCCA runoff championships.

Oval racing returned to greater Los Angeles in 1970 with the opening of Ontario Motor Speedway. Virtually identical in layout to the Indianapolis Motor Speedway and seemingly well financed, the track couldn't miss as "Indy of the West." In the first year OMS hosted a NASCAR and USAC Champ car 500-mile race and Formula 1/Formula-5000 cars in 1971.

Opened as a ¾-mile paved oval in 1969, Pocono International Raceway, near Long Pond, Pennsylvania, was completed as a 2.5 mile paved tri-oval in 1971.

In 1971 the Pocono International Speedway was opened in eastern Pennsylvania. Designed for Indy and sports cars alike, the track now hosts two NASCAR races annually. Courtesy of the EMMR collection.

At the end of 1971 there were sixteen paved oval tracks of at least one mile in length and eleven professional level road courses. Indeed, in the words of Brock Yates, it looked like motorsports was to be "the sport of the 70s."

63

THE UNFAIR ADVANTAGE
Roger Penske and Mark Donohue

No team, in any series, in any era, has enjoyed the success of Penske Motorsports. Since 1966 the teams of Roger Penske have won and often dominated every form of racing in which they were involved.

The Penske record as of 2003: USRRC, two driver's titles; Trans-Am, three manufacturer's titles; Can-Am, two driver's titles; NASCAR, 50+ victories; F-5000, two victories; Formula 1, one victory; USAC/CART/IRL, 110+ victories, 10 driver's titles; Indianapolis 500, 13 wins; Daytona 24-hour, one win.

Success brings the best drivers, which brings more success. Winning Penske drivers have included: Mark Donohue, Peter Revson, George Follmer, Gary Betten-

hausen, John Watson, Bobby Allison, Tom Sneva, Mario Andretti, Rick Mears, Bobby Unser, Al Unser, Danny Sullivan, Emerson Fittipaldi, Rusty Wallace, Al Unser, Jr., Jeremy Mayfield, Paul Tracy, Ryan Newman, Gil deFerran and Helio Castroneves.

Not bad for a guy whose four-car race team once had to leave one car outside because the garage only held three cars.

The Detroit-based Penske Corporation is a conglomeration of automotive businesses that, at this writing anyway, employs 34,000 people worldwide and takes in up to $11 billion in annual revenues. A small but important part is Penske Racing. Penske formerly owned the tracks at Michigan, Homestead-Miami, Nazareth,

Roger Penske, "The Captain," intense, demanding and analytical, has been involved in almost every aspect of his race team. Courtesy of the EMMR collection.

Rockingham and California. Roger was a founder of the IROC series and an original partner of CART. In addition, he sits on the boards of Philip Morris, GE and Gulfstream Aerospace.

Shaker Heights, Ohio, was a community of wealth in the 1950s. The senior Penske was a corporate vice president. Still, Roger worked his way through Leigh University, restoring sports cars to graduate with a BA in business in 1959. After racing a Corvette he bought a Porsche from Bob Holbert's dealership, beginning a Penske/Holbert relationship and winning a national SCCA title in 1960. The first "Unfair Advantage" came in 1961. His theory was that to win, a team had to have something the competitors didn't have. He bought a wrecked Formula 1 Cooper Climax. Adding a body made the car eligible to race against sports cars, most of which were modified street Ferraris and Corvettes. Another Penske idea was having Zerex antifreeze sponsor the car at a time when sponsors' names only went on Indy cars. With funds and a specially built race car Penske dominated professional sports car racing in 1962 and 1963 and began a trend that culminated in the Can-Am cars of the late 1960s. Soon he was driving Corvette Grand Sports and Jim Hall's Chaparral. At 26 years old he was Sports Car Driver of the Year in 1964. Then abruptly he retired to start a race team.

At the funeral for driver Walt Hangsen in 1965 Roger met Mark Donohue. They found they had common goals and a partnership was born.

Donohue had no great plans to be a race driver and didn't see his first race until he was a sophomore in the engineering program at Brown University. But in a progression of cars he quickly built a reputation among amateur racers culminating with a ride on the factory Ford GT team.

He was supremely analytical but also a very private person. In his autobiography Donohue wrote about every car and team member but never once mentioned his family, including his son David who now carries on the racing tradition.

With funding from the Sun Oil Company Penske bought a Lola T70. At the 1966 Nassau Speed Weeks Group 7 race Penske

Mark Donohue, "Captain Nice," was liked by everyone yet showed a skill and drive matched by few others. Courtesy of the EMMR collection.

made a critical strategy decision. Everyone had to make a pit stop, but when Mark came in he jumped out of the car then jumped back in, taking on neither fuel nor tires, to the astonishment of most of the great sports car teams of the time. Donohue roared back out to take the win, putting everyone on notice about Penske racing. The Donohue Penske Lola took the 1966 USRRC championship and won a Can-Am race in the inaugural season.

Donohue was quiet yet polite, traits that earned him the nickname "Captain Nice," even from those drivers whom he had beaten.

In 1967 Penske became the semi-factory team for Chevrolet in the new Trans-Am series. With two race teams, four cars, and a three car garage in Reading, Pennsylvania, Penske Racing consisted of only four full time employees, Penske, Donohue, Karl Kainhofer, and a Leigh engineering student, Al Holbert. Extra crewmembers were added as needed for each race, and Roger farmed out specialty and engine work.

The first Trans-Am season was mediocre until mid-season when the car became a dominating factor. Then in 1968 Donohue won eight in a row. At the end of the 1968 season Donohue ran the Riverside race for Champ cars, staying with eventual winner Dan Gurney until mechanical problems ended his run. Still it was a notice that Penske racing was heading to Champ cars and Indianapolis.

Penske needed an advantage, and it was not to be found running what everyone else ran. In late 1968 Penske Racing signed to race and develop Lola cars. The partnership reaped immediate rewards as Donohue and Chuck Parsons won the 24-hour Daytona race in a T70 mk III coupe. But at Sebring the car and trailer were stolen. The chassis was recovered but not the motor and support equipment, and Penske ended the program.

Donohue drove a 4-wheel drive Lola T150 to Rookie of the Year and a seventh place finish at the 1969 Indianapolis 500. With a 2-wheel drive version, the Lola T154, Donohue took second in the 500 in 1970.

The T163 Can-Am car was a major disappointment. The McLaren cars were so dominant that the race, even for a Penske prepared car, was for third unless McLaren entered a third car. Penske withdrew from Can-Am competition before the season was completed.

Although facing stiffer competition from Bud Moore's Mustangs, Donohue and the Camaro again were the best of the Trans-Am.

American Motors Corporation (AMC) was trying to get a performance image, but in two years of competition the Javelin had not been victorious and American Motors had not been a factor in NASCAR since the days of the Hudson Hornets in the early 1950s. American Motors turned to Penske. By mid-season the Trans-Am Javelin was winning over the best field of factory backed cars in the history of the series. While Javelin was second to Mustang in 1970 Donohue came back to take the manufacturer's and first driver's title for 1971. At Riverside, 1973, Donohue in a Matador gave AMC its first NASCAR victory. It was not the last as Bobby Allison drove the restyled Matador to more victories. Still, even Roger Penske could not make a Matador into a champion.

One advantage Donohue had in his Matador was a superb set of four disc brakes. These came from a new association Penske had made with Porsche. With the 917 legislated out of international racing Porsche needed a next step. Adding a turbocharger to the 917 motor Porsche had the car to dethrone the McLarens in the Can-Am. But while testing at Road Atlanta Donohue crashed and was hospitalized. Former Penske Can-Am driver George

Penske, center, always looking for an edge, modified a McLaren M16 specifically for USAC short ovals in 1972. Courtesy of Dudley Evans.

Follmer was brought in and won the 1972 championship. At the end of the season McLaren withdrew from the series. Donohue returned as driver for 1973 in the Porsche 917-30, the ultimate Can-Am car. He easily won the title, setting records for lap speed and poster sales that stood for years.

While the Penske (Sunoco Oil) and McLaren (Gulf Oil) teams were competitors in the Can-Am series they were partners in open wheel racing. Donohue drove the McLaren Grand Prix car to a third place finish at the Grand Prix of Canada in 1971, and Mark was the only non–McLaren factory driver to have a revolutionary M16 for the Indy 500. The motor failed in the 1971 race, but Donohue brought the car home to victory in 1972.

At the end of the 1973 season Donohue won the inaugural IROC series, then retired. But it was not a long retirement as he returned to driving with the Penske PC-1 Formula 1 car at the Canadian Grand Prix. The car was not a great success despite Donohue's best analytical skills though he did earn four points. At a qualifying session for the Austrian Grand Prix Donohue went off the road. In the impact he was hit on the helmet by a wood post. He emerged,

unsteady but under his own control. Still there was hidden brain damage and, despite brain surgery, he died by mid-week. John Watson came in to drive. Watson took a single win in the Penske PC-4. At the end of the 1976 season the team withdrew from international racing.

When AMC dropped the Matador and withdrew from NAS-CAR the Penske team changed to a Mercury and a Monte Carlo but with very limited success. Most of the Mercury equipment and cars were sold to the newly formed Elliott family race team. Penske was going to concentrate on Indy Cars and the new CART series.

Penske's team was already dominant in the Indy car series. In 1977 and 1978 Tom Sneva had won the driver's title, the latter without winning a single race. But Roger needed more than titles, he needed victories, and Sneva was replaced by Bobby Unser. But it was the new kid, Rick Mears, who upstaged them all. In only his second year Mears took the pole and victory at Indianapolis, then hung in to win his first driver's title. Mears would win the 500 three more times (1984, 1988 and 1991) and was named "Driver of the Decade" for the 1980s.

Penske developed his own Indy car based on the original Grand Prix PC-1. With the PC-7 ground effects were added to the PC-6, keeping Penske drivers on the leading edge. In 1986 Al Unser drove the first Ilmor-Chevrolet in the Indianapolis 500. Penske had helped two engineers from Cosworth start their own company with a contract from Chevrolet. The highlight came at the 1988 Indianapolis 500 when, for the first time, the front row was made up of a single team (Mears, Danny Sullivan, Al Unser, Sr.).

By 1989 Penske had international

tobacco brand Marlboro as primary sponsor. The top team with the best drivers and the largest financial support, a true "unfair advantage."

In 1994 with Chevrolet withdrawing from CART competition, Penske arranged for Mercedes to replace them at Ilmor. The partnership yielded immediate benefits as Ilmor engineers developed a Mercedes motor that exploited a loophole (an unfair advantage) in the USAC rulebook that allowed a pushrod motor more cubic inches than an overhead cam type. Penske drivers Emerson Fittipaldi and Al Unser, Jr., easily dominated the 1994 race with Unser taking his second win. Unser went on to post eight wins and take the season's title. At Milwaukee Penske drivers Unser, Fittipaldi and Paul Tracy finished first, second and third.

Penske's Indy car program hit bottom in 1995 when, unable to qualify the Marlboro Penskes, it was not able to get cars loaned from Bobby Rahal up to speed and missed the last CART race at the speedway. Courtesy of Dudley Evans.

The power of the Ilmor motor, listed as a Mercedes beginning in 1995, hid the poor handling of the Penske chassis. In 1994 Bobby Rahal's new Honda-powered cars were unable to find qualifying speed for the 500 so Penske made two Penske cars available to him. Rahal was sponsored by the Miller Brewing Company, the sponsor of Penske's NASCAR team for Rusty Wallace and part of the Phillip Morris empire that also included Marlboro. The tables were turned for 1995 as Rahal made his Lolas available to Penske drivers when the team cars were not up to qualifying speed. It was not to be, and neither Penske driver made the field. For the remainder of the decade Penske cars were only also-rans.

Penske South fields Wallace's car #2 in NASCAR. In 1998 Penske merged with Michael Kranefaus' team and driver Jeremy Mayfield in the #12 car. For 2002 Ryan Newman replaced Mayfield.

At the conclusion of 1999 Penske reorganized the CART team, replacing his own chassis, Al Unser, Jr., and

Penske Racing had the best of everything due to lucrative sponsorships. Penske was on the board of directors for Phillip Morris (Marlboro).

Mercedes power with Reynard, Gil deFerran and Helio Castroneves, and Honda power. Results were immediate in 2000 as both new drivers won, with deFerren taking the driver's title, and repeating in 2001.

In 2001 Penske returned to Indianapolis. Rookie Castroneves led deFerren to Penske's first 1-2 finish. Castroneves repeated in 2002 and in 2003 deFerren, now with Toyota power, reversed the 2001 results for his first 500 win and Penske's second 1-2 in three years.

To satisfy the advertising needs of sponsor Marlboro for 2002 Team Penske switched to the IRL.

64 I Can Go Slow Faster Than You Can
Bracket Racing

By the early 1970s drag racing was enjoying unimagined popularity. Sponsors were lining up to put their decals on cars of the professional drivers in order to be seen by the thousands in the stands at the Nationals and millions watching on TV. That is if a professional driver was doing great. The local amateur was being left behind. Even local strips were becoming involved in horsepower races as exotic racing equipment was made available, at huge cost to find that extra tenth of a second reduction in elapsed time. Drivers were spending more time in technical inspec-tion than racing, the slightest infraction meaning disqualification. Something had to be done before the local run-for-fun driver left the sport.

In the late 1960s several California tracks tried racing with an informal set of rules where handicaps were allotted to slower cars. With the use of the "Christmas Tree" starting lights a slower car began before the faster car, the handicap based on past performance. The ideal was that both cars would arrive at the finish line at the same time. This put the emphasis on consistency rather than all-out top speed. The cars were organized by performance potentials called brackets. By the mid 1970s this alternative form of drag racing had spread across the country and the term Bracket Racing took hold.

Drivers made several preliminary runs "dialing in" the car to a time that could be repeated consistently. Then the time was painted on the side window. With each run the time was recorded, the drivers trying to stay within a tight margin of their time bracket. If

A locally prepared Monza prepares for a run at Mason Dixon Dragway, Maryland. Courtesy of J.A. Martin.

a car went faster, beyond the bracket, they had "broken out" and were disqualified. To remove the inconsistency of shifting, most bracket racers used an automatic transmission.

To win, the driver needed to come off the light at the earliest possible moment. Called a "hole shot," driver reaction time was the best beginning for a consistent run. Another requisite was keeping the power tuned to optimum performance. Driver skill, not horsepower, was the key to success.

Publicists, strip operators and drivers hailed the new form as a return to fun racing. In 1974 the United States Bracket Racers Association (USBRA) was formed with a separate national championship. The NHRA established bracket rules in 1976. And in 1980 the Championship Bracket Racing Association (CBRA) ran a series of sixteen races.

By the end of the century bracket racing had become the dominant form of local amateur drag racing.

65 THIS TIME WITH MORE RULES AND MORE COMPETITION
Can-Am Reborn

After a two-year absence, responding to fan apathy for the F-5000 series that had replaced it, the Can-Am returned. This time rules were employed that curtailed some of the creativity and unlimited power of the original incarnation in the hope that the series would be less vulnerable to domination. The Group 7 requirement for a passenger seat, useless for anyone bigger than a baby anyway, was eliminated. Power was limited to non-turbocharged motors of five liters or less.

In the first three years almost all of the cars were full-bodied F-5000 cars. Continuing the domination from the F-5000 series, the Haas/Hall team won the title in 1977 (Patrick Tambay), 1978 (Alan Jones), 1979 (Jackie Ickx) and 1980 (Tambay again), the first three in the Lola T333CS a full bodied T332. Brian Redman,

the F-5000 champion, had been injured in a pre-season testing accident and retired before the series began. Other full-bodied variations of the Lola T332 were the Prophet, Schkee, Newman Spyder and the Frisbee, the latter with crude ground effects. The first Can-Am car designed with true ground effects was Lee Dykstra's HR-1

A full field of new Can-Am racers lines up for the start of the Road Atlanta Can-Am race, 1980. From the collection of J.A. Martin.

driven by Al Holbert for Carl Hogan. Lola won in 1980 with the ground effects T530.

For Tambay, Rosberg and Jones the Can-Am was a stepping stone back to F1. Jones (1980) and Rosberg (1982) won World Driving championships in Williams cars, proving that the foreign drivers were the equals of the first group from a decade earlier.

By 1981 the quality of the field behind champion Geoff Brabham was as good as any year of the series, though the best years were still ahead. Teo Fabi began with the Can-Am in America before moving to the CART series. Al Holbert, Brabham, Bobby Rahal and Danny Sullivan had risen in American sports cars before winning the IMSA titles for the former two and Indy/CART titles for the latter two.

Al Unser, Jr., drove a Frisbee to a championship for the Galles team in 1982, preparing him for CART in 1983. Jacques Villeneuve, uncle of the future World Champion, won the 1983 title in another Frisbee. The following year Irishman Michael Roe, driving the former Brabham VDS-002, won seven of the ten races for the title.

By the mid 1980s the Can-Am was again barely existent. Many of the cars were Indy cars with full bodies and stock block motors. Rick Miaskiewicz won three races and the 1985 title. The Can-Am finally died at the end of the 1986 season.

When the SCCA dropped the series it was reintroduced as Can-Am Teams (CAT) using Indy cars with stock block motors and fenders. From the collection of J.A. Martin.

The final champion was Horst Kroll. The last winner was a seventeen-year-old Canadian, Paul Tracy.

There were several series that tied onto the Can-Am name and formula. Bill Tempero organized the Can-Am Teams. When the SCCA objected to the name he shortened it to CAT. Then the series evolved into the American Indy Car Series. The low cost, power and performance made the cars a good training series for CART.

In 1998 the SCCA, within the reborn USRRC, applied the name to the open prototype cars in the ongoing conflict with SportsCar.

At vintage meets Can-Am cars, especially from the first era, are consistently the most popular racers of the event.

66 DIRT ON DIRT

After World War II the only big paved track was Indianapolis. Local racing was all on dirt ovals and new types of race cars were evolving to be practical for this environment. Originally there were two types of local dirt racers, Late Model and Modified. Late Model cars were strictly stock; nothing was done to the engine or chassis.

With the Modified class changes in engine size were allowed.

Stock car classes were originally very similar from region to region. But as racing grew in the 1950s each region took on an identity of its own. The most notable regional series was NASCAR, which went from strictly stock vehicles to, by the 1990s, specialized vehicles that had only the general appearance of a stock car.

In the 1960s the concept of a stock car began to change. For safety roll cages were added and doors welded shut. Improvements in fuel tanks were incorporated. The term "stock" was loosened up to mean stock parts from any type of car, of any year. A good junkyard became crucial for a successful race car. This caused a drain on quality used parts, many of which had been prewar. To continue to prepare a quality race car approved non-stock parts were used.

In the 1970s racers found that subcompact bodies fit Modified chassis. Of special interest was the AMC Gremlin with slab sides on top and sides, a contour that was very easy to duplicate in sheet metal. Pennsylvanian Dick Tobias took the next step and began producing a tubular steel chassis, roll cage and all, for other racers.

While oval track dirt racing stayed close to stock through the 1960s specialized performance parts were being made for drag racing. As the drag market stabilized in the 1970s suppliers looked for new markets, and found local oval racers. By the early 1980s all manner of specialized parts were accepted for the Modified class. By the late 1980s the Modified of the northeast was a unique specialized race car. The only body part that resembled a specific street car was the rear window configuration.

While the cars had evolved, sanctioning for the cars was random, with each

The DIRT series turned the New York state love of modified racing on dirt into a profitable series for driver and promoter alike. Courtesy of DIRT.

track often having slightly different rules. In 1976 Glenn Donnelly of Weedsport Speedway, along with Don Petrocci and Bob Petrocci, Jr., of Rolling Wheels Raceway, formed the Driver's Independent Race Tracks of Central New York, or DIRT. A third track, Canandaigua, was included for the inaugural season. Will Cagle won at Rolling Wheels Raceway, the first DIRT sanctioned race. Cagle went on to win the first DIRT season's championship, making him Mr. DIRT.

From the three New York tracks DIRT grew over the next two decades to include dirt ovals throughout the northeast and expanded with a winter series in Florida and DIRT South in Texas. National cable TV channels have featured DIRT races. Not all the DIRT events are on dirt. A DIRT-Asphalt series puts the DIRT Modifieds on hard surface tracks, including the one-mile Pennsylvania track at Nazareth. None of the paved tracks, except for Flemington Speedway that was forced to be paved, were DIRT tracks but instead featured DIRT sanctioned events.

In 1996 the series name was officially changed to DIRT, dropping Drivers Independent Race Tracks.

By 1998 DIRT included 21 full-member tracks with another six at associate tracks.

There are three classes of DIRT cars; Modified, 358 Modified and Sportsman. All three look identical, but there are big differences in lap times. Modified allows the motor to be up to 467 cid with a four barrel carburetor, about 750 horsepower. Modified 358 uses a maximum motor size of 358 cid with the four barrel for about 550 hp. Sportsman is the least powerful and uses the greatest number of stock parts. Limited to a two barrel carburetor and a stock ignition, power is only about 400 hp.

Even within a region fan preferences vary. In Maryland the Late Model Stocks are popular while just over the line in Pennsylvania Sprint cars rule. In New York the favorite series is still the Modified.

---

67 A GREAT IDEA SOLD OUT
International Race of Champions

A Holy Grail of racing is a series to prove who is really the best driver in the world. If the element of unequal cars were removed it would be driver skill that made the difference, that determined who was best. Like the search for the Holy Grail this pursuit is more symbolic than realistic, but it does drive men to search deeply as to what they feel constitutes a real race driver.

In reality drivers, by necessity, become specialists in one or another form of racing, an arena where they do best and feel most comfortable. Still the idea for a series of races where all drivers are equal with equal equipment persisted.

By the mid 1960s racing was becoming more internationalized with American and European drivers winning in each other's arenas, and, due to television, American fans were able to appreciate foreign drivers.

In 1973 the idea became reality with Roger Penske's International Race of Champions. For the first year the cars were the new Porsche Carreras, drawing upon Penske's ties with the Porsche factory from the Can-Am 917-30K. There were four races, all on road courses. The first three were held at Riverside, the first two on Saturday with the third the next day. From the initial lineup of twelve drivers the top six went on to the final race on the infield road course of the Daytona International Speedway.

ABC picked up the series as part of Wide World of Sports, though in later years the series moved to live and tape delay broadcasts independent of WWS.

The lineup was everything the promoters could have wanted. From NASCAR came Richard Petty, David Pearson and Bobby Allison. From the USAC Indy car ranks were Bobby Unser, A.J. Foyt, series champion Roger McCluskey and Indy winner Gordon Johncock. Former world champions Emerson Fittipaldi and Denny Hulme represented Formula 1. Rounding out the dozen were previous Can-Am champions Peter Revson, George Follmer and Mark Donohue.

Donohue took three of the four races including the championship. Follmer won the second Saturday Riverside race.

Almost immediately it became apparent that the format was not perfect. The nimble rear engine Porsches on road courses gave a decided advantage to the sports car drivers. The second series began in the fall of 1974 on the oval at Michigan International Speedway and concluded on the oval at Daytona, but with two races at Riverside. The driver lineup was altered to include four each from NASCAR, Indy cars and sportscars, which included Formula 1.

And the car had changed. The Porsches had been replaced with Chevrolet Camaros modified by

In 1986 the Camaros of IROC raced on the Watkins Glen road course. From the collection of J.A. Martin.

Jay Signore to safety regulations similar to NASCAR with a full roll cage. To make the cars as equal as possible Dave Marcis and George Follmer, later Jim Sauter, set up all twelve race cars so that they felt all were identical.

Bobby Unser won the two oval races and the series title. Fittipaldi and Bobby Allison took the two Riverside races.

The format remained the same as A.J. Foyt won the third and fourth series title, though he did not win a race. Al Unser won series five. For 1978 three qualifying races were held, one each for the road, Indy and NASCAR drivers, then one race each was held at a road course (Riverside) and an oval (Atlanta). Series six went to Mario Andretti. Then, breaking the hold the Indy car drivers had on the series, Bobby Allison won the oval final race and the seventh title.

The series was interrupted after that because of declining TV ratings and waning enthusiasm

by spectators and sponsors. But it was reborn three years later with the new generation Camaro and a decided NASCAR slant. Neil Bonnet won two races but was edged out by Cale Yarborough for the title. Darrell Waltrip and Benny Parsons finished third and fourth in the points. The format had returned to four races with three on ovals.

Dale Earnhardt won two races and the title for IROC 14. The series had only three races, with endurance driver Martin Brundle taking the Cleveland race.

Dodge made the biggest change by

Mark Martin leads a trio of NASCAR drivers on the Michigan high banks in 1990. Courtesy of John Whipple.

Mark Martin prepares to go out for practice in an IROC modified Dodge Avenger. By the 1990s IROC had become the domain of NASCAR. Martin won four IROC titles. Courtesy of John Whipple.

becoming a sponsor of the series in 1990, with highly modified Dodge Daytonas. The Daytona was to remain the car of choice until 1994 and IROC 18 when Dodge changed to the Avenger body that continued through IROC 19.

General Motors returned in 1996 with Pontiac Firebirds which were used into the new century.

All four IROC 16 races were held on oval tracks, the last two at Michigan. Since then all IROC races have been held on oval tracks. With the NASCAR style cars the series has come full circle from the all road racing series of 1973. For 2000 the series was comprised of nine NASCAR and three IRL drivers, all oval and all American drivers. It's not international anymore and very few are major series champions.

IROC, now a separate company with Jay Signore president and Les Richter CEO, makes the series commercially viable with cars as equal as humanly possible.

Al Unser, Jr., is the winningest IROC driver with eleven wins. Mark Martin has won the most titles with four, including three in a row. Except for Al Unser, Jr.'s title in 1986 and 1988 a NASCAR driver has won the series every year since 1980. Martin and Unser, Jr., have both won over a million dollars. Michigan has had the most races with 25. Thirteen different tracks have held IROC races, four of which were road courses. Through 2003, over 100 drivers have accepted invitations to participate.

68 AMERICAN FORMULA ONE
Shadow, Penske and Parnelli

There had never been such a sight as the Grand Prix of Canada in 1974. Included in the field were three different makes of cars from the United States. Two had American drivers as well. The Shadow, driven by Jean-Pierre Jarrier of France, was senior while the Penske with Mark Donohue and the Parnelli with Mario Andretti were making their race debuts. All three cars failed to finish.

The first American car designed to compete in the modern Formula 1 series was from Reventlow Automobiles Inc. called the Scarab. The blue with white front engine cars were the creations of wealthy sportsman Lance Reventlow. Lance and mechanic/driver Chuck Daigh qualified for the 1960 Belgian Grand Prix but neither finished, Reventlow completing only one lap. Daigh finished 10th at the 1960 Riverside race, the team's only other qualification.

The cars were already obsolete as new cars were rear engined and the formula was changing. The program was cancelled at the end of the season.

Dan Gurney's All American Racers Eagle competed from 1966 to 1968.

The three new teams of 1974 had their origins in other series. Don Nicholls' Shadow team had been in the Can-Am series since 1970. The UOP Shadow DN1A Formula 1 car debuted at South Africa in 1973, taking sixth place for the first points for that make of car. American driver George Follmer finished fifth in Spain, and Jackie Oliver took a fourth in Canada. Other than the black team cars there was later a white Shadow with Embassy sponsorship for the fledgling team of Graham Hill. Hill and driver Tony Brise later ran a Hill Cosworth until their deaths in a plane crash.

Jarrier and Peter Revson were the Shadow drivers for 1974. Revson won two races for McLaren in 1973 but at the 1974 South Africa Grand Prix he was killed in a qualifying accident. Bertil Roos took the second seat. The highpoint of the season was a third at Monte Carlo by Jarrier.

After winning the Can-Am and IROC championships in 1973 Mark Donohue retired, or so he thought. Roger Penske was ready to move to Formula 1 and Mark came out of retirement to develop the car.

First National City Bank Traveller's Checks sponsored the team, hence the red, white and blue paint scheme on the PC-1.

With team championships in Indy cars, the Vels Parnelli Jones team added a F-5000 program in 1974. This gave the team road racing experience. The Parnelli VPJ4 was the next step. Visually similar to the Penske, both cars were standard state of the art designs built around the Ford Cosworth motor and twin side radiators.

Neither team completed a race in 1974.

Mark Donohue debuted the Penske PC-1 at Mosport in 1974. From the collection of J.A. Martin.

Tom Pryce joined Jarrier at Shadow for 1975. The best finish was a fourth at Germany.

Donohue earned the first Penske team points with a fifth at Sweden. The car just in front of him was Mario Andretti earning the first Parnelli points. Andretti, who had previously been in Formula 1, earned a fifth at France in the only other finish of the season.

To get a better baseline Penske replaced the PC-1 with a March 751 for the British GP where Donohue took another fifth. Then, in practice in Austria, Donohue had the accident that took his life.

Pryce and Jarrier continued in the Shadow for 1976 with two fourth place finishes highlighting the season.

Penske continued with a new car, the PC-3, and a new driver, John Watson. When they returned to Austria Watson already had a fifth and two thirds to show for the season. The new PC-4 showed promise. When the favored Ferraris dropped out Watson took the lead for the lone win by a Penske in F1. It was a grand salute to Donohue.

The Parnelli team didn't seem to be going anywhere. Andretti picked up a sixth at South Africa. After the 1976 U.S. Grand Prix at Long Beach the program was terminated.

The Parnelli chassis, however, with the first turbocharged Ford Cosworth, became a pacesetter in Indy cars through the end of the decade.

While at Long Beach, Andretti met with Colin Chapman of Lotus, another racer on the low side. Andretti signed to race and develop the previously unloved JPS77. By season's end Lotus was a front runner again with two third place finishes and a win in the rain-soaked season's finale at Japan. It was the start of a beautiful friendship that led to the 1978 World's Driving championship.

Austria was the scene of both lows and highs for American teams. After Donohue's death and Watson's victory it was Shadow DN8A driver Alan Jones who set the next mark. After taking only a fifth as best result Jones roared to victory in Austria in 1977, the first and only win for an F1 Shadow. By season's end Shadow had 23 points, the most of any American car.

Jarrier took a private Penske to a sixth at the 1977 Long Beach Grand Prix. Roger Penske had turned his full attention to his Indy car program. Jarrier continued to compete with the PC-4 but Italy was the last race. The English F1 base became the construction shop for the Penske Indy cars that dominated the 1980s and early 1990s.

For 1978 it was again the Shadow that alone carried the U.S. banner, but there were American drivers trying to break into F1. Brett Lunger had raced since the mid–1970s as a privateer in various Surtees, March, McLaren, and Ensign cars but earned no points. In 1977 and 1978 Danny Ongais raced a non-team Penske, Ensign and Shadow, also to no points. Eddie Cheever began 1978 in a Theodore before moving to a Hesketh. Cheever's F1 career would culminate with a seat in the turbo Renault alongside Alain Prost. Bobby Rahal had two F1 drives for the Wolf team at the end of 1978.

Tragedy struck the Shadow team again at South Africa when driver Tom Pryce was killed when he hit a fire marshal trying to attend to a disabled Shadow. The marshal's extinguisher fatally hit Pryce in the head. The marshal was killed as well.

In 1977 several members of the Shadow team left to form a new team — Arrows. When the Arrows A1 debuted there were so many design similarities to the Shadow DN9 that Nicholls took them to court and won forcing a new Arrows car.

For the 1978 season Ted Field sponsored Danny Ongais in the Interscope Shadow, the last American Shadow driver.

Elio deAngelis earned the marque's last points with a fourth at Watkins Glen, 1979.

Hong Kong businessman Teddy Yip took over the team for 1980 but, with little success, closed the doors at season's end.

69 A True "World" Champion
Mario Andretti

As young boys the Andretti twins, Mario and Aldo, loved to go to the racetrack at nearby Monza, in Italy, to watch the great Alberto Ascari and the other Grand Prix drivers. Their dreams to join their heroes seemed to have ended when their family immigrated to America, only to discover that their new home town of

Nazareth, Pennsylvania, had a one-mile dirt track.

Aldo's promising career was cut short when he was injured in a racing accident and retired. It was up to Mario to carry on the dream, and carry on he did. Through the early 1960s Mario moved up from jalopies to sprint cars and in 1965 arrived in the American Mecca of speed, the Indianapolis 500. He was an instant sensation, setting a new lap record and becoming the highest placed rookie on both the grid

Andretti on his way to leading Holman Moody Fords to a 1-2 at the Daytona 500, 1967. Courtesy of Holman Moody.

and in the finishing order, taking third. With a victory on the road course at Indianapolis Raceway Park and consistently high finishes, he earned the 1965 USAC driver's title. He repeated as driver's champion in 1966 and finished second in 1967 and 1968. With wins at NASCAR's Daytona 500 and the 12-hour race of Sebring (his first of three) Mario was ready to try the Holy Grail of racing, Formula 1.

For 1969 Mario was slated to drive for Andy Granatelli who had supported the Lotus team in Indy racing since 1966. With those connections Mario was hired to drive the Gold Leaf Team Lotus at the 1968 U.S. Grand Prix at Watkins Glen, his first grand prix where he took the pole position but dropped out early. The following year he returned to Watkins Glen with a 4wd Lotus 63 but with less spectacular results.

Sponsored by STP, Mario ran most of the 1970 Grand Prix season in a March 701. At season's end Mario fulfilled one dream by signing to drive for Ferrari. He had driven for Ferrari in endurance racing. At Sebring 1970, after his car fell out, he was put in the fourth place 512S with less than an hour to go. As he stated, "I was on a mission." In the night he pounded the track and

competition and gave Ferrari the first endurance win for the make since 1967. Though driving on a limited basis he made the most of the F1 opportunity by winning the first race of the season at South Africa then taking the Formula 1/Formula-5000 race at Ontario Motor Speedway, the Questor Grand Prix.

After joining the Vels/Parnelli Jones Indy car team Andretti, with Viceroy cigarette sponsorship, raced in the SCCA/USAC sanctioned Formula-5000 road racing series. The sponsorship led to the red chevron on his helmet that became so familiar for both Mario and son Michael.

In 1974 Mario won the USAC dirt car

Mario's original Midget racer shares a museum spot with his 1969 Indy winning Hawk. From the collection of J.A. Martin.

championship while also driving for the Alfa Romeo endurance team.

Through 1974 and 1975 Mario and the Vels/Parnelli F-5000 team gained experience in open wheeled road racing. At the Canadian Grand Prix at Mosport in the fall of 1974 they debuted the Parnelli Cosworth Grand Prix car. The car was campaigned for portions of three seasons. The chassis, with a turbocharged Cosworth motor, went on to become a front runner in Indy car racing for the rest of the decade.

It began to look like Mario's Grand Prix goals were to be unrealized until he met Colin Chapman at Long Beach in 1976. Ronnie Peterson had left what he considered to be an unstable race car, the black John Player Special Lotus 77. At the race Parnelli announced that he was disbanding the F1 team. Both Chapman and Andretti were at career low points, so they joined. By the race at Mosport Mario, the development driver, had the car stable and finished third. At the season's finale, in a rain storm, Andretti took the pole and then the win in what he has described as the best F1 drive of his career.

Chapman had some interesting ideas about race car design and now he had a driver with whom he could easily commu-

nicate. When the Lotus 78 first appeared in the spring of 1977 it was noticeable for its width. Inside the extra wide side pods were ground effect wings. At the 1977 Long Beach Grand Prix Mario fought with Jody Schecketer and Niki Lauda. With the end of the race in sight Mario slipped past Schecketer and took the win. The season was followed with wins at France and Italy. Unfortunately the Lotus was as likely to DNF as win so Mario had to settle for third place in the driver's points, but the ground effects car had proven to be the way to go.

Ronnie Peterson returned to Lotus to join Andretti for the 1978 season. Mario began the season with a victory at South Africa. The real fun for Mario and Lotus began at Spa. There was a new Lotus, the model 79, a brilliant refinement of the 78. With the 79 Mario took the pole and the win, Ronnie Peterson in the 78 came second. Peterson got his own 79 and the Lotus pair "won two, one-two." It was now apparent that the Lotus duo were in a class by themselves. The brilliant technician and the master of control made the team unbeatable. Mario won again to easily lead the points, only challenged by Peterson.

Mario returned to Monza ready to take the crown on the grounds of his childhood dreams. He had the pole, but the day would go all wrong. At the start Peterson's car balked and was hit from behind. The fiery crash would lead to his death a few days later. On the restart Mario and front row partner Giles Villeneuve, mindful of the first start, were tense at the flag. There was a discrepancy between the flagman and the lights so the field moved at the first flag motion. Mario easily led the race only to be given a one-minute penalty for starting early. The victory was given to second row starter Niki

Mario Andretti and the Lotus 78, the winning combination that led to the 1978 World Driver and Manufacturer title. From the collection of J.A. Martin.

Lauda who hadn't crossed the start line before the lights went green.

Mario, like Phil Hill seventeen years before, won his world driver's title at Monza while losing his teammate.

Andretti raced for Lotus again in 1979 and 1980 but the new Lotus cars seemed to show that Chapman had gone too far in exotic aerodynamics, and the other teams were understanding ground effects. For 1981 Mario moved to the Alfa Romeo team but the car

Quietly the "Driver of the Century" waits for practice to begin at Watkins Glen in 1979. From the collection of J.A. Martin.

was too heavy to be competitive. After that he secured occasional rides with Williams and Ferrari. For 1983 Mario recommitted himself to Indy cars with the Carl Haas/ Paul Newman Lola team. The fire had not gone, however, and he took the CART driver's title, his fourth, in 1984. When he won the Phoenix race in 1993 he became the only driver to have won a major race in four different decades.

The competitive fire still burned, and in 2000 Mario joined the Panoz Le Mans team. After a violent crash into a wall resulting from a deflated tire, he finished sixteenth.

The title "World Champion" was never more appropriate than for Mario Andretti. Mario seemed to be doing things different from what was expected of a race car driver. The Champ car series had

been the domain of senior experienced drivers, yet Mario had won three titles before he turned thirty. Young drivers were Grand Prix aces, yet Mario took up the challenge at an age when many Grand Prix drivers had already retired.

Mario Andretti and sons Michael (left) and Jeff (right) raced together in the Indianapolis 500 twice, 1991 and 1992. This photograph came from the 1991 Texaco press kit, the year Michael placed 2nd, Mario 7th and Jeff 15th.

70 ROAD RACING GOES PROFESSIONAL
John Bishop and IMSA

The question of whether motorsports should remain pure and be contested by amateurs who drive because of their love of the sport or should include professionals, whose only vocation is to make a living by excelling in a sport, goes back to the chariot races of ancient Rome.

The question arose in American sports car racing in the 1950s. While the AAA/USAC open wheel series had been the domain of the professional drivers since the foundation of the sport, there had been insufficient financial and spectator support for sports car racing in America, and the amateurs were left to race for the fun of the sport. Amateur did not mean being less than a top driver as John Fitch was talented enough to be a part of the Mercedes-Benz endurance team of the mid 1950s.

But on the west coast a new type of road racer was coming of age, hot young drivers who were holding their own against the best of Europe and wanted to race for a living. Men like Phil Hill, Dan Gurney, Richie Ginther and the transplanted Texan Carroll Shelby. Using experience gained in SCCA races and financed by patrons who owned the Ferraris and Maseratis, these drivers went on to drive for the best European factory teams.

As more American drivers were racing for a living the SCCA inaugurated the United States Road Racing Championship in 1963. The USRRC was a series of races at the best American tracks leading not to the SCCA runoffs but to a winner's purse. This was exacerbated as the new one-off hot rods, like Roger Penske's Zerex Special and Jim Hall's Chaparral, were regularly beating the Ferraris and Maseratis. A gen-

tleman driver could no longer purchase a contending car.

In 1966 the SCCA initiated three new professional series, all based on the five liter American V-8. The Trans-Am was for stock "pony cars," Formula-5000 for open wheeled, and Can-Am for sports racers. Within the SCCA there was now a professional and amateur department.

The SCCA Executive Director during the 1960s was John Bishop, a former ergonomics engineer who had become involved with the club by painting covers for programs. Under Bishop's leadership the USRRC was created, followed by the three 1966 series. Still there was conflict. Recalled Bishop, "The old guard wanted to keep the club on an amateur course and it was getting nigh impossible."

There was no reconciliation. It came to a head at the 1969 Board of Directors meeting. Bishop quit.

Bishop had been talking with Bill France of NASCAR. France had created NASCAR as an entirely professional series with one-man rule, no second-guessing by a board of directors. From discussions between the two men came the seed for a second sports car organization, one entirely professional. France assisted in financing and organization, and by the end of the year the International Motor Sports Association (IMSA) was in business.

But what kind of business? The first IMSA event was a Formula Ford race at Pocono. Some 348 people showed up and, despite the negative press by the SCCA, they had a race. Bishop knew that IMSA needed an identity, an IMSA type of car. For inspiration he turned to Europe and the Group 4 class of cars. These were race modified Porsches, BMWs and Alfa Romeos. These were pure race cars, yet affordable and maintainable by most private teams.

The first champions of the GT series were Peter Gregg and Hurley Haywood with the Brumos Porsche 914. Gregg was a veteran of both the Trans-Am and an expert on Porsches. Haywood was young, having just returned from being a helicopter pilot in Viet Nam.

Early on Bishop decided that every participant would receive part of the winning purse. This insured that teams where racing was part of the advertising/promotion budget that there was income as well as expenses.

Another decision was to make races long enough that co-drivers were needed. As many drivers paid for a drive, the more drivers, the more income to the team.

The big break financially came in 1972 when Camel cigarettes came on as title sponsor.

By the early 1970s the FIA's World Manufacturers series was coming apart. For 1973 the two American endurance races, Daytona and Sebring, were no longer

on the international calendar and there was a good chance both were about to cease. Seizing the opportunity IMSA took over sanctioning for the two races. The thundering Porsche 917s were replaced by the GT class Porsche Carerras. The first winners were Gregg and Haywood. By 1974 the IMSA GT series had more events than the rival Trans-Am.

So successful were the European Group 4 cars that American cars, even the Corvettes, were becoming uncompetitive. IMSA needed a balance that included American sports cars. Technical inspector Mark Raffauf stated, "We wanted to put an international flavor and we constantly had to fight the FIA and the homologation system. We wanted rules to make a mass-produced car competitive with a limited run race car for viable competition and entertainment." The result in 1975 was the All American GT series. The premier car of the series was the Chevrolet Monza that was tricked out with aerodynamic devices and a big V-8 on a tube frame. Al Holbert won the GT championship in 1976 and 1977 in a Lee Dykstra designed Monza.

Porsche was pressuring both IMSA and the SCCA to allow the new turbo Porsche. Reluctantly both agreed, and by the end of the decade the Porsche 935 was dominating the series. The SCCA responded by returning to stock based sports cars.

A quick solution was to allow one-off racers that only had to look like production cars, sports cars equivalent to Funny Cars. Known as GTX, they were virtually cars without rules. But IMSA was glad to have the manufacturers participate so the cars were allowed, although they were still outclassed by the 935s.

The long-term solution

To encourage less funded teams and women drivers IMSA created support series like the Kelly American Challenge. Lyn St. James' Capri ride led to the Ford GTO and Probe GTP teams. Courtesy of Ed Clayton.

The All American GT class was the first step by IMSA to create fan interest by making American cars equal to the special European models. A Monza GT leads a Porsche through the corkscrew at Laguna Seca in 1976. From the collection of J.A. Martin.

a GT Prototype formula that was straight forward and sensible, hopefully using a wide variety of different production engines."

IMSA and Europe wanted similar cars but there was a fundamental difference in execution. IMSA favored a sliding scale of engine size to keep the cars competitive. Europe, still feeling the effect of the 1979 oil crisis favored a formula based on fuel consumption.

The differences were fundamental between American and European racing. In Europe racing is used by the factories to prove their cars. In America racing is entertainment. Domination by a single make or an economy run by exotic cars is not marketable in America.

The GTP series was a success, growing to sixteen races a season in the late

was an all-new series. Working with the *Auto Club d'Ouest*, the organizers of Le Mans, IMSA officials came up with a new type of sports racer. Recalled Bishop, "We had the same problem. Car builders here and around the world supported the idea of

With the GTP series IMSA took the world lead. A balance was created between an extraordinary variety of chassis and motors by means of regulating engine size to car weight. Courtesy of Ed Clayton.

1980s. The first chassis suppliers were Lola and March with the customer supplying the power. Then Porsche introduced the 962, and those with big enough checkbooks could have a race-winning car. Porsche sold cars and provided support services from motor maintenance to body parts.

Beginning with BMW in 1981 other manufacturers became involved. Over the length of the series Jaguar, Ford, Chevrolet, Buick, Nissan, Toyota, Pontiac, Mazda and Honda/Acura had factory-supported teams. Unfortunately for the series these cars were not available to the private teams, and in 1993 the GTP series came to an end.

John Bishop had already left IMSA. Following heart surgery in 1987 Bishop sold IMSA to Mike Cone and Jeff Parker for a reported $9 million in 1988. Subsequently IMSA has been resold several times and even had its name changed to SportsCar in 1996, then back to IMSA in 2001.

71 UNITED STATES GRAND PRIX, POSTWAR

When the World Drivers and Manufacturers Championship for Formula 1 was established in 1950 there was no United States Grand Prix as such although the FIA granted championship points to the Indianapolis 500 through 1960. North America was shut out through the era of Juan Fangio, Alberto Ascari, the Mercedes Silver Arrows and Vanwall. By the time America was reintroduced to Grand Prix racing the days of the front engine car were past.

Sebring: 1959

Alec Ulman brought Grand Prix racing back to the United States at the site of his 12-hour race using the same layout used for the endurance classic. Bruce McLaren won his first Grand Prix in a Cooper, at the time the youngest driver to ever win a Grand Prix. His teammate Jack Brabham secured the driver's title. Rodger Ward, optimistic from his victory in the Formula Libre race at Lime Rock over several top European cars, came in an Offy powered Midget racer, but did not find success this time.

Riverside: 1960

Located east of the automotive hot bed of Los Angeles, Riverside seemed like a good idea at the time, but the track did not offer the facilities needed for Formula 1. There was little shade and the pits were primitive, even by 1960 standards. Dan Gurney started on the front row in a BRM but had his car fail before the race concluded. Stirling Moss braved the hot sun to win in a private entry Lotus.

Watkins Glen: 1961–1980

"The Glen" quickly became synonymous with Grand Prix racing in the 1960s and 1970s. The western New York state course was as beautiful as any on the circuit, especially on race weekend in early October with the leaves brightly colored.

For two decades Watkins Glen was Formula 1 to most Americans. Jimmy Clark qualified his #1 Lotus in front of John Surtees' #7 Ferrari for the 1964 race. From the collection of J.A. Martin.

For many years Watkins Glen offered the largest purse on the circuit and so drew large entries. While most of the great drivers won at Watkins Glen, none were Americans. Mario Andretti entered his first Grand Prix there in 1968, winning the pole in a Lotus 49B. A decade later he arrived back as World Champion only to have a failure in his Lotus 79 during qualifying.

By the late 1970s debts by the organizers and larger purses at European tracks were financially more than the track could bear. The year 1980 was the last race, won by Alan Jones. By then the entire track looked like the infamous Bog. A year later the track went bankrupt.

A group headed by nearby Corning Glass and the France family (NASCAR) reopened the track in 1984 to IMSA prototypes and NASCAR.

In the 1960s the United States Grand Prix at Watkins Glen had the largest purse of the series. With Long Beach the U.S. had a second race. This was an exception to the "one country, one race" precedent as the two were almost 3,000 miles apart. But in 1981 and 1982 there was a Grand Prix at both Long Beach and Las Vegas, only 236 miles apart. And in 1982, with the inception of the Detroit race, there were three U.S. Grand Prix races.

After Phoenix was removed from the schedule several tracks and cities submitted proposals for a Grand Prix. The most serious efforts were from Road America in Wisconsin and a street race in lower Manhattan. But nothing came to fruition until the Indianapolis Motor Speedway added an infield road course and a lot of money.

Long Beach: 1976–1983

In 1974 Chris Pook approached Dan Gurney to help him stage a Grand Prix through the streets of the Los Angeles port city of Long Beach. There was no model to work from but they persuaded the Long Beach City Council, the California Coastal Commission, local elderly residents and the FIA that it would help revitalize the area. In 1975 an F-5000 went off well and the Grand Prix arrived the following year.

In 1977 Mario Andretti, in the new Lotus 78, won over Jody Scheckter and

Tom Pryce, in a UOP Shadow, negotiates the streets of Long Beach (California) for the 1976 Grand Prix. Courtesy of the Freda Otto collection.

Niki Lauda to signify that he was coming of age as a Grand Prix driver and ready to take the crown in 1978.

For 1981 and 1982 Long Beach began the F1 season that ended nine months and hundreds of miles later at Las Vegas.

By 1983 the town's image had improved, but Formula 1 was asking for more appearance money than Pook was willing to pay. John Watson won the last Grand Prix, and for 1984 Long Beach became a CART event. Mario won three more times, the only driver to compete at Long Beach in F-5000, F1 and CART.

Las Vegas: 1981–1982

To the land of Elvis imitators and Wayne Newton came the best drivers in the world. If that seems unnatural, the course was even worse. A track layout was devised using barricades in the parking lot of Caesar's Palace. In the first race Alan Jones won but Nelson Piquet won the World Championship over Jones' teammate Carlos Reutemann. Michelle Albereto won the 1982 race in a Ferrari.

For 1983 CART replaced Formula 1 with Tom Sneva winning his only road course victory.

Detroit: 1982–1988

Detroit, Michigan, is the home of the American auto industry. But in 1982 the Motor City was in a severe recession. Foreign cars were often vandalized, simply for being foreign. But in the seven years of the race there were no American drivers of cars.

The races were held on the streets through downtown Detroit. The 1983 race was significant as Michelle Albereto earned the last win for the Ford of England DFV motor (the first was in 1967). Ayrton Senna

For seven years the international Formula 1 series ran through the Motor City. From the collection of J.A. Martin.

won the last three races with three different engine/chassis packages.

Beginning in 1989 the race was sanctioned by CART featuring American drivers and sponsors.

Dallas: 1984

It seemed more like a TV movie than a race. The stars of the TV show *Dallas* often upstaged the drivers. The Texas fans knew J.R. Ewing, they didn't know Keke Rosberg. But it was the 100+ degree heat that stole the action on the street circuit. Rosberg won the July race, but the most memorable sight was an exhausted Nigel Mansell, in a black driving suit, pushing his disabled Lotus over the finish line.

The streets of Dallas, Texas, were as hot as the Grand Prix cars in the 1984 race. Teams adjusted by adding extra radiators, as in the nose of a Brabham. From the collection of J.A. Martin.

Phoenix: 1989–1991

As if no one learned from Dallas, another U.S. Grand Prix was held on city streets in the desert. The 3.8 km course had no beauty or even character. Of the three races, Ayrton Senna won two after Alain Prost won in 1989.

There was no second Dallas Grand Prix, but the Trans-Am ran at Addison and Reunion Stadium for several years.

Alain Prost acknowledges winning the 1989 U.S. Grand Prix at Phoenix, Arizona. From the collection of J.A. Martin.

Indianapolis: 2000–Present

In 1998 Indianapolis Motor Speedway president Tony George signed an agreement with Bernie Ecclestone to bring Grand Prix racing back to America. A course was built in the infield of the famed brickyard. Grand Prix style pits were built under traditional turn 1 seats. The event was run clockwise, opposite to the direction of the 500 and the Brickyard 400.

At the inaugural race in September 2000 Michael Schumaker led a Ferrari 1-2 before the largest crowd ever to see a Grand Prix live. There were no American cars or drivers among the entrants.

72 UNSER, THE FIRST CLAN OF RACING

No family has accomplished more in racing than have the Unsers of Albuquer-que, New Mexico. For three generations of sons, brothers and cousins the Unsers have won in almost every form of racing they have entered. Yet they have never strayed far from their roots, all still residing in the area of their western heritage.

Brothers Louis, Jr., Jerome (Jerry), and Joseph (Joe) were born in Alton, Illinois. Their father, a German butcher, had a bad heart, and in 1909 he moved the family to Colorado in the shadow of Pikes Peak. The three boys soon fixed up a motorcycle that even the police could not catch. In 1915 the boys took the cycle with sidecar up the mountain. Louie and his brother Joe returned in 1926 for their first official run. Joe took second while Louie did not finish. Joe finished second four times before being killed in a testing accident just after the 1929 race. It wasn't until his eighth trip in 1934 that Louie won. He went on to eight more wins (setting six records), the last win in 1953, though he continued to compete thirty-six times, through 1967. When the organizers told him he was too old to compete he paid the entry fee with his Social Security check.

The third brother, Jerry, was considered a mediocre driver with a third as his best finish. His major contributions were his four sons. Twins, though not identical, Jerry, Jr., and Louis were born in 1932. Two years later Bobby was born with Al following in 1939. When the Depression hit Colorado Jerry moved his family to Albuquerque, New Mexico.

While serving in the Navy in Hawaii, Jerry, Jr., dominated local jalopy races to the point that he was given a special send-off by the fans when his tour ended. On return to the States he drove for the Ford factory stock car team.

Jerry, Jr., and Louis assaulted Pikes Peak in 1955. Louis was third with Jerry fourth. For 1956 and·1957 Jerry won his class. It wasn't until 1960 that Louis first won his class, which he repeated in 1961. Louis' last race was in 1964. He developed

multiple sclerosis and turned to building engines for Bobby.

Jerry was the first Unser to make it to Indianapolis but he paid the price. He was killed during practice for the 1959 race.

Bobby first went to the Peak in 1955 and won the following year. Through 1997 Bobby took thirteen wins and never failed to finish. His first three years at Indianapolis were with the final wails of the Novi, in 1964 with the four wheel drive car. He made 74 laps cumulative. His fortunes greatly improved when he teamed up with Jud Phillips and finished third in the 1967 championship points.

In the early running of the 1968 Indianapolis 500 Bobby was the only driver to stay with the leading turbine of Joe Leonard. Leonard's car quit but Bobby's didn't, resulting in his first 500 victory. He culminated the season by taking the 1968 driver's championship.

When Dan Gurney retired in 1970 he immediately hired Bobby to drive the factory Eagle. While 1971 was at best a good year 1972 was historic, and frustrating. With the all new Eagle Bobby won four races, seven poles, led every race and set eight qualifying records. But the new car was fragile, and he dropped out of more races than he finished. By 1974, though the car was becoming more reliable and Bobby won the California 500 and his second driver's championship. He was also named Martini and Rossi Driver of the Year. In addition he won the 1974/1975 IROC series. In 1975 he took his second Indianapolis win. After a brief stint with a Lightning and back with the Eagle, Bobby signed on with Roger Penske in 1979. He won the 1980 500-mile races at Pocono and Ontario, California, and the 1981 Indianapolis race, the latter after a five month appeal board review over a potential passing infraction during the race. At the end of the season he retired.

He came back in 1993 for the Fast Master's Tournament against other past racing

Bobby Unser pulls his Penske Ford into victory lane at Trenton in 1979. Courtesy of Dave Kneebone.

styles were almost opposite. Bobby was fast, the charger setting lap records and getting the most out of the car. When needed Al was able to put out a competitive lap, but he was more likely to keep the car in control, to not extend it beyond its capabilities. He won four Indianapolis 500s, two by finishing races when the faster drivers, including Bobby, fell aside, and three USAC/CART driving championships by not extending the car.

champions over age 50 in identically prepared Jaguar XJ220s. He took the title in the only year for the series.

As soon as he put down his helmet he took up a microphone as an expert commentator for ABC Sports' coverage of Indy car races.

It is ironic that Al Unser, Sr,. is now called "Big Al" since he was the baby of the Unser brothers. As competitive as Al was towards his brother Bobby, their driving

Al came up to Indianapolis and the Champ car series in 1965, finishing second at Indy in 1967. In 1968 he signed with the Vel's/Parnelli Jones team, winning the 500 and the driver's championship in 1970. He won the 500 again in 1971. Through 1977 he was part of the Super Team with Joe Leonard and Mario Andretti, his teammate in the SCCA/USAC F-5000 series. Al joined with Jim Hall in 1978 with the new Lola. Not only did he win his third 500, but he also won the Pocono 500 and Ontario 500, the only time a driver won three 500-mile Champ car races in one season.

Bobby Unser prepares for the CART race on the high banks of the Atlanta Motor Speedway in 1979. Courtesy of Ed Clayton.

Al Unser debuted the Porsche Indy car at Laguna Seca (California). Courtesy of Cliff Morgan.

As if to prove that it was the driver, not the car, he won the 1978 IROC title. It looked like Al had the winning car for Indianapolis in 1979 when Jim Hall brought out the ground effects Chaparral 2K, but a failed motor ended his run.

After a few seasons with the Longhorn team Al signed with Penske racing in 1983, replacing his brother Bobby who had retired. Al responded by winning his second driver's title. Al was brought out of semi-retirement in 1985 as a replacement driver for the injured Rick Mears. Although he won only one race, he won his third driver's title, this time over his son by a single point. The hugs between the two competing drivers showed the bonds of father and son.

With the return of Mears, Al was back on the sidelines until Penske driver Danny Ongais was injured in practice for the 1987 Indy 500. Again Penske called upon Al. Driving a year old former show car Al patiently waited while the faster drivers fell out to come home with his fourth Indy 500 win.

Al doesn't seem like an innovator, yet he was the first driver to race and win with the Cosworth Ford motor, the first driver to race the Ilmor Chevrolet, Indy Porsche, and the first at Indianapolis with the Alfa Romeo motor. In 1992 he finished third at Indianapolis with the Menard Buick, the highest any stock block rear-engine car ever finished.

When Tony George began the IRL he hired Al to assist the young drivers. Those who listened were wise, for few drivers understand a race car better than Big Al.

The first third generation Unser driver was Bobby, Jr., in 1976, winning his class. Bobby, Jr., continued through 1985.

Al Unser, Jr., says that everything he knows he learned from his dad, but that he doesn't know everything his dad knows. Still the younger Unser learned enough to win a Super Vee and Can-Am title plus two CART (1991, 1994) driver's titles and two Indianapolis 500s (1992, 1994). Both Sr. and Jr. have won the Daytona 24-hour sports car race.

Little Al's racing education was grounded in what helped his elders and what was best for racing in the 1980s and beyond. "Junie" first went to Pikes Peak in 1979 at age 17, winning in 1983. Before moving up to Champ cars in 1983 Little Al won in sprint cars on dirt, ASA stock cars and in Super Vees. In 1982 he signed to drive a Frisbee in the Can-Am series. Though it was his first full season in sports cars he took the title. He made an impact at Indianapolis in 1983 when he ran closely behind his father to ward off a charging Tom Sneva. Running competitive laps, Little Al kept an eye ahead and an eye behind. After Sneva passed him and very quickly disposed of Al, Sr., to win the race, Little Al readily acknowledged his efforts to help his father. Two years later he took his father to the last race before the elder won the driver's title.

In 1994 Little Al signed to drive for Roger Penske who had fielded cars in

Al Unser, Sr. (l) and Jr. (r) were as caring to each other off the track as they were competitive on the track. 1983. Courtesy of Dave Kneebone.

Hardly more than a kid, Al Unser Jr., was already enjoying racing as a winner, as at Road Atlanta in 1982. Courtesy of Ed Clayton.

which his father and uncle had "500" victories. The three Unsers have nine Indy 500 wins and seven Champ car driver's titles.

One Indy 500 he did not win was 1989. When engine failure ended Michael Andretti's dominant performance the race was left to Little Al and Emerson Fittipaldi. As the laps were winding down the two were as close as any pair ever. Two laps from the end, neither giving an inch, they came together and Al hit the wall. When Fittipaldi came by on the white flag lap Unser jumped out to give an enthusiastic thumbs up to show that he was fine and thanks for some great racing. It was an Unser style display.

Junior dominated the 1994 CART season, winning both Indianapolis and the season's driving title with eight wins. But racing fortune can turn very quickly. Bad luck and inferior cars contributed to a dry spell in which Al did not win another CART race and was released by Penske after 1999. Al, Jr., was burned out. Events off the track and the years of competition had taken their toll.

He reunited with Rick Galles for a 2000 IRL effort. Results were immediate with a win at Phoenix. Though he holds Indianapolis in the highest regard, his return was emotional but less than memorable with a mid-field starting position and an early exit.

Junior's competitive drive and skill at his height showed in the IROC series though it has favored the NASCAR drivers since the 1984 rebirth. Al, Jr., won the title in 1986 and 1988 and is still the winningest driver in series history with eleven race wins.

The IRL gave two more Unsers the opportunity to get to Indianapolis. Johnny Unser, Jerry's son, began racing at Indianapolis in 1996, the first year of the IRL.

Under his dad's leadership, Robby has tried the IRL but has never lived up to his potential as anticipated when he was picked in the early 1990s as one of the ten most promising drivers in the world. His brother, Bobby, Jr., had raced in the 1980s but never pursued it as a career.

Bobby Unser said about his family, "Dad and both my uncles sought new challenges and racing gets to people. They felt that there was not much romance and very little money. We kids have had a little of both. We got in because it was exciting. It's like a feeding frenzy. You have to have desire to win, a big desire."

The Unsers like things that are fast. In the summer they race dirt bikes. When the snow falls the bikes are replaced by snowmobiles, but the competition continues. They are also practical jokers who play as hard as they race.

73

AWESOME BILL FROM DAWSONVILLE
Bill Elliott in 1985

NASCAR is successful because it fosters the illusion that everyone is equal and has a chance to win. Rule changes are often made during mid-season when one car seems to have an advantage. But occasionally one car comes along that defies the rules. Worse yet is one driver that defies even the drivers who share his brand of car. So it was in 1985 for the redhead of racing, Bill Elliott.

The Elliotts, like the Pettys, made racing a family affair. Bill was the driver with brothers Ernie and Dan preparing the car. Their home was in the Georgia hill town of Dawsonville, northwest of Atlanta. Way northwest.

The Melling team works to keep Bill Elliott's Ford in the championship hunt. Courtesy of Ed Clayton.

Their father George Elliott had fielded stock cars for several years, and when young Bill learned to drive, he helped set them up, though they were raced by a hired driver. But by 16 Bill was behind the wheel and ready to race. The first Elliott family effort was in 1976. When Roger Penske withdrew from NASCAR the Elliotts bought his Mercury, the team's first quality car. Financial support arrived in 1981 from Henry Melling. After a one race trial Melling bought the team, freeing the Elliotts to do the racing.

The first win came at the final race of the 1983 season at the Riverside road course when late race troubles sidelined the early leaders.

In 1983 Ford redesigned the Thunderbird, turning a box into one of the most aerodynamic cars on the road. Despite the slippery shape, Ford teams were having trouble taking advantage of the new pack-age. By the summer of 1984 the Elliotts seemed to be coming to grips with the car, and near the end of the season Bill won three superspeedway races. While not faster in a straight line, the Elliott Ford held speed through the corners better and had superior acceleration out of the corners.

Not everyone was ready for what happened at Daytona. Bill took the pole then roared off to such a lead that NASCAR had to make a creative use of the yellow flag to keep the Coors Ford within sight of the field. Towards the end officials held Elliott in the pit on the pretext of an unsafe crack in the plastic light housing until Lake Speed, in second, was able to get in sight of Elliott. Still it was an easy win.

Wins followed at the superspeedways of Rockingham, Darlington and Atlanta. Under pressure from the Chevrolet teams NASCAR added a height restriction to the Thunderbirds for Talladega. The Ford teams responded by taking the top three spots. Elliott won in one of the most amazing races

Bill Elliott was all smiles in the early part of the 1985 season. Courtesy of Ed Clayton.

in NASCAR history. Early problems put Elliott two laps down on the two and two-thirds mile track. On the track, without benefit of yellow flags, Elliott ran faster than anyone, even the other Fords, to make up both laps and handily win the race. Winston Cigarettes, sponsor of the series, began a new promotion for 1985. Any driver that was able to win three of the four premier races of the tour, the Daytona 500, the Winston 500 at Talladega, the World 600 at Charlotte and the Southern 500 at Darlington, would win a $1 million bonus. Elliott had taken the first two races on his way to the Winston Million.

Charlotte did not happen so it was all up for grabs at the Southern 500 at Darlington. Coming into the race Elliott was enjoying a lead in the driver's championship over Darrell Waltrip, the driver of Junior Johnson's #11 Chevrolet. Waltrip and Johnson had already won driver's titles in 1981 and 1982, and Waltrip was the winningest driver in 1984. Waltrip was grabbing wins and points at the short tracks where Elliott was not a factor.

The race did not

look that good for Elliott's #9 Coors Ford. Dale Earnhardt led the early part of the race until he hit the wall in turn 2. Then Harry Gant took over the lead and was pulling away from the field until a cylinder failed. Elliott took the lead with 44 laps to go, but Cale Yarborough was closing the gap in his #28 Thunderbird. Slowed by a failure in his power steering, Cale was still able to get within .6 seconds of Elliott but had to settle for second. For the afternoon's work he earned $1,857,253.

Bill Elliott was the Million-dollar kid. While other drivers have won two of the four races no other driver took the million until Jeff Gordon did it in 1997, the last year of the promotion.

The magic of the season seemed to have peaked at Darlington. Waltrip had a bad day and finished 17th, leaving Elliott with a 206 point lead. But Elliott won just one more race as one small problem after another plagued the team through the fall. They were just not big enough to keep up with the NASCAR rule changes and the stress from racing every weekend. By the season's finale Waltrip had the driver's title wrapped up. Elliott was second with eleven

At Atlanta Elliott's #9 Thunderbird comes up on Neil Bonnett, #12, and Cale Yarborough, #28. It was another Elliott win. Courtesy of Ed Clayton.

victories, all on tracks of one mile or greater. That was a record. The public and press recognized his achievement. He was Driver of the Year for the National Motorsports Press Association, Auto Racing Digest and the Jerry Titus Memorial award.

The latter part of Elliott's 1985 season was a series of accidents and component failures that reduced his points lead to a second place finish. Courtesy of Ed Clayton.

While his was faster than the other Fords, Elliott's success caused many teams to rethink Ford as a winning race car. Over the next few years many teams switched to Ford from GM cars, including Junior Johnson.

For 1987 Ford redesigned the Thunderbird and Elliott promptly used the new car to win his second Daytona 500. But the rest of the year was not a repeat of 1985 and he finished with six wins.

Realizing the team's shortcomings in 1985, the Elliotts began a short track program. The work came to fruition in 1988 when Bill Elliott won six races, including a short track win at Bristol, and the driver's title. In 1992, driving for Junior Johnson, he nearly won the driver's title again only to fall five points shy to Alan Kulwicki, although taking the season's final race.

Following a major accident at Talladega in 1996 Elliott has not enjoyed the same success he found in the late 1980s when he was the ESPN Driver of the Decade. Still he won the Most Popular Driver's title 15 times and through the 2002 season has had 43 victories and 55 pole positions.

The year 2001 was a rebirth for Elliott. Dodge and Ray Evernham signed him to lead the reintroduction of the brand to Winston Cup racing. Bill responded at Daytona by taking his first pole position in several years. He finished fifth. In 2002 he won Pocono and the Brickyard 400.

74 WORLD OF OUTLAWS

Sprint car racing is as American as apple pie and a relatively low cost way to race on the edge. From the first sprint cars in the early years of racing through the 1950s Sprint cars were the way to prove an ability to handle power and were the step toward the Olympus of Indianapolis.

Sprint cars are open wheel with no compromises for body shape. For most of the period sprint cars raced on local dirt tracks of a half of a mile or less. The competition was close and rough. For many years sprint car champions were the best America had. With a power to weight ratio

The World of Outlaws tour ran through dirt tracks, like Lincoln Speedway (Pennsylvania) across the country. From the collection of J.A. Martin.

equal to Formula 1 or Indy cars, sprint cars took real drivers to handle them. And with the mud slinging slides through the corners they were crowd favorites.

The rear engine revolution that changed Indy car racing directly affected sprint cars. The skills needed to handle the little rear engine racers were different than those acquired in sprint car racing. Tom Sneva was the last USAC sprint car winner to make it to the top of Indy car racing. Lacking a goal, sprint car racing lost direction.

Enter Texas race promoter Ted Johnson. In 1978 he organized drivers who wanted to race in this form into a series. Playing on the renegade image of the tour that raced across the continent and calendar and the conflict that developed with the Sprint Car establishment within USAC, Johnson called his series the World of Outlaws (WoO).

The big conflict between USAC and the WoO was in regard to wings. USAC outlawed wings while WoO specified their size. Wings serve as two safety factors and one marketing purpose to the racers. The 25 square foot mid-body wing keeps the car stable by increasing traction. And if a car flips, the break-away wing absorbs much of the initial shock of the crash.

Marketing is very different. Wings are giant billboards where sponsors can display ads, logos or decals.

In 1998 WoO drivers competed in 92 races at 49 tracks from February through November, with 12 races televised. This allowed no time for testing or servicing a car back at the shop. Once the tour starts it is survival of the fittest.

Two names have dominated the series since inception. Steve Kinser won the first championship in 1978 and has repeated thirteen times. In all Steve has 424 victories. His cousin Mark won the title in 1996 and has 100 wins. The biggest challenger is Sammy Swindell who has three series titles and 236 wins.

There are as many as thirty touring teams, and part of the appeal of the WoO series is that local drivers compete against the pros. Many of the local drivers are excellent, with top equipment, and often win the events, to the delight of the fans.

The premier Outlaw, Steve Kinser, getting ready to go on the job. From the collection of J.A. Martin.

75 TRACKS LOST
1971–1986

The heady days of track construction in the 1960s abruptly ran into the realities of the 1970s. It seemed that everything was conspiring against the growth of motorsports.

At the end of the 1970 season the big three American automakers announced that they were withdrawing from all forms of auto racing. Virtually overnight the quantity and quality of cars dropped noticeably. There were fewer races and these decreased the financial viability of existing tracks.

Federally mandated emissions standards were beginning to take hold. To comply companies added cleaners and catalytic converters thereby reducing mileage and horsepower. As the average mileage had to also improve the only option was to produce smaller, lighter cars.

In October 1973 the mideast war led to the oil embargo and fuel cost increases. GTOs and Road Runners were no longer practical. Companies discontinued large V-8 powered cars so there was no need to race in order to sell these cars. The era of the muscle car was over.

To the public racing was a conspicuous consumption of oil, and there were serious proposals to ban racing. In response major races were reduced in length, despite the fact that the entire Daytona 500 used less fuel than powering the lights for the Orange Bowl for one football game. This consumption was seen compared to the unseen consumption (a powerplant outside of view) of the game.

The first casualties were two historic Pennsylvania oval tracks. In 1971 the circular track at Langhorne was closed, ending racing that began in 1925. Then in 1979 the last race was held at Trenton; the first race was in 1914. The land was worth more for a shopping center than for a race track. To keep a full schedule CART put races onto road courses from Riverside to Mid-Ohio. The versatility of the drivers was shown off and open wheel racing survived.

Watkins Glen was no better off than the oval tracks. It had not been kept up to international standards and in 1980 hosted its last United States Grand Prix. CART ran there in 1981 just before track operators went bankrupt.

The remainder of the road courses fared better. Because of having lower expectations than for an oval race and hosting many amateur events with volunteer workers they did not require the financial input needed elsewhere. And road courses were generally out in the country, not having land coveted by developers.

There is a happy ending to Watkins Glen. In 1983 a group headed by nearby Corning Glass and the France family bought the track, reopening it in 1984. The crowds are greater than ever but for NASCAR and sports cars, not the expensive European competitors.

The queen of western racing, Ontario Motor Speedway, also had serious financial problems. Everyone, from the county to traffic control police, expected great financial rewards from the track and they wanted their share. Several ownership groups, including one by Parnelli Jones, tried to keep costs in line but mismanagement and heavy financial burdens were too much so they gave up in 1980 and the track was bulldozed under.

Up north the last USAC Champ car race was held at Hanford in 1969.

Southern California had a third setback in 1988 when Riverside was closed. The track was still doing fine but population sprawl closed in and the land became more valuable for building houses.

The sole bright spot in racing was nearby in the sleepy Los Angeles suburb of Long Beach. City fathers were interested in using a car race to enliven the city and its image. Chris Pook, supported by Dan Gurney and Phil Hill, organized a race using city streets with temporary barricades and seating. They would put on a race without a race track. The first race was a F-5000 event in 1975. The following year the Grand Prix was held there.

By the late 1980s no fewer than eight cities held street races. While not artistic successes they were good races with a minimum of expenses.

With the loss of four major oval tracks and no new tracks to compensate it is fair to say that road racing saved American open wheel racing.

Top: In 1977 Ontario (California) seemed to have it all including a NASCAR, drag, and Indy car race. By 1981 the track was a pile of broken concrete and broken dreams. Courtesy of Cliff Morgan. *Bottom:* Riverside (California) was one of the first true permanent road courses in America. The course run by IMSA GTPs here cut across the arid countryside east of Los Angeles. Due to pressures from housing development the track did not last out the 1980s. Courtesy of Cliff Morgan.

76   EIGHT IN A ROW, NISSAN GTPs

By the spring of 1988 the IMSA GTP series was ready for a change of champions. The all-conquering Porsche 962, winner of the last three manufacturer's championships, was beginning its seventh season of racing, a Methuselah of race designs. BMW, Ford, Chevrolet and Nissan had challenged the German model but to little effect. Jaguar, through Bob Tullius' American Group 44 team, had made the contest interesting but never successful. Now the English company was preparing to send TWR, the World championship team of Tom Walkinshaw, to win the title. Nothing stood in their way, or so it seemed.

The season began as planned. In the fall of 1987 TWR had opened an American headquarters and began testing three of the all-conquering XJR-9s. The work showed immediate results as two TWR Jaguars finished first and third at the 24-hour race at Daytona. Porsche came back to edge out Jaguar at Miami and another Porsche won at Sebring, but when the sprint season began at Road Atlanta the Porsches could not match the new Jaguars for speed. The championship was all but in Walkinshaw's pocket.

Two TWR Jaguars finished 1-3 in their first IMSA race, the 24-hour race at Daytona. It looked like the start of a memorable year. Jaguar did not win again until the last race of the season, after Nissan had won nine races. Courtesy of Dudley Evans.

A funny thing happened over the red clay of northwestern Georgia. Jaguar was beaten, and badly, by the upstart Nissan team. Nissan lead driver Geoff Brabham had elected to start his backup car and was relegated to start from the rear. Jaguar started from the front. Yet within laps Brabham caught and passed John Nielsen in the lead XJR-9. A mishandled Nissan pit stop put the Jaguar back in the lead only to have the flying Nissan retake the lead and go on to victory. To Jaguar this certainly had to be an aberration. It was instead a preview of races to come.

The Nissan GTP was the effort of Don Devendorf, a brilliant engineer with Hughes Electronics who raced as a sideline. Through the 1970s he had raced stock small sedans. For the turbocharged 280ZX he developed an electronic engine management system that was far better than any available from the factory team of any make. Starting with the 280ZX motor and limited support from Nissan, Devendorf's Electromotive group entered the GTP series in 1985 with a car built and developed in southern Cal-

ifornia, but to no great success. Through 1985 and 1986 the car became faster, but one failure after another caused it to drop out.

Devendorf was good but not a great driver, but he was a methodical engineer. At the start of the GTP program he made a checklist of what would be required to make a winning car. He began checking off items.

In 1986, realizing that he could not be both team and development manager, Devendorf was able to get Nissan to hire Kas Kastner to run the race operation. Kastner, nicknamed "the Prussian" for his autocratic style, took over and effectively isolated the race team from outside influences like the marketing department.

Lola built the original chassis, model 810, based on the 1981 T600. Trevor Harris designed a new chassis that, while visually almost identical, was much stiffer and easier to work on.

Geoff Brabham, son of three-time World Driving champion Jack Brabham, agreed, reluctantly at first, to drive the Nissan GTP 300 ZX-T. While Geoff and co-driver Elliott Forbes-Robinson won the 1987 Miami race the rest of the season was marked with DNFs.

At the beginning of the 1988 season Geoff Brabham committed to drive full time for Nissan. At the end of the season he had the first of four GTP drivers' titles. Courtesy of Kas Kastner.

Nissan's success at Road Atlanta caught everyone by surprise, including Nissan. The 1988 racing budget had not included a full season, yet they were suddenly confronted with supporting the best sports car on the planet. Between Road Atlanta and Lime Rock, a race that was not in the budget, marketing scurried to find additional funds.

Jaguar's nightmare got worse at West Palm Beach. Brabham took the pole and, with John Morton, the race. All the two Jaguars could do was fight for second.

Lime Rock Park was the race nearest Jaguar U.S. headquarters in New Jersey so

Through 1987 the Bridgestone tires had been a major problem, causing several accidents when a tire blew, destroying a chassis and reducing driver confidence. At the end of the 1987 season Kastner asked Bridgestone to pay for lost chassis due to tire failures. Bridgestone refused and the team switched to Goodyear tires. At the first test the car was noticeably faster. This was critical because IMSA had reduced the size of turbocharged motors like the Nissan. This should have been another advantage to non-turbocharged Jaguars, yet the new Nissan was even faster than the previous year's version.

Every change was a check on Devendorf's list. "We analyzed every failure and every one of them offered a properly engineered solution to the problem," says Devendorf. As the 1988 season began all the items on Devendorf's list had been checked off. "We had received copies of their (TWR Jaguar) PR announcing that in '88 they were coming over as world champion and wipe the slate clean."

Top: In 1987 the Lola based Nissan was the fastest GTP car in IMSA. But it was also the most fragile, winning only one race. Courtesy of Ed Clayton. *Bottom:* The Nissan was an assembly of a turbo V-6, electronics, aerodynamic body panels and Goodyear tires, the fastest road racing machine on the planet. Courtesy of Kas Kastner.

all the Jaguar supporters saw the Nissan's superiority first hand. Brabham won, Jaguars finished second and third.

At the next five races the top step of the winner's podium was occupied by Geoff Brabham. At Portland a second 300 ZX-T was entered for John Morton. Nissans finished first and second. From April through September the series belonged to Brabham and the Electromotive Nissan.

Nissan's winning streak ended at eight races in the streets of San Antonio, Texas. Brabham dropped out and James Weaver won in a Porsche. Brabham came back with another win at Columbus. He also won the non-points race at Tampa, Florida.

Jan Lammers and Martin Brundle won the season's finale at Del Mar (San Diego), the first Jaguar win since Daytona. By then the titles were already decided. Brabham easily won the driver's championship. Nissan, though skipping two of the first three races, lost the manufacturer's championship to Porsche by a single point. Jaguar was third. "They underrated our performance," says Devendorf. "They always thought that the European cars were better."

For the next three seasons Jaguar won Le Mans twice and the world title three times, but they never won an IMSA GTP title. Brabham and Nissan were the champions.

---

77 THE NEW FUEL OF RACING
Sponsorship

America's most unique contribution to racing has been not in the cars, but what was on the outside of the cars, the sponsor's name. While the European teams were financed by automotive companies American racing was about independent manufacturers who sold cars to a team that had to find ways to finance their sport. The best way was to tap into American capitalism and use the car as an advertising medium. Let sponsors pay for the racing.

Sponsorship in America is as old as racing itself, part of Indy car racing since the 1920s. NASCAR did not actively seek sponsors until the 1970s but has done so with a vengeance since then to fuel its phenomenal growth.

There have been sponsors in NAS-CAR since the 1950s but they have been limited in scope to auto related activities

such as a car dealership or a service station. Sponsors, more like patrons, had their name put on the car to show participation, and less to use the car as a sales tool.

By the 1960s auto related companies, such as oil and oil products, became involved. However the graphics of the car did not reflect the sponsor's involvement; visual themes remained just a name on the tail.

The first sponsor to influence the look of the car was STP. Andy Granatelli's fuel additive company became involved in 1971 with a large decal on the Plymouth of Pete Hamilton. They increased their visibility in 1972 with the STP red #11 Dodge of Buddy Baker. When Petty Engineering reduced their effort to a single car STP moved to Richard's #43. The deal was almost lost when STP wanted an all red car while the Pettys wanted to remain all Petty

Trailers with every conceivable racing souvenir create a carnival atmosphere at races, especially with NASCAR. Cash from the trailers is often a greater source of income than race winnings or direct contributions from the sponsor. From the collection of J.A. Martin.

blue. A compromise led to the familiar red and blue.

Coca-Cola adorned Bobby Allison's various cars from 1970 with the logo wave and Coke colors. When Cale Yarborough returned to NASCAR with Junior Johnson the car was sponsored by Holly Farms. Gatorade followed with the DiGard team. These sponsors were aimed at the fans in the stands and were items they could purchase at the track.

City Bank Financial service took the next step in sponsorship. They used racing as a way to advertise sponsoring the USAC Indy car series, the Penske Formula 1 car and Junior Johnson's #11. Consumer awareness had to extend beyond the track.

By the mid–1970s other Formula 1 teams were adorned, not in national colors, but in the colors of corporate sponsors. Lotus, which had brought Formula 1 style chassis design to America, took American style sponsorship back to Europe. In 1968 the English racing green of Team Lotus became the red and white of Gold Leaf Team Lotus. Only Ferrari retains its national color, and then only because sponsor Marlboro is red.

Most sponsorship was still directed to the male fan. The big surge in NASCAR sponsorship came in 1988 when Tide laundry detergent picked up the #17 car of Darrel Waltrip. Tide had no direct tie to racing and was used more by women than men. Other non-male oriented products soon followed. Marketing was including women as Purex sponsored Patty Moise and Secret deodorant sponsored the Trans-Am car of Lyn St. James.

When Snickers candy bars and M&M picked up the sponsorship of a car it was an acknowledgement that racing is a tool for reaching kids. Food is still a major sponsorship group, but with McDonalds and Burger King the orientation is for the family, especially young members. Kelloggs and General Mills also use race cars, putting the sponsor's name on the car and the car on the cereal box.

Since the 1980s sponsor names have been added to event titles, quickly becoming the event name. The next step came when sponsors took over track names: Charlotte became the Lowe's Motor Speedway, Mazda was added to Laguna Seca and Sears Point became Infineon Raceway. Every time the race location was used it was another sponsor ad.

The three stages in NASCAR sponsorship: #33 tobacco and oil products, #31 general men's products, #10 family products. Courtesy of Ed Clayton.

Car sponsorship means more than putting a sponsor's name on the hood and rear quarter panel. The car's graphics give a personality to the individual cars as NASCAR racers have become more generic in shape. This personality is translated to commercial tie-ins like collectable cars for kids ($1.99) to adults ($75 and up).

New sponsors reflect changes in the types of business that increasingly look at racing as a way to connect with a very loyal fan/customer base.

This diversity in sponsorship reflects the diversity of race fans. Gone is the image of beer drinking young men that the public associated with racing, especially NASCAR. Today NASCAR is a successful spectator sport with kids and women coming with the men as a family. Race attendance records at Daytona of 90,000 are easily eclipsed at every event, even half-mile tracks like Bristol with

In the earl 1980s the Red Lobster restaurant chain pioneered family products through racecar (an IMSA GTP March) sponsorship. Through clever graphics, hospitality tents, and store promotions they created programs that became the norm in all forms of racing a decade later. From the collection of J.A. Martin.

Toys became a very big income source for NASCAR. Hot Wheels, sponsor of Kyle Petty, was a natural. Courtesy of Ed Clayton.

stands holding 130,000 fans.

Big sponsor bucks (in the tens of millions of dollars) have allowed teams to invest in fully equipped mobile trailers and in-house development programs. These have led to innovations of speed and safety that were unimaginable even in the 1980s.

International TV coverage led to foreign products (Tecate beer of Mexico) as sponsors at American races. Courtesy of Dudley Evans.

78 IT'S MORE THAN JUST AN OLD CAR THING
Vintage Racing

Vintage race cars are often placed on pedestals in museums like artifacts. Only by putting a race car on the track can you hear the motor and feel the excitement to understand why that car exists. Vintage racing puts these machines where they belong.

"What's old is what's new" is never so true as in vintage racing. Beginning in the 1980s and accelerating in the 1990s, racing vintage cars has become one of the fastest growing segments of American motorsports.

To the English, vintage racing is nothing new. Since the 1920s old race cars have been kept in race condition in Britain. This tradition has continued through meets like the Goodwood Festival of Speed.

But in the U.S. people have just recently discovered the fun of old cars. Postwar England produced a cornucopia of relatively low cost sports cars that they exported to America such as the MG, Triumph and Jaguar, plus low cost race cars from cottage shops like Lola and Lotus. These were easy to buy and easy to maintain. The addition of the American Corvette in the 1950s and the Cobra in the 1960s included a national flavor.

In the 1960s sports car racing gained an aura with American cars like the Ford GT and Chaparral challenging the best of Europe driven by American stars like Dan Gurney, Phil Hill, Peter Revson, Mario Andretti and Carroll Shelby. Entranced by the cars and heroes behind the wheel were young boys who dreamed of being out there but had other directions for their lives.

By the 1970s there were thousands of older sports cars dropping in price as their place on the grid dropped. But the cars were still in good condition and support equipment was available.

The young boys were growing up and beginning to have the means to buy the car of their dreams whether it was a "Bug Eye" Sprite or an original Ferrari Testa Rossa.

Most vintage racing groups began as local clubs and expanded, though most stayed within a region, thereby foregoing the cost of cross country freight. VARA, Vintage Auto Racing Association, began in Southern California while SOVREN, Society of Vintage Racing Enthusiasts, was established in the northwest. Sportscar Vintage Racing Association, SVRA, originated in Sebring, Florida.

In 1977 several members of the Atlanta Jaguar Club created the Walter Mitty Challenge at Road Atlanta. From the Mitty came the east coast Historic Sportscar Racing (HSR).

A second type of vintage group began in the 1980s, those based on a specific type of car. Groups now center on Can-Am or Trans-Am cars and more recently Winston Cup or Champ Cars.

Not all vintage clubs race. Some are a center for enthusiasts for a specific marque where members can find parts or to show off to other admirers.

Sports cars are meant to be moving works of art, mobile examples of form and function. And like other works of art they need to be put in their proper environment, in this case a racetrack, not a museum. And only on a track can the full range of senses be excited from a race car.

Vintage racing has moved beyond sports cars. At one end are collections of Formula 1 cars; at the other are vintage NASCAR racers, though few here go back further than the 1970s. As the century ended there were nearly one hundred such groups with seventy or so national groups for special marques and interests.

The premier vintage meet is the Monterey Historic races held each August at the Laguna Seca track and nearby Pebble Beach resort. Organized by Steve Earle in 1974 the event features one marque each year, but the finest race cars from around the world compete against cars of similar performance and vintage. Often adding to the vintage feel are retired drivers like Phil Hill or David Hobbs.

Lime Rock Park has held the Vintage Festival on Labor Day. Tracks as big as Daytona and Sebring to special road sections through city parks like in Pittsburgh have hosted vintage races. In the tradition of General LeMay, military air bases have also hosted vintage events.

For real authenticity, efforts have been made to reopen abandoned race tracks. Virginia International was closed in the 1970s only to be refurbished and reopened in the late 1990s for vintage racing.

At Summit Point (West Virginia) a Corvette Grand Sport (1963) chases a Lola T70 Mk III (1969). From the collection of J.A. Martin.

Aerial photos located the Latrobe Valley 1930s quarter mile dirt track near Gettysburg, Pennsylvania. It was rebuilt to 1930s standards and is host to sprint cars and jalopies from prewar to the 1950s.

Special magazines, *Victory Lane* and *Vintage Oval Track*, have the highest readership percentage to the audience for any national magazine in America.

The term vintage has even changed. In the 1970s a vintage car was one from late prewar or early postwar. By the end of the 1990s a vintage racecar is one that is no longer competitive and retired.

Vintage racing is the closest thing yet to time travel.

Right: Poster for Baltimore Concours d' Elegance. From the collection of J.A. Martin.

79 THE OPEN WHEEL SCHISM
CART, the IRL and All Those Egos

By the mid 1970s Champ car racing was a very different sport than it had been in 1960. The advent of the rear engine cars had opened the way for more foreign drivers. At first the successful cars were foreign built until American designers came to the forefront. Soon the days of the car built in a shed by a single mechanic had passed. Companies were building cars. Designers like Bob Riley, Gordon Coppuck, Maurice Phillippe and Roman Slobodynskj were becoming as necessary to a winning effort as a crew chief.

The new rear engine cars were different from the old roadsters and the techniques learned from sprint cars were fast losing relevance.

The nature of the series was also changing. Beginning in 1965 Champ car races were being run on road courses in addition to oval tracks. The last dirt race was held in 1970. By the late 1970s the ovals of Langhorne, Hanford and Trenton were closed with Ontario soon to follow.

New sponsors were entering and the growth of TV coverage made racing more accessible to fans, fans to support the sponsors. More money with everyone wanting greater control and "their share."

In 1977 Tony Hulman, the man who had founded USAC and led the IMS for thirty years, died. His leadership would soon be sorely missed.

Several championship teams were

With the demise of many ovals Indy car racing found salvation on the road courses. In 1979 the CART series came to Watkins Glen. From the collection of J.A. Martin.

becoming frustrated that the USAC governing board of 21 was not addressing the needs of the champ car teams. Early in 1978 Dan Gurney composed a "white paper" analyzing the situation. He called for the teams to work together and with USAC for the growth of the sport, first using the name CART. The paper called for growth by sponsorship and media exposure rather than cost containment.

The 1978 spring race at Trenton had just concluded when a private plane took off heading back to Indianapolis carrying the USAC officials that ran the Champ car races. They never made it as the plane crashed and all were killed.

The leadership void for the series was filled by USAC with officials from the Midget and Sprint car series. While well intentioned they were not familiar with the costs of operating a Champ car team or the amount of sponsorship money needed to support the teams. They tried to run the series like a big sprint car race, putting the

emphasis on cost restraints. A disagreement soon developed between USAC officials and the Champ car teams. The owners knew that a Champ car was expensive to run so the effort was in getting more team income. With no resolution in sight the owners formed Championship Auto Racing Teams (CART). Headed by Pat Patrick, Dan Gurney, Roger Penske and Carl Haas, CART would conduct the races for 1979.

The first battle was over the Indy 500. The Hulman family stayed with USAC but knew that they needed the CART teams. A compromise was reached and a full field entered the race.

USAC countered with a separate Champ car series. Only A.J. Foyt of the major teams stayed with USAC. He won the championship in 1979 over virtually no opposition.

The two groups seemed to find an agreement for the 1980 season with the formation of the Championship Racing

Not everyone was happy with road races and other CART changes. Tony George created the IRL with normally aspirated engines, mostly Oldsmobile, as here with Scott Goodyear at Indianapolis, 1997. Courtesy of Dudley Evans.

League. All was fine at Indianapolis, but after the race the CRL fell apart and CART was back in charge for the remainder of the season.

The technical sticking point in the 1980s was the amount of boost allowed in turbocharged motors. USAC and the Indianapolis Motor Speedway allowed higher boost (more horsepower) for stock-based motors. This helped the Buick V-6 that was not competitive in CART races.

USAC made several attempts to conduct a series mixing points from Indianapolis with the USAC Silver Crown series, known as the Gold Crown series. The season ended with the Indy 500 then began the next season at the following race. The series never caught on and USAC finally gave in. USAC would conduct the Indianapolis 500 with CART cars and drivers. A representative of IMS sat on the CART board as one of many voices.

Through the 1980s CART grew with new race venues at road courses and took over the Formula 1 dates at Long Beach and Detroit. Without the road circuits CART would have been reduced to a series of four oval tracks. The road courses saved Indy car racing. By the early 1990s the CART series raced on road courses, small and large

ovals, and temporary street circuits. They also raced outside the U.S.

New sponsors were coming on and Ford, Honda, Mercedes-Benz and Toyota were building engines especially for the series. CART seemed in fine shape.

In the early 1990s Tony George, grandson of Tony Hulman, became president of the Speedway. With George the IMS again spoke with a single voice, replacing the various representatives of the past. George wanted a bigger say in how the series was run and how profits of merchandise were distributed. His contention was that the teams were worth more because they were racing at his speedway. CART members felt that the Memorial Day race was the best part of the series, but without the series Indy had reduced meaning.

George reduced the dependence of the speedway on the Indy 500. In 1992 he had a six car NASCAR test session. Winston Cup came in 1994 for the Brickyard 400. George had a second golden goose.

Several attempts had been made by George to create an international oval racing series with additional races in Europe and Japan, but nothing came of it. Still it showed that George was trying to get along without CART. In 1994 he announced that, beginning in 1996, the Indianapolis 500 was to be sanctioned by the Indy Racing League (IRL). Initially the cars would be identical to CART but beginning in 1997 power would come from non-turbocharged four liter OHC motors based on production motors. Oldsmobile had such an engine which had been developed for IMSA, taking the Daytona 24-hour and Sebring 12-hour races in 1996. Nissan also developed a motor.

George fired the first shot by restricting all but eight places in the 1996 race to

IRL regulars. Rather than fight for these spots CART teams held a separate Memorial Day 500-mile race at Michigan. The public did not buy it, nor did they buy the IRL race as the "Greatest Spectacle in Racing." The split had been made.

The basic differences in CART and the IRL can be seen in the names. CART is based upon the competing teams. The IRL is a support series for the Indianapolis 500.

IRL was an all-oval race series. This was now practical

The last winner at Indianapolis (1995) before the split was Jacques Villeneuve in a turbo Ford powered Reynard. Courtesy of Dudley Evans.

because of the infusion of new tracks ready to host a NASCAR event. IRL, except for the new track at Disney World, would go to new NASCAR ovals. Only Phoenix and New Hampshire of the oval tracks left CART for the IRL.

The stated purpose of the IRL was to return American oval racing to a golden past that probably never really existed. Indianapolis was the pinnacle for an American driver who started from the local sprint tracks building and racing his own car, the way Vukovich had done in the 1950s. Teams would buy the motor then prepare it themselves. This was in contrast with the CART practice of teams leasing race-prepared motors from the manufacturers. The little guy was to have a chance against the high buck teams that dominated CART.

It was soon apparent that sprints were no longer the best training ground for Indianapolis. Except for Tony Stewart and Sam Hornish the sprint trained drivers were not ready for the high speed ground effects machines. The top IRL drivers came from the CART support series, were midfield CART drivers, or were former Formula 1 drivers from Europe. In 1998 the IRL champion was Kenny Brack of Sweden. The most nationalistic of car owners,

Foyt, chose a foreign driver who had never driven a sprint car in competition.

The IRL was a benefit to NASCAR. To stay solvent a track needed multiple big races and the IRL provided a second race series.

Although both series expanded to new tracks, interest dropped off at existing tracks. For 1998 Indianapolis changed qualifying to a single weekend and were still not able to pull 40,000 spectators for pole day, that in the past drew in excess of 200,000 spectators. Attendance for the Indianapolis 500 remained strong though TV ratings were in decline, but the rest of the IRL played to under capacity houses. Tracks that hosted 150,000 fans for the Winston Cup race looked virtually empty with 10,000 IRL spectators. The Indianapolis Motor Speedway and NASCAR were subsidizing the IRL.

CART attendance was more balanced but still did not show the spectacular gains made by NASCAR during the same period. CART moved to race in South America, Australia, Japan and Europe. This made the series viable for advertising by companies in those countries. The sponsors reflected the international character with beers from Brazil (Brahma) and cigarettes from Canada (Players) and Colombia (Hollywood).

Publicly both groups declared that the public would support two series as they were so different, but they weren't that different to the public. Fans and sponsors alike wanted one series.

Both sides agreed to discuss but the problem for possible reunification continued to be the motor. CART engine companies said they could build a normally aspirated motor but to insure protection for innovations they put into the motor they would have to keep control by leasing complete motors. IRL insisted on individual teams having responsibility for their motors as George Biognotti had. However, the top IRL teams were already buying prepared motors from a few engine specialty shops.

The CART/IRL disparity in skill levels became apparent in 2000 when Target Team Ganassi returned to Indianapolis. Rookie Juan Montoya was the easy winner. The following year CART teams entered seven cars. At the end of the delayed race the CART teams made up the top six positions, lead by another rookie.

Neither series was able to have a stable schedule as they moved in opposite directions. Pulling in crowds of 150,000 at the Monterrey, Mexico, road course, CART left the oval tracks of Homestead, Gateway and Michigan while IRL began racing at all three plus the new ovals at Kentucky, Chicago and Kansas City while leaving Atlanta, Charlotte, Disney World, Dover, Las Vegas and New Hampshire for poor attendance.

New CART inner-city street races were crowd favorites though failing to attract large TV audiences. ABC, long the Indy 500 broadcaster, and ABC-owned ESPN signed to exclusively broadcast the IRL.

In 2001 CART announced that for 2003 teams would use the same 3.5 liter non-turbo motor as the IRL. Toyota then Honda, at first declaring they did not have time to make a new motor, announced they would go with the 3.5 and the IRL in 2003, with Toyota leasing motors.

Rebuffed by the IRL for a common motor CART, with support from Ford, continued with the turbo motor, seemingly abandoning any efforts for commonality with the IRL.

For 2003 Michael Andretti/Team Green, Team Ganassi and several drivers with Japanese motor contracts followed Penske to the IRL as sponsors and engine suppliers needed to be visible at Indianapolis.

After multiple CEOs and rules bickering by team owners/board members CART selected Long Beach promoter Chris Pook to lead, providing the body's first single voice, leadership it had long needed. Pook moved to strengthen CART by maintaining an emphasis on hi-tech cars. From his success at Long Beach, Pook sought more street races, thereby opening the road course races to the IRL and USAC. Pook also had to build a better financial base for the publicly owned company.

Both series expanded development series; CART with "Stars of Tomorrow" go-karts through Formula Dodge to Toyota Atlantic, and IRL with the Pro Infiniti series.

Both series continued with no attempt to end the split, the egos still battling for supremacy in the world of American professional open wheel racing while NASCAR blew right past them.

After the conclusion of the 2003 series CART filed for bankruptcy. The assets were bought by Open Wheel Racing Series LLC, a group of team owners who plan to continue the road/oval/street circuit series.

80 GORDON DOESN'T TAKE LANIER

Jeff Gordon has done about everything there is to do and taken about every award possible in NAS-CAR. While still in his twenties, in a sport dominated by mature seasoned veterans, he won three driver's titles, his first in only his third Winston Cup season, two Daytona 500s (youngest ever winner) and three Brickyard 400s.

To make it seem more unfair, he has been confused at celebrity events for actor Tom Cruise. He has done so much there are even anti–Jeff Gordon clubs, a sure sign of success in NASCAR.

Jeff Gordon and the Baby Ruth Ford at Lanier, 1992. From the collection of J.A. Martin.

Although born in Vallejo, California, he was raised in Pittsboro, Indiana. His heroes were the stars of the Indy 500. By eight years old he was winning quarter midget races. He won three midget championships and four national go-kart championships. On his sixteenth birthday he received his USAC competition license and by age twenty he was named by the American Auto Racing Writers and Broadcasters Association to the All-American Team. Before he could vote he had over 600 victories.

Though courted for Indy cars and even considered for a Formula 1 training program, by three-time world champion Jackie Stewart, Gordon abruptly left the open wheel racers for NASCAR. Bill Davis signed "the Kid" to drive his Thunderbird in the Busch Grand National Series where he took the Rookie of the Year title in 1992.

In late April 1992 the series pulled into the three-eighths mile oval at Lanier National Speedway, north of Atlanta, Geor-gia. Gordon was in the same white Baby Ruth T-Bird he had driven to three pole positions and one win in the first nine Busch races. A record run of 14.709 seconds gave him another pole over a field that included Jeff and Ward Burton.

When the green flag dropped Gordon took off, easily leading every lap. Then on lap 117, soon after a yellow flag series of pit stops, Gordon had to pit again to replace a deflated tire. With fifteen second laps, even a quick stop results in a loss of several laps and Gordon returned five laps behind, the race two-thirds complete.

Kenny Wallace held the lead for the next hundred laps followed by Bobby Labonte. But all eyes were on Gordon, who was cutting through the field. Twice he came upon the leaders and passed them at will. But the laps were running down and Bobby Labonte, after gaining the lead with 23 laps to go, took the win. Gordon was still two laps down, having just passed Ricky Craven in the #99 DuPont Chevrolet for tenth place.

Young Jeff Gordon took his first tentative steps in NASCAR as here at New Hampshire in the 1991 Busch race. From the collection of J.A. Martin.

His career after Lanier is well documented. At the end of the 1992 season he and his crew chief Ray Evernham signed with the Rick Hendrick Chevrolet team, a move that did not sit well with Ford which

The view seen most often by competitors of Gordon and the Hendrick-prepared Dupont #24. They were the dominant team of the mid through late 1990s. Courtesy of Ed Clayton.

was grooming him for Winston Cup. Ford executives wanted Gordon to have one more season in the Busch series, but Gordon felt he was ready for the big league and Hendrick offered the opportunity. He was still less than 21 years old.

In 1993 he took Rookie of the Year, winning the first race of the year, a qualifier at Daytona, the youngest driver to win at Daytona. In 1994 he won two of the toughest on the circuit at the 600 mile Charlotte race and the inaugural Brickyard 400 at Indianapolis, plus the non-points Winston and Busch Clash.

Led by Evernham, the crew developed into the standard for NASCAR. With the colorful DuPont color scheme the crew took on the identity of "the Rainbow Warriors." The crew's esprit de corps gave Gordon the support to put him in position to win, to give beyond "a little extra" that was expected in NASCAR. In 1995, while still the youngest driver at almost every race he entered, Gordon won the Winston Cup driver's title and was, as usual, the youngest driver to do so. The year 1996 was an off year as Gordon finished second to Hendrick teammate Terry Labonte but still took ten wins. Better years were 1997 and 1998 with Gordon winning the driver's title twice again plus the Daytona 500. Gordon was also only the second driver, after Bill Elliott in 1985, to win the Winston Million. When he won the fall Atlanta race he tied Richard Petty for most wins in a modern (post 1972) season with thirteen. The 1999 season began with another Daytona 500 win. Though 1999 and 2000 were off years by his standards, he still won races, taking the title again in 2001.

81   THE VIPER STRIKES FOR DODGE

In the early 1990s the Chrysler Corporation, especially the Dodge division, was in need of an image boost. The company had been saved in the 1980s by the utilitarian K car and the innovation of the mini-van, but more was needed to grow in the 1990s.

The design and concept folks presented a thoroughly outrageous idea, a two-seat sports car. The Viper was a throwback to the muscle cars of the sixties. There was little apparent finesse. The car was built

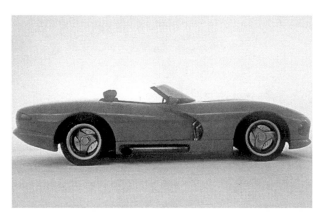

In 1990 Chrysler Corporation introduced the Viper as an idea car. It was with the introduction of the coupe that the Viper found its racing destiny.

around a front mounted eight-liter aluminum V-10 motor that produced enormous power. It looked like half the car was under the hood, and surely 90 percent of the soul was. The interior was less than comfortable with little attention to airflow. This car was all testosterone, an engine with a driver hanging off the back, and the public loved it. The reaction was so great that it was soon ordered into production.

A coupe was shown in 1995, and public reaction was again so positive that production soon followed. Adding a roof added 15 mph to the top speed.

Despite road tests that showed the Viper to be the king of acceleration, no factory attempt was made to race the car.

Enter the French ORECA (*Organisation et Exploitation des Courses Automobiles*) team in 1996. They prepared a pair of Viper GTS-R coupes for international racing. (In Europe the Viper was sold under the Chrysler brand). In the first season (1997) the team easily won the GT-2 man-

ufacturer's and driver's title (Justin Bell) over established turbo Porsche teams. The big win was Le Mans where Vipers finished first and second in class for the first win of any kind by an American car since the glory days of the Ford GT in the 1960s.

A second team, Chamberlain Engineering, entered Vipers midway through the season.

Vipers won again in 1998 with Olivier Beretta taking the driver's title. The team included American drivers David Donohue, son of Mark Donohue, and Tommy Archer, who had been racing Chrysler cars since the company acquired his services in the Renault Jeep purchase. Even with an FIA mandated weight penalty, Vipers won nine of the ten GT-2 races, including the class title at Le Mans.

Vipers GTS-Rs won again at Le Mans in 1999 and took a third straight GT-2 title, over the wails of many Porsche teams. Olivier Beretta and Karl Wendlinger co-won the FIA-GT driver's title.

A pair of Vipers lead a lone Corvette at the 2000 Petit Le Mans. Courtesy of Ed Clayton.

With the American Le Mans Series using the rules from the French race it was only natural that the winning Vipers would come home to win more races. Despite not competing in the first race, Dodge Vipers won the remaining six races to take the 1999 American Le Mans Series GTS manufacturer's title with the driver's title going to Beretta. In addition Bobby Archer won the driver's championship with a stock Viper in the Speedvision Cup for production sports cars over Corvettes, Acura NSXs and all those turbo Porsches.

The ultimate prize came in the first race of the 2000 season. Three Oreca Vipers, plus a pair from Chamberlain Motorsports, were entered in the Daytona 24-hour race. By Sunday morning the No. 91 Viper of Olivier Beretta, Karl Wendlinger and Dominique Dupuy passed the ailing Dyson Sports Racer to take the lead. At the finish Vipers were first, third, fifth, sixth and seventh. The winning trio accented the win with another class victory at Le Mans three months later for another Viper year.

82 WHO'S THIS GUY PANOZ?

Don Panoz came into motor sports fairly late in life, but when he arrived he made a major stir that many think will be felt well into the 21st century. In three years he has bought three race tracks, developed a new race car and created a new

road racing series, all of which challenged the existing order of sports car racing.

He is a man who earned his wealth not from the auto industry but in pharmaceuticals, founding Mylan Laboratories in 1960 in Morgantown, West Virginia,

Don Panoz went against conventional wisdom to create a Reynard built racer with a front mounted stock car motor, and was successful. Courtesy of Ed Clayton.

(a DNF good for 9th in GTS-1), but dissatisfaction with race management led "The Don" to his next challenges. He bought the tracks of Road Atlanta, Sebring, and Mosport and immediately began making improvements in safety and fan comfort. And he organized a new series, the American Le Mans Series (ALMS).

The GTR-1 was a serious challenge to contemporary race car design. As the street car was front engine the race car had to be front engine. No prototype racer since the 1983 Mustang GTP had the driver behind the motor. But by placing the driver low in the chassis the car presented no more frontal area than a rear engine racer. Similar to the Mustang GTP, this allowed the entire rear of the car to work as ground effect tunnels.

The year 1998 was a great year for the Panoz team with seven wins, including the class win at Sebring, in the Professional SportsCar Championship. Internationally the team took seventh at Le Mans and two third place finishes, all against factory supported GTs and open prototype cars.

and Elan Pharmaceutical in Ireland in 1969. Looking for a U.S. location for Elan in 1980, he resettled his family in Georgia, at the same time going into winemaking with his own vineyards in Gainesville. In 1985 he opened Chateau Elan, a golf resort and winery near Road Atlanta in Braselton. In 1990 he helped his son Danny establish a company to build limited edition sports cars, and when he retired from Elan in 1996 he threw his energy into establishing a racing heritage for Panoz Auto Development. He had Reynard Cars design and build a body to fit the front engine chassis. Roush Racing supplied the normally aspirated 620 horsepower Ford V-8 motors. The car was called the GTR-1 and it was to race in the GT class against the exotic production-inspired cars like the turbocharged Porsche GT1 that won the 1998 Le Mans race. That's a major challenge for anyone.

Their first race was the 1997 Sebring 12 Hours

For 1999 the Panoz LMP-1 retained the motor and location of the GT counterpart. Running against the prototypes of Ferrari, BMW and a bunch of private teams, Panoz picked up the American Le Mans Series manufacturers title. Courtesy of Ed Clayton.

Don Panoz, seated at center, gave a press conference to the French Le Mans partners prior to the start of the 2001 Sebring 12-hour race. From the collection of J.A. Martin.

To win the big races Panoz had to move up to challenge the prototype racers. The weapon debuted in 1999 at Road Atlanta. Like the GTR, the LMP-1 had the Ford V-8 in front of the driver. The driver, in the open cockpit, sat just in front of the rear wheels. The first race resulted in a fifth place finish as it was as much a test session as a race. Le Mans was the goal.

Two LMP-1s were taken to France for the 24-hour race. By the checkered flag on Sunday afternoon LMP-1 #12 was in seventh place with #11 in eleventh place. Three weeks later Johnny O'Connell and Jan Magnussen led an LMP-1 sweep of the Mosport endurance race over the Riley-Scott and Ferrari World Sports Cars.

The 2000 season was not the follow-up that was planned. Only at the Nurburgring did the LMP-1 find victory, and despite the addition of Mario Andretti to the lineup finished only fifth best at Le Mans.

In 2000 Panoz/Ralph Sanchez acquired the rights to the Trans-Am series, often run as a support race for the ALMS feature. The race package made both series more viable for TV.

Don Panoz has changed the nature of American sports car racing as no one has since John Bishop.

83 THE LUCK OF BEING EARNHARDT

Dale Earnhardt was the dominant NASCAR driver from the early 1980s to the mid–1990s. In that stretch he earned seven Winston Cup driver's titles and the nick-name "The Intimidator." He was named Rookie of the Year after winning two races in 1979. The son of Sportsman champion Ralph Earnhardt, "the man in black" seemed to have won everything there is in NAS-CAR.

Since the first race in 1959 the premier NASCAR race has been the Daytona 500. A victory here made a successful season, regardless of how the remainder of the year went. Richard Petty, the other seven time NASCAR champion, won the Daytona 500 seven times.

Earnhardt and Daytona should have been naturals, and they almost were. Coming into the 1998 Daytona 500 Earnhardt had won thirty races at the 2.5 mile France family track in every type of event. He had won qualifying races, Busch Grand National and IROC races and the summer Firecracker 400. But there was always something that prevented him from finding the checkered flag for the February 500-mile race.

He first came to Daytona in 1979 as a rookie with the Rod Osterlund team. His #2 Buick was one of the few cars able to stay in sight of Buddy Baker in 1980 but a slow final pit stop, then a broken motor, ended his assault.

In 1984 Dale was fast in Bud Moore's Thunderbird, but Cale Yarborough was faster, taking the win with Dale second. There was only one front runner in 1985, Bill Elliott on the beginning of a super year. Dale was a DNF to start a year that couldn't pass soon enough.

In 1986 he was again a factor in Richard Childress' #3 Wrangler Chevrolet, running with Geoff Bodine. With three laps remaining Earnhardt ran out of fuel and the race belonged to Bodine.

A long final pit stop wasted the 1987 drive in a fifth place finish. The following year Dale was not a factor, leading only two laps to finish tenth. By 1989 Earnhardt had three driver's titles and had been trying for the 500 for ten years, but it was Darrell Waltrip's year and Dale's carburetor problems resulted in a third place finish. It looked like Earnhardt was going to take the #3 Goodwrench Chevrolet to victory lane in 1990. Dale took the white flag ahead of Derrike Cope only to run over debris and cut a rear tire virtually within sight of the finish line. Cope took the first of his two career wins.

Earnhardt was leading Ernie Irvan as the end of the 1991 race was nearing. Early in the race the gods sent an omen as #3 and a seagull met on the backstretch. Though

Earnhardt quickly showed his potential by winning the driver's title in 1980 in only his second full season at Atlanta in the Osterlund Monte Carlo. Courtesy of Ed Clayton.

The "Intimidator." Black was as much an attitude as marketing color choice for Dale Earnhardt's #3. Courtesy of Ed Clayton.

Chevy of Dale Jarrett. Dale J. got a good run on the backstretch to swing under for the lead and hold off Dale E. to take the checkered flag.

Dale was not a factor in 1994, fading to seventh as Sterling Marlin took the win. Marlin was again in the lead in 1995 when he used a slower car as a pick keeping the black #3 again in the runner-up spot.

Marlin was not a factor in 1996 but that other Dale was back, now in a Ford. DJ just plan outran DE for his second Daytona 500 win. Earnhardt was in the lead in 1997 as the pack passed lap 190 of the 200 lap race. Then, with only five laps to go, Dale got caught up in an accident sending him to 31st position in the final order. "The Kid," Jeff Gordon, led a Hendrick Motorsports first, second and third finish.

Even those who normally wished Dale Earnhardt nothing but bad luck, and there

the damage was superficial to the Chevrolet it was a sign of Dale's luck. On lap 197 the gods denied Dale again when he came together with Davey Allison, allowing Ernie Irvan to take the win.

It was a Ford year in 1992 and Dale's Chevrolet finished ninth.

Chevrolets were in front again in 1993. After leading for much of the race Dale was leading at the white flag. But hanging on his tail was the Interstate

Before drivers faced the black #3 on the track they had to face the steely look of Dale Earnhardt. Courtesy of Ed Clayton.

were many, acknowledged that he should win the 1998 Daytona 500. He had certainly proved worthy of the reward. In qualifying he had taken a 125-mile race, something he did almost every year. Though he led 107 of the 200 laps no one could say Earnhardt dominated the race. When the second yellow flag came out on lap 174 he led the field into the pits. The Richard Childress Racing pit crew put in gas and changed only two right side tires, allowing Earnhardt to exit still in the lead. Right behind him was his teammate Mike Skinner, but in third and fourth were Penske teammates Jeremy Mayfield and Rusty Wallace. The Ford pair quickly hooked up to challenge the black Chevrolet for the win. On lap 179 Skinner lost the draft and Earnhardt was on his own. Pole winner Bobby Labonte made a run, passing the pair of Penske Fords and easing the pressure on Earnhardt. When John Andretti, Jimmy Spencer and Lake Speed came together in a bump-up the yellow flag came out with one plus laps remaining. Whoever took the yellow flag first would win. Earnhardt was not to be denied.

On his twentieth attempt he had won the Daytona 500. He drove down the pit lane where opposing teams lined up to offer congratulations. It was *déjà vu* of two weeks before when opposing teams had applauded Gianpiero Moretti who had finally won the 24-hour race, an event he had first entered in 1970. In both cases it was a genuine expression of admiration by the competition for perseverance. And in both cases the driver showed an emotional side that few had seen before, acknowledging what the win meant. Then if anyone questioned what it meant to Earnhardt he made an abrupt right turn and began making donuts in the grass. It was his only 1998 win, and he probably wouldn't have traded it for a twenty-win season.

In 1999 he caught Jeff Gordon's draft in the final laps to finish second again. Be-

yond NASCAR the season was a success as he took three of the four IROC races and his third series title.

The final laps of the 2001 Daytona 500 were shaping into a Dale Earnhardt benefit. He was running third, protecting the two cars he owned, Michael Waltrip (first) and son Dale, Jr. (second). The most aggressive driver of the last two decades was playing defense. On the last lap, when it became apparent that the pair would finish first and second, and facing a multi-car assault, Dale surrendered third. Then on the last corner he made contact with another car, causing him to turn into the wall at 185 mph where he was hit by Kenny Schrader. The medical examiner concluded that he had died instantly. The last lap had again undone what should have been the greatest day of an illustrious career.

After his death anything with the Earnhardt image was up for sale. Only a secure location kept this Earnhardt-faced Coca-Cola machine from being stolen. Many others were. From the J.A. Martin collection.

84 Sports Car Split
IMSA/SportsCar/USRRC/ALMS/Grand Am

In 1988 John Bishop sold IMSA, and the world of professional sports car racing has yet to return to stability.

In 1992 IMSA announced that 1993 would be the final year for the GTP cars. Beginning in 1994 the championship was to be for World Sports Cars (WSC). To reduce costs the cars were limited to non-turbocharged engines with a parity scale on horsepower. Flat bottom designs virtually eliminated ground effects. And the cars were open so the fans could see the drivers, as in the days of the Can-Am series.

In the first year (1994) most of the cars were former GT Lights cars, mostly Spices, with the roofs removed. Riley-Scott produced a new race car, the Mk III, but the great surprise occurred when Ferrari debuted the 330SP with a win at Road Atlanta. However, with regular top finishes but no wins Wayne Taylor took the driver's championship in a Jim Downing

Kudzu Mazda. Taylor won again in 1996 in an Oldsmobile Aurora powered Riley-Scott.

The series originally did not attract the crowds that the Can-Am or GTP cars had, though the racing was excellent with well-prepared proper race cars. The battle continued with the Rob Dyson team in a pair of Ford powered Riley-Scotts and the Ferraris of Momo founder Gianpierro Moretti and the Scandia team of Andy Evans. The emotional high point came when Moretti, who had been racing at Daytona since 1970, won for the first time in his last race there, and the first 24-hour win for Ferrari since 1967.

In 1997 the IMSA became a part of the International Motor Sports Management Group. IMSG also bought the Sebring and Mosport tracks. The name IMSA was retired to be replaced by SportsCar. Management's feeling was that the organization's name should reflect what the series was about.

The Ford powered Riley and Scott Mk III of Dyson Racing was the premier private WSC team and first champion of both the USRRC and Grand Am series. Courtesy of Ed Clayton.

Encouraged by Bill France, Jr., of NASCAR the SCCA stepped in for 1998 with a separate series for World Sports Cars (WSC). Going back to the 1960s, the series was called the United States Road Racing Championship (USRRC). The WSC cars were listed as Can-Am racers. The goal of the USRRC was to encourage private teams to fill the field. Cars and equipment had to be available to all competitors. The primary cars were the Ferrari 330SP

The Indiana built Riley and Scott Mk III, shown in wind tunnel model, was the first car specifically designed for the World SportsCar series. With various motors it was a winning chassis through 2002. Courtesy of Riley and Scott.

Petit Le Mans Poster. From the collection of J.A. Martin.

and the Riley-Scott Mk III, with a variety of power plants.

Most teams raced in both the USRRC and SportsCar series, with the Dyson Racing team taking the driver's championship in both.

In 1997 Don Panoz began a race team with the GTR-1 race car based on the Panoz sports car. While the Panoz was competitive at the first race at Sebring Panoz was dissatisfied with the way the race was regulated, especially when the winning car was owned by Andy Evans, owner of both SportsCar and the Sebring race. Panoz also disagreed with the rules that did not allow prototype GT cars like his to compete on an equal basis with the open racers like the Ferrari 330SP. He preferred the rules for the 24-hour Le Mans race where the two classes competed on a fairly equal basis. In 1998 he founded the American Le Mans Series (ALMS) within SportsCar, with the premier race (Petit Le Mans) at his Road Atlanta circuit in August 1998. By the end of 1998 Evans was out of Sports-Car.

For 1999 the ALMS series was comprised of eight races, beginning with the 12-hour race of Sebring. Unlike the USRRC, the ALMS encouraged factory teams with one-off prototype cars. At Sebring in 1999 BMW and Audi debuted new race cars. BMW won, with Audis finishing third and fifth. Three months later an identical BMW won at Le Mans. In 2000, 2001, and 2002 Audi duplicated at Sebring and Le Mans, then finished with a win at Petit Le Mans.

The American Le Mans Series was built around factory prepared prototypes, like the 2000 champion Audi that won Petit Le Mans (shown), Sebring and the Le Mans 24-hour race. Courtesy of Ed Clayton.

By 2000 there were more American manufacturers in international sports car racing than at any time since the 1960s. Cadillac, as shown at Petit Le Mans 2000, used racing to change its stodgy 1950s image to one of a hi tech performance company. Courtesy of Ed Clayton.

The USRRC lasted less than two seasons. By the summer of 1999 the SCCA announced that, due to lack of marketing capital, they were ending the series.

In its place Bill France, Jr., and brother Jim created the Grand American Road Racing Association for WSCs to conduct eight races, four on tracks owned by the International Speedway Corporation, also France family owned, that began with the 2000 Daytona 24-hour race. The ALMS is directed to the factory teams while the Grand Am is centered on the privateers.

At Petit Le Mans 2001 SportsCar was renamed IMSA.

Beginning in 2003 the aesthetically challenged closed cockpit Daytona Prototypes replaced WSCs as the premier Grand Am series. By regulation the cars were hardly faster than the small bore GT cars, with a Porsche 911 winning the 24 hour Daytona race.

So buy a program, because you can't tell who's racing without one.

85 THE NEW SPEEDWAYS
1986 On

By the late 1980s the conditions that had killed the muscle cars had passed. Despite claims of impossibilities the auto industry was building cars that were meeting and exceeding corporate mileage and safety regulations. Performance cars were faster than even before the early 1970s. And while Iraq and Iran, then Iraq and everybody, were fighting the oil market the gas prices stabilized. The economy had been sustaining stable growth and sporting events were profiting from leisure spending. NASCAR was on the verge of a growth spurt unsurpassed in racing history.

In 1987 Roger Penske got the boom in new tracks started in a sedate way when he purchased Nazareth Speedway, a one-mile

dirt oval in eastern Pennsylvania. Penske kept the five-turn elevation change layout but paved it over and added up to date amenities, renaming it Pennsylvania International Raceway. The name was later changed back to Nazareth Speedway.

Heartland Park Topeka is a road course where the front straight is used for drag races. Built in 1989, the Kansas track has hosted IMSA, NASCAR and NHRA events.

Another new speedway was not a new track at all. As a way to bypass regulations for building, Bob Bahre converted the existing Bryar sports car ⅝ oval track in southern New Hampshire. He was allowed to modify and improve the track, which he did with great enthusiasm creating the one-mile New Hampshire International Speedway. In 1990 the NASCAR Busch Grand National cars came to race. Soon the track was host to CART, then IRL events, and Winston Cup cars plus motorcycles and sports cars on an infield road course.

Richmond International Raceway had gone through several versions since the half-mile dirt oval was opened in 1953. In 1968 the surface was paved over. The biggest change came in the summer of 1988 when almost the entire track was bulldozed. Richard Petty was given the honor of knocking down the first wall, and a new .75 mile track was built in its place. The track is now more of a stadium with grandstands completely surrounding the racing surface.

In 1992 Hurricane Andrew blew through the southern Florida community of Homestead. As a way to rebuild the financial base of the community a one-mile race track was built. When the track opened in 1995 it had four corners, like a downsized Indianapolis Motor Speedway. While the CART drivers could handle the track, the corners were too tight for NASCAR so for 1998 the shape of Homestead-Miami Speedway was remade to two half-circles and two straights.

A single race, even a Winston Cup event, cannot support a race track year round, opening the way for NASCAR Busch and the Craftsman Truck Series even if many of these tracks were already scheduling Winston Cup and CART events. That made the timing right for Tony George to unveil his Indy Racing League with open wheel oval track events. Open an oval track and the IRL would come. With three NASCAR series plus CART or the IRL, a new track could have a good chance to be financially sound.

And build new tracks they did. In 1996 the IRL was the opening race for a one-mile oval on the Disney World land in central Florida.

Bruton Smith had rebuilt his financial

The one-mile track at Homestead, Florida, was one of the first new speedways. It was built on the site of the damage from Hurricane Andrew and began the track building boom of the 1990s. Courtesy of the Homestead-Miami Speedway.

empire since the early debacle at Charlotte, and he was back building race tracks as Speedway Motorsports. He bought North Wilkesboro, then removed the track from the Winston Cup schedule, opening dates in 1997 for his new 1.5-mile Texas Motor Speedway between Dallas and Fort Worth, Texas. He also bought Sears Point and the Atlanta Motor Speedway and regained ownership of Charlotte. After he purchased Bristol he expanded its capacity from 30,000 to a stadium holding over 130,000. The term "Thunder Valley" was never truer of the northeastern Tennessee area.

Roger Penske, ever on the edge of motorsports, believed that it was time to reenter the southern California market. In Fontana, within sight of the land where Ontario once stood, he built a two-mile track virtually identical to his track in Michigan. Before the decade ended Penske sold his tracks to the France-family controlled International Speedway Corporation.

In 1996 new race complexes were built. The 1.5 Las Vegas oval is center to a racing complex of two small ovals and a drag strip and an infield road course. Pikes Peak International Raceway has a one-mile oval and a 1.5-mile road course.

St. Louis International had been a combination road/drag track in Illinois within sight of downtown St. Louis. Chris Pook of Long Beach fame bought the track then made the same "improvements" as done in New Hampshire. What emerged was the 1.25 mile oval of Gateway International Raceway.

In 1999 CART team owner Chip Ganassi built the Chicago Speedway on the north side of the windy city. A CART race kicked off the racing schedule in August 1999.

The first new track of the 21st century is the Kentucky Speedway just south of Cincinnati, Ohio.

New oval tracks were built near Kansas City, Kansas, Nashville, Tennessee, and Chicagoland south of Chicago. American style oval tracks were also being built in England and Germany to add to the ovals in Brazil, Australia and Japan that were built in the 1990s. American racing is moving into countries that have long looked down upon the American style of racing.

New road courses were built, but not all for professional series. Thunderhill near San Francisco was opened when Sears Point and Laguna Seca could not handle the demands for track time from car clubs. A course for similar purpose was built near New Orleans, Louisiana. Virginia International was reopened in 2000.

In 2003 a Grand Am event highlighted the inaugural season for the Barber Motorsports Park in Alabama.

86 LO TECH WITH HI EXCITEMENT
NASCAR Trucks

By the early 1990s success had brought a new problem to NASCAR. There was more, a great deal more, demand for NASCAR races than there were dates for races. New tracks were being planned and everyone wanted a Winston Cup race with the stars that the fans had taken to so strongly. The Busch series, long the minor leagues, had grown to where race attendance was almost on an equal basis with the Cup cars of a few years ago. Busch races were able to handle some of the demand but tracks needed more top events.

Stock cars used to be stock, not only based on a production car, but built from a street car. But the cars of the early 1990s bore only a superficial resemblance to a street car. A four door street Ford Taurus has a V-6 driving the front wheels. A racing Taurus had a 350 cubic inch V-8 driving the rear wheels.

But there was one type of vehicle that was still built parallel to race conditions. In the early 1990s pickup trucks, long viewed as work vehicles, were becoming the favorite of suburbanites. Many stock cars were running with truck engines.

Racing with pickup trucks had been tried before. Pickups have been central to off road races since the 1970s. In the mid–1980s the SCCA had tried a semi-pro series with compact pickups on road courses. GATR, Great American Truck Racing, experimented with several types of trucks on courses from local dirt tracks to speedways. Neither found an adequate market.

Enter Dick Landfield, Jim Venable, Frank Vessels and Jimmy Smith. In 1993 the four off-road racers built a pickup truck specifically for closed course racing and in early 1994 applied to NASCAR for sanctioning to race their trucks. No dummy, Billy France, Jr,. jumped on the proposal and in May 1994 announced the creation of the Super Truck Series.

By July plans were in place for a demonstration race. P.J. Jones, son of Parnelli Jones, won the first race at Mesa Marin Raceway in a Vessels-owned Ford. Three more races were held by the end of the year, and the response was very positive. A twenty race schedule was announced for 1995. To create additional interest a three race preview series was held in late 1994 and televised by TNN.

Though using truck sheet metal, the

Before NASCAR thought of trucks as racers the SCCA had a truck series fought by light pickups from many manufacturers. Two Nissans are about to finish a lap at Road Atlanta. Courtesy of Ed Clayton.

construction methods were tried and true NASCAR. Under the skin was a tube frame and full roll cage virtually identical to a Busch or Winston Cup car. There was no compromise in driver safety.

Craftsman Tools announced in late 1994 they were joining with a $1.6 million package. The following year they became series title sponsor.

Initially there were two makes; the Chevrolet Silverado and the Ford F-150. Both trucks were popular with the buying public, outselling the companies' most successful cars, the Lumina and Taurus. The popularity of trucks with the general public was a prime motivator for the manufacturers to put factory support behind the respective teams.

The NASCAR Craftsman Truck Series

1997/1999 champion Jack Sprague's 2001 Silverado is typical of the top racers in the NASCAR Craftsman Truck Series. Courtesy of Hendrick Racing.

(NCTS) was officially inaugurated at Phoenix International Raceway on February 5, 1995. Mike Skinner won the race with Dale Earnhardt's Goodwrench Service Chevrolet. Skinner went on to take the first title over Joe Ruttman. The first season saw races at tracks too small to host a Winston Cup race, like the .33 mile Santa Clarita, California, plus new venues like the Heartland Park Topeka road course. The boxy truck shape made the trucks slower on the superspeedways but was not a handicap on short ovals or road courses.

Ron Hornaday won the title for the second season in the NAPA Auto Parts Chevrolet owned by Dale and Theresa Earnhardt.

The boost to the series and to NAS-CAR came at Portland Speedway when Rich Bickle qualified a Richard Petty owned Dodge Ram. It was the first entry by a Chrysler Corporation vehicle in NASCAR since the late 1970s and a rejoining of the Petty and Dodge names. At I-70 Speedway in May 1997 Tony Raines took the first Dodge victory. Less than four years later Dodge reentered Winston Cup competition.

Each year the series has grown, providing a springboard for drivers, teams, and tracks culminating in the Winston Cup series. Mike Skinner, Mike Bliss, Kenny Irwin, all went from the trucks to the premier series.

Jack Sprague won the 1997 title in a Rick Hendrick prepared Chevrolet. Hornaday came back to win the 1998 title with Sprague again in 1999. Greg Biffle won the most 1999 races (nine) helping Ford to its first manufacturer's title, then followed in 2000 as series champion.

For 2001 the Dodge Boys finally found their way, winning the manufacturer's championship with Jack Sprague taking a third driver's title.

Toyota will enter NASCAR in 2004 with a truck program based on the full size American built Tundra.

The trucks have become everything NASCAR, the manufacturers and the TV networks hoped for.

87 A DAY FOR HISTORY
John Force, Kenny Bernstein and Shirley Muldowney

November 10, 2002, was a typically beautiful southern California day at the historic Pomona drag strip, but it wasn't the sun that made the day special. Two men were creating drag racing history at the concluding race for the 2002 NHRA season. John Force won his record tenth straight Funny Car championship and

Kenny Bernstein was retiring after one of racing's great careers.

John Force gave little early indication of becoming a dominant figure in drag racing. Born in 1949, Force decided that he was too slow to move from high school to college quarterback. With a tax refund he bought a Vega Funny Car, then talked his way to Australia for an exhibition run, turning the first 200 mph run down under. Having to augment his racing career financially, he turned to the other thing he does well, promotion. He often has said that only his car is faster than his mouth. He shilled on TV for a truck driving school and wore a clown suit for his sponsor, Wendy's. "Anything for gas money," declared Force. The reasons have changed but the mouth has not slowed, as Force is always good for a TV sound bite that shows his enthusiasm for the sport.

The big break in Force's career came in 1985 when he joined with crew chief Austin Coil and picked up Castrol Oil as primary sponsor, pairings that have continued to this date. John won his first Top Fuel race in 1987, then his first championship in 1990, repeating in 1991. In 1992 he finished second, but he regained it in 1993 and won every year through 2002, ten straight. No one in any professional sport has ever been so dominant for a full decade. His total of 109 wins is second in professional motorsports only to Richard Petty's 200. In 1996 he won 13 times with 16 final appearances in 19 events, all NHRA records, and is the only drag racer ever named as Driver of the Year for all motorsports.

Force cut back on driving in 2003 with his driver Tony Pedregon winning the Top Fuel title.

Bernstein, born in 1944 in Clovis, New Mexico, also began racing in the 1960s but left the sport in 1973 to build a financial base. He opened a restaurant, the Chelsea Street Pub, and was so successful that he soon had 16 operating units.

He returned to earn his first national win in 1979 then won four straight Funny Car titles (1985–88) plus another in the IHRA. In 1990 he moved to Top Fuel and in 1992 became the first driver to break 300 mph (301.70) at Gainesville, FL. In 1996 he won the Top Fuel title.

The "King of Speed" in drag racing is also the only owner to have also won events in NASCAR (Ricky Rudd) and Indy cars (Roberto Guerrero).

The year 2002 was the end of a storied career. At Pomona he concluded the "Forever Red" tour with a second round loss but still had sufficient points for the runner-up spot in the Top Fuel championship.

Fate intervened at Englishtown, NJ, in June 2003 when Bernstein's son Brandon was injured. Kenny had turned driving the Budweiser car over to Brandon but had to reenter the cockpit for the remainder of the season. He responded by winning the final four events, bringing his career total to 69. Highlighting the season, Brandon was named NHRA Rookie of the Year.

Kenny's last run at Pomona on November 9, 2003, was to take the overall win over Cory McClenathan. Earlier Cory had defeated Shirley Muldowney in the second round. It was her last drive. Pomona was the culmination of "Last Pass," her retirement tour. She and Bernstein were leaving the sport at the same event after having faced each other so many times over the last three decades.

No woman driver had ever reached the top level of drag racing and no woman had ever won a top level championship in any form of racing, until Shirley. Born (in 1940) and raised in Vermont, Shirley found that she was able to handle speed better than her husband or any other driver in the area. As shown in the movie *Heart Like a Wheel*, she left both behind to become the first woman to earn an NHRA license to drive what are now called Funny Cars.

After four serious fires in three years,

John Force, winner of ten consecutive Funny Car championships and the dominant figure in drag racing since the early 1990s.

one needing 18 months of recovery, Shirley decided Funny Cars were too dangerous, with the driver sitting just behind a hyperstressed motor inside a plastic shell, and in 1973, after a fire at the US Nation-als, she moved to the safer (open and rear motor) and faster Top Fuel.

Though she never plays down being a woman, as witnessed by her early nickname of "Cha Cha" and the pink parachute, she has won by beating the boys at their own game, winning an equal amount of respect from those she has beaten and lost to. Along the way she became the first woman to win a national event and the first to win a championship. She won three championships (1977, 1980, 1982) in Top Fuel, the first woman in any form of motor sports to do so.

With her accomplishments have come public acknowledgements. In 1977 the U.S. House of Representatives honored her. She was named fifth among NHRA's greatest drivers and in 2003 was inducted into the International Motorsports Hall of Fame. After the Pomona event Shirley was given a special presentation at the NHRA awards dinner for a historic career.

EPILOGUE

Racing is ever changing, and many of the changes are the same that affect all aspects of society. Communication and transportation advances have made world economies more interdependent and global. Products are designed for a world market with only a few modifications for local conditions.

Formula 1 races are beamed live to American TVs via satellite. European and Asian viewers can watch NASCAR and CART as it happens. Advertisers realize this. Sponsors that sell to the world, from Fosters Beer and Marlboro cigarettes to Compaq computers and FedEx, adorn racecars of many nations and series.

But the U.S. market is big enough that a series can still be developed with no support from outside American borders, NASCAR, the World of Outlaws, and the NHRA being the most notable examples. As shown by the growth spurt in the 1990s most Americans prefer oval track racing to road racing.

Indeed, Americans have yet to truly embrace road racing. Formula 1 returned to the United States only because of the Indianapolis Motor Speedway, and even there tickets went unsold. While many superspeedways have road courses on the same property, it is the NASCAR races that continue to be the most popular.

Part of the reason that Americans have not taken to the kind of racing accepted by the rest of the world is that Americans don't need it. America didn't need Formula 1 because there were already open wheeled championship cars. Stock cars and drag racing were open to anyone. There was always a place for racing, at any budget.

Many of our homegrown motorsports have gained worldwide audiences. Places like Martinsville and Milwaukee are as well known in Japan and Europe as in America. American style oval tracks have been built in South America, Japan, Australia and Europe.

Some aspects of the American racing image are no longer a part of racing. The backyard mechanic is no longer a factor at the top level. NASCAR teams employ dozens of computer-directed engineers. The IRL was created in part to return racing to individual teams but the winners now get their power from specialty motor shops, the same ones used by their competitors. It is doubtful we'll see another Harry Miller, A.J. Watson or Don Devendorf.

And racing, like all sports, has become so specialized and time consuming that versatility is not practical. A young driver has to decide whether to race stock cars, open wheel or sports cars. Gone are the days of open schedules when a driver could race Formula 1 one weekend then hit a Trans-Am the following. John Andretti and Tony Stewart have shown that American drivers are still capable and versatile.

America has had great success in racing and has produced many great innovations and drivers that have become legendary in the history of motorsports.

J.A. Martin

BIBLIOGRAPHY

Abodaher, David J. *The Speedmakers: Great Race Drivers.* New York, NY: Julian Messner, 1979.

Batchelor, Dean, and Albert R. Bochroch. *Cunningham: The Life and Cars of Briggs Swift Cunningham.* Osceola, WI: Motorbooks International, 1993

Bentley, John. *The Devil Behind Them.* Englewood Cliffs, NJ: Prentice-Hall, Inc., 1958.

Bochroch, Albert. *American Automobile Racing: An Illustrated History.* New York, NY: The Viking Press, 1974.

Borgeson, Griffith. *The Golden Age of the American Racing Car.* New York, NY: W. Norton, 1966.

British Petroleum Co., Ltd. *The BP Book of World Land Speed Records.* London: Baynard Press, 1963.

Brown, Allan E. *The History of America's Speedways Past & Present.* Comstock Park, MI: America's Speedways.

Burgess-Wise, David. *The Ultimate Race Car.* New York, NY: D K Publishing 1999.

Coffey, Frank, and Joseph Layden. *America on Wheels: The First 100 Years: 1896–1996.* Santa Monica, CA: General Publishing Group, 1996.

Crabb, Richard. *Birth of a Giant: The Men and Incidents That Gave America the Motorcar.* Philadelphia, PA: Chilton Book Co., 1969.

De Geer, Stanley L. *The Pikes Peak Race, 1916–1990.* Albuquerque, NM: Peak Publishing Co., 1992.

de Paolo, Peter. *I Drove the Boards.* Originally published in 8 parts in *Speed Age* magazine, 1951-52, republished in *The Bulb Horn,* 1980–83, now available in one volume from Thomas F. Saal, 1488 West Clifton, Lakewood, OH 44107.

Dillon, James. *The Short but Dramatic Racing History of Mercer,* in 3 parts, *The Bulb Horn,* VMCCA, 1-3/90, 4-6/90, 7-9/90.

Donohue, Mark, with Paul Van Valkenburgh. *The Unfair Advantage.* New York, NY: Dodd, Mead and Co., 1975.

Doyle, Gary D. *King of the Boards: The Life and Times of Jimmy Murphy.* Sedona, AZ: Self-published 2002, www.king-of-the-boards. com.

Fielden, Greg. *Forty Years of Stock Car Racing.* Surfside Beach, SC: The Galfield Press, 1989.

Fisher, Jane. *Fabulous Hoosier: The Life of Carl Graham Fisher.* New York, NY: Robt. M. McBride & Co., 1947.

Fox, Charles. *The Great Racing Cars and Drivers.* New York, NY: Grosset & Dunlap, 1972.

Fox, Jack C. *The Illustrated History of Sprint Car Racing.* Indianapolis, IN: Carl Hungness Publishing, 1985.

Fox, Jack C. *The Illustrated History of the Indianapolis 500, 1911–1994.* Speedway, IN: Carl Hungness Publishing, 1994.

Genst, Robert, and Don Cox. *The Birth of Hot Rodding — The Story of the Dry Lakes Era.* Osceola, WI: Motorbooks International, 2003.

Golenbock, Peter. *The Last Lap*. New York, NY: Macmillan Publishing, 1998.

Golias, Bernard J., and Thomas F. Saal. *Famous but Forgotten: The Story of Alexander Winton*. Twinsburg, OH: Golias Publishing, 1997.

Goodman, Roland. *Mexican Road Race: Carrera Pan-Americana Mexico*. Los Angeles, CA: Floyd Clymer, 1950.

Gunnell, John A. *100 Years of American Cars*. Iola, WI: Krause Publications, 1993.

Helck, Peter. *Great Auto Races*. New York, NY: Harry N. Abrams, Inc., 1975.

Hunter, Don, and Ben White. *American Stock Car Racers*. Osceola, WI: Motorbooks International, 1997.

Keyser, Michael. *The Speed Merchants*. Englewood Cliffs, NJ: Prentice-Hall, 1973.

Kirby, Gordon. *Unser: An American Family Portrait*. Dallas, TX: Anlon Press, 1988.

Levine, Leo. *Ford: The Dust and the Glory: A Racing History*, vol. 1. New York, NY: Macmillan, 1968.

Levine, Leo. *Ford: The Dust and the Glory: A Racing History*, vol. 2, 1968–2000. Warrendale, PA: Society of Automotive Engineers, 2001.

Lord Montagu of Beaulieu, research by Michael Sedgwick. *The Gordon Bennett Races*. London: Cassell & Co. Ltd., 1963.

Ludvigsen, Karl. *Gurney's Eagles*. Minneapolis, MN: Motorbooks International, 1976.

Lyons, Pete. *Can-Am*. Osceola, WI: Motorbooks International, 1995.

Martin, J.A., and Ken Wells. *Prototypes*. Phoenix, AZ: David Bull Publishing, 2000.

Motor Racing Year 1967-68. West Wickham, Kent, UK: Knightsbridge Publication, 1967.

Peters, George, and Henri Greuter. *Novi, The Legendary Indianapolis Race Car*, vol. I. Hazelwood, MO: Bar Jeans Enterprises, 1991.

Petty, Richard, and William Neely. *King Richard I*. New York, NY: Macmillian Publishing, 1986.

Post, Robert C. *High Performance: The Culture and Technology of Drag Racing, Revised Edition 1950–2000*. Baltimore, MD: Johns Hopkins University Press, 2001.

Rendall, Ivan, and Gau, John. *The Power and the Glory*. London: BBC Books, 1991.

Ruiz, Marco. *The History of the Automobile*. New York, NY: Gallery Books, 1984.

Scalzo, Joe. *The Unbelievable Unsers*. Chicago, IL: Henry Regnery Co., 1971.

Shaw, Wilbur. *Gentlemen, Start Your Engines*. New York, NY: Coward-McCann, 1955.

Shelby, Carroll. *The Cobra Story*. Osceola, WI: Motorbooks International, 1965.

Shoen, Michael L. *The Cobra-Ferrari Wars*. New York, NY: CFW, 1988.

Taylor, Rich. *Lime Rock Park*. Sharon, CT: Sharon Mountain Press, 1992.

Wallen, Dick. *Board Track, Guts, Gold & Glory*. Glendale, AZ: Self-published, 1990.

INDEX